A Concise Companion to
Shakespeare and the Text

Blackwell Concise Companions to Literature and Culture
General Editor: David Bradshaw, University of Oxford

This series offers accessible, innovative approaches to major areas of literary study. Each volume provides an indispensable companion for anyone wishing to gain an authoritative understanding of a given period or movement's intellectual character and contexts.

Published

Chaucer	Edited by Corinne Saunders
English Renaissance Literature	Edited by Donna B. Hamilton
Shakespeare and the Text	Edited by Andrew Murphy
Shakespeare on Screen	Edited by Diana E. Henderson
Milton	Edited by Angelica Duran
The Restoration and Eighteenth Century	Edited by Cynthia Wall
The Victorian Novel	Edited by Francis O'Gorman
Modernism	Edited by David Bradshaw
Postwar American Literature and Culture	Edited by Josephine G. Hendin
Twentieth-Century American Poetry	Edited by Stephen Fredman
Contemporary British Fiction	Edited by James F. English
Feminist Theory	Edited by Mary Eagleton

Forthcoming

Postwar British and Irish Poetry	Edited by C. D. Blanton and Nigel Alderman

A Concise Companion to
Shakespeare and
the Text

Edited by Andrew Murphy

Blackwell
Publishing

© 2007 by Blackwell Publishing Ltd
except for editorial material and organization © 2007 by Andrew Murphy

BLACKWELL PUBLISHING
350 Main Street, Malden, MA 02148-5020, USA
9600 Garsington Road, Oxford OX4 2DQ, UK
550 Swanston Street, Carlton, Victoria 3053, Australia

The right of Andrew Murphy to be identified as the Author of the Editorial
Material in this Work has been asserted in accordance with the UK Copyright,
Designs, and Patents Act 1988.

First published 2007 by Blackwell Publishing Ltd

2   2008

Library of Congress Cataloging-in-Publication Data

A concise companion to Shakespeare and the text / edited by Andrew Murphy.
    p. cm.—(Blackwell concise companions to literature and culture)
  Includes bibliographical references and index.
  ISBN: 978-1-4051-3528-3 (alk. paper)
  1. Shakespeare, William, 1564–1616—Criticism, Textual.   2. Shakespeare, William,
1564–1616—Bibliography.   3. Transmission of texts—History.   4. Drama—Editing—
History.   I. Murphy, Andrew.

PR3071.C66 2007
822.3'3—dc22

                                                                    2006025798

A catalogue record for this title is available from the British Library.

Set in 10/12.5pt Meridien
by Graphicraft Limited, Hong Kong
Printed and bound in Singapore
by Markono Print Media Pte Ltd

The publisher's policy is to use permanent paper from mills that operate
a sustainable forestry policy, and which has been manufactured from pulp
processed using acid-free and elementary chlorine-free practices. Furthermore,
the publisher ensures that the text paper and cover board used have met
acceptable environmental accreditation standards.

For further information on
Blackwell Publishing, visit our website:
www.blackwellpublishing.com

Contents

Contents

Notes on Contributors

Thomas L. Berger is Piskor Professor of English at St. Lawrence University in Canton, New York. He is the co-editor of *An Index of Characters in English Printed Drama to the Restoration* (1975) and the editor of facsimile editions of *2 Henry IV* and *Titus Andronicus* for the Malone Society, of which he is the USA secretary-treasurer. Currently he is assembling, with Sonia Massai, an edition of *The Paratexts of Early Modern English Printed Drama* for Cambridge University Press.

Michael Best is professor emeritus at the University of Victoria, British Columbia. He has published books on Renaissance magic and on the English housewife in seventeenth-century England, and two CD-ROMs on Shakespeare. His current work is focused on his role as coordinating editor of the Internet Shakespeare Editions (ISE), which he founded in 1996. The ISE is publishing quality, peer-reviewed electronic texts and performance materials on Shakespeare, making them freely available on the internet at www.ise.uvic.ca.

David Bevington is the Phyllis Fay Horton Distinguished Service Professor Emeritus in the Humanities at the University of Chicago, where he has taught since 1967. His studies include *From "Mankind" to Marlowe* (1962), *Tudor Drama and Politics* (1968), and *Action Is Eloquence: Shakespeare's Language of Gesture* (1985). He is also the editor of *Medieval Drama* (1975); *The Bantam Shakespeare*, in 29 paperback volumes (1988), currently being re-edited; and *The Complete Works of*

Shakespeare, fifth edition (2003); as well as of the Oxford *1 Henry IV* (1987), the Cambridge *Antony and Cleopatra* (1990), and the Arden 3 *Troilus and Cressida* (1998). He is the senior editor of the Revels Student Editions, and is a senior editor of the Revels Plays and of the forthcoming Cambridge edition of the works of Ben Jonson. He is senior editor of the recently published *Norton Anthology of Renaissance Drama* (2002).

Roger Chartier is professeur at the Collège de France and Annenberg Visiting Professor at the University of Pennsylvania. His main works in English are *The Cultural Uses of Print in Early Modern France* (1987); *Cultural History: Between Practices and Representations* (1988); *The Cultural Origins of the French Revolution* (1991); *The Order of Books: Readers, Authors, and Libraries in Europe between the Fourteenth and Eighteenth Centuries* (1994); *Forms and Meanings: Texts, Performances, and Audiences from Codex to Computer* (1995); *On the Edge of the Cliff: History, Language, and Practices* (1997); and *Publishing Drama in Early Modern Europe* (1999). His latest book, *Inscrire et effacer: Culture écrite et littérature XI–XVIIIe siècle* (2005), will be published in English translation in 2007.

John Drakakis is professor of English studies at the University of Stirling and director of the Scottish Institute for Northern Renaissance Studies. He is the general editor of the New Critical Idiom series, has written widely on Shakespeare and literary theory, and has just completed the Arden 3 edition of *The Merchant of Venice*.

Leah S. Marcus has authored four books, the most recent, *Unediting the Renaissance* (1996), on editorial practice and early modern texts. She has co-edited the writings of Queen Elizabeth I and edited *The Merchant of Venice* for Norton (2006). She is currently working on an edition of *The Duchess of Malfi* for Arden.

Sonia Massai is a lecturer in English studies at King's College London. Her recent and forthcoming publications on early modern drama in print include an essay in *Textual Performances*, her book on *Shakespeare and the Rise of the Editor*, and an edition of *The Paratexts of Early Modern English Printed Drama*, which she is preparing with Thomas L. Berger.

Andrew Murphy is professor of English at the University of St. Andrews. He is the author, most recently, of *Shakespeare in Print:*

A History and Chronology of Shakespeare Publishing (2003) and the editor of *The Renaissance Text: Theory, Editing, Textuality* (2000).

Neil Rhodes is professor of English literature and cultural history at the University of St. Andrews. He is the author of *Shakespeare and the Origins of English* (2004) and has also edited (with Jonathan Sawday) *The Renaissance Computer: Knowledge Technology in the First Age of Print* (2000) and (with Stuart Gillespie) *Shakespeare and Elizabethan Popular Culture* (2006).

Helen Smith is a lecturer in Renaissance literature at the University of York. She has published on early modern women stationers and on the clothing of the early modern book, and is currently completing a book, *Grossly Material Things: Women and Textual Production in Early Modern England*.

Peter Stallybrass is Annenberg Professor in the Humanities at the University of Pennsylvania, where he directs the seminar on the history of material texts. His 2006 A. S. W. Rosenbach Lectures in Bibliography are published under the title *Printing for Manuscript*. In 2006, he also curated exhibitions with Heather Wolfe on "Technologies of Writing" at the Folger Shakespeare Library and with James Green on "Benjamin Franklin, Writer and Printer" at the Library Company of Philadelphia.

Paul Werstine is professor of English at King's University College at the University of Western Ontario. He is co-editor, with Barbara A. Mowat, of the Folger Shakespeare Library edition of Shakespeare (1992–), and co-general editor, with Richard Knowles, of the Modern Language Association's New Variorum Edition of Shakespeare.

Anthony James West, an independent scholar, started and directs the First Folio Project. His publications include the first two volumes in the series, *The Shakespeare First Folio: The History of the Book* (2001, 2003). Research is underway for the third volume.

Acknowledgments

This volume evolved from conversations held with Emma Bennett in two very different locations: over coffee and bagels in New Orleans and over tea and biscuits in Stratford-on-Avon. I am grateful to Emma for her advice and guidance and to Blackwell's advisers for the enormously helpful feedback which they have provided. My thanks also to Fiona Sewell for her eagle-eyed and astute copy-editing. I am grateful to the contributors to the volume, from whose work (here and elsewhere) I have learned a very great deal. Finally: thanks to Gerard and Charonne for ongoing support and encouragement.

Note on Texts

When quoting from the 1623 First Folio edition of Shakespeare's plays, contributors use Charlton Hinman's facsimile edition, using Hinman's "through line number" (TLN) referencing system. When using modern texts, contributors indicate individually which edition they are quoting from. Contributors use standard referencing of F for Folio and Q for Quarto, numbered according to edition (e.g. F1 = First Folio; Q2 = Second Quarto). When quoting from texts which lack page numbers, signature numbers are used instead.

Introduction: What Happens in *Hamlet*?

Andrew Murphy

One of the most tiresome questions faced by Shakespeareans on a regular basis is, without a doubt, "But did he *really* write the plays?" In some respects, this is not at all a difficult question to answer. While conspiracy theorists and cryptologists may well combine to unearth secret codes in the texts which demonstrate that Francis Bacon or Queen Elizabeth I took time out of their busy schedules to knock off somewhat more than three dozen substantial plays, the actual documentary evidence which survives from the time clearly indicates that it was indeed the grammar-school boy from Stratford who was the author of the works ascribed to him and not, say, some modest aristocrat with a surplus of time on his hands. But the issue might, more interestingly, be approached from a different angle. If we agree that Shakespeare wrote the texts that are ascribed to him, then exactly what do we mean by that? If, for example, we walk into a bookshop and buy a copy of *Hamlet*, can we confidently say that Shakespeare is the author of the words of the play that sit between the covers of the edition?

To bring this question more clearly into focus, it will be helpful to look at an extended sequence from *Hamlet* in a particular modern text. One of the most highly regarded editions of the play from the latter half of the twentieth century was Harold Jenkins's Arden 2 text, first published in 1982. I would like to examine here an extended section of Jenkins's Act III, scene i, which includes, of course, what is conventionally Shakespeare's best-known piece of writing,

1

the "To be, or not to be" soliloquy. Immediately before the soliloquy, the king, queen, and Polonius discuss Hamlet's strange behavior, with Ophelia in attendance, largely silent. At the end of his soliloquy Hamlet engages in an exchange with Ophelia, which culminates in his "Get thee to a nunnery" outburst.

How does Jenkins's edition square with the texts we have inherited from Shakespeare's own era? We do not, of course, have any manuscript edition of *Hamlet* from the Renaissance – indeed, no manuscript of any of Shakespeare's plays has survived. We do, however, have three early printed texts. The first of these, the First Quarto (Q1, published in 1603), is quite an odd text, and it is difficult to square it with the other two. It is one of a small number of early editions that present attenuated (and sometimes rather garbled) versions of some of Shakespeare's plays. The Second Quarto, Q2 (variously dated 1604 and 1605), provides a longer and more coherent text, as does the version of the play included in the First Folio (F1) collected plays volume, published in 1623, seven years after Shakespeare's death. Q2 and F1 are generally very similar to each other, though there are significant differences between them in some sections of the play.

The first thing we notice in turning back to the earliest editions is that Jenkins's designation of this section of text as Act III, scene i, is nowhere to be found. Q1 and Q2 have no act or scene markers at all. The F1 text of the play begins with *"Actus Primus. Scæna Prima."* and it provides a "Scena Secunda" and "Scena Tertia" for the first act before moving on to "Actus Secundus," then "Scena Secunda." Beyond this scene, there are no further divisions in the text; in effect, the entire remainder of the play is Act II, scene ii. Jenkins tells us in his textual notes that he takes his act and scene designation from a quarto published in 1676 – this is a theatrical text of the play prepared by Sir William D'Avenant. So, the particular division of the text that we find here dates from sixty years after Shakespeare's death.

Immediately after the act and scene designation, Jenkins provides a stage direction: *"Enter* King, Queen, Polonius, Ophelia, Rosencrantz, Guildenstern." Q1 has no equivalent of this stage direction, partly because it compacts a number of scenes into a condensed presentation at this point in the play. Q2 and F1 do have an equivalent direction, but both add *"Lords"* to the list of characters to be brought on stage. Where have the Lords gone, in Jenkins's text? In omitting them, he tells us that he is following Edward Capell's 1768 edition, and he explains in a note that "The *Lords* of Q2 and F presumably originated with Shakespeare, who then omitted to make use of them.

There is no appropriate . . . point at which they could retire" (274). For Jenkins, then, the Lords are superfluous and, if Shakespeare was responsible for inventing them, Jenkins believes he subsequently forgot that he called them into existence. We might say, however, that their absence or presence does make a difference to the text. With the Lords (albeit silently) present the scene provides a more social and less private vision of the world of the play: they make it less a "domestic" drama, we might say.

As we move forward through the text we find further variations in the stage directions. The immediate next direction is uncontroversial: Rosencrantz and Guildenstern exit at line 28 of Jenkins's text, and they have an equivalent exit in Q2 and F1 (Q1 lacks an exit largely because of the way its narrative is reconfigured). However, after his line 42, Jenkins indicates an exit for the Queen and no such exit is included in either Q2 or F1. Checking Jenkins's textual notes, we find that he has taken this stage direction from Lewis Theobald's edition of 1733. Intuitively, the change does make sense, in that, at Jenkins's line 28 (following Rosencrantz and Guildenstern's exit), the King has said "Sweet Gertrude, leave us too" and the Queen responds "I shall obey you." Since Ophelia's "Madam, I wish it may" at line 42 is addressed to the Queen, Jenkins, following Theobald, has indicated the earliest (and most natural) point at which she can exit the stage. However, it is worth noting in the current context that the direction is again a departure from the text as it has come down to us in the earliest editions.

Next we come to the sequencing of exits and entrances at the point where Hamlet arrives on the stage. Here we find a high level of variation. Jenkins brings the King and Polonius off immediately after Polonius's line "I hear him coming. Let's withdraw, my lord." He is following F1 here, as Q2 marks no exit at this point. Hamlet's entrance is then differently configured in F1 and in Q2: in F1 he comes on after Polonius's line (and, therefore, after Polonius and the King have exited), whereas in Q2 he comes on before Polonius's line (and, therefore, presumably, just as Polonius and the King are starting to leave, though, as we have seen, Q2 gives them no explicit exit). In one sense, this is a rather trivial point, but it could be said to resonate with traditional debates over the question of the extent to which Hamlet suspects that Ophelia has been set up by the King and her father – a question which much exercised John Dover Wilson in the book from which this introduction takes its subtitle (see also references to Wilson's edition of *Hamlet* below).

We have seen that Jenkins takes his exit for Polonius and the King from F1, but, in fact, F1 offers just a blanket *"Exeunt"* and Jenkins adds to it *"[King and Polonius]."* Here, he tells us in his notes, he is again following Capell's text, though he registers that Nicholas Rowe's edition of 1709 expanded F1's *Exeunt* to *"all but Ophelia."* In one way, of course, this again makes intuitive sense, since Ophelia needs to be on stage to pick up Hamlet's cue of "Soft you now, / The fair Ophelia!" and she has no re-entrance in any of the texts in advance of this line. But there is a strange ambiguity here too in that all four characters (the King, Polonius, Ophelia, and Hamlet) are, in fact, somewhere within the stage space for the duration of both "To be, or not to be" and the nunnery exchange. In F1, we might say, the King, Polonius, and Ophelia are all equally withdrawn from Hamlet, whereas Jenkins, following the editorial tradition dating back to Rowe, leaves Ophelia in a kind of "limbo" where, if we read her exclusion from the exit direction in a strictly literal sense, she may perhaps be placed to hear his depressed musings on death and self-destruction.

Returning to the very beginning of the scene again, we will remember that Jenkins's first stage direction calls for the entrance of "KING, QUEEN, POLONIUS, OPHELIA, ROSENCRANTZ, GUILDENSTERN" and, during the course of the scene, the Queen is specifically named in the dialogue (by the King) as "Gertrude." However, if we track the character names back through the earliest editions, we find a different picture emerging. Polonius is absent from Q1; his equivalent in that text is called "Corambis." Likewise, in Q1, Hamlet's student friends are named "Rossencraft" and "Gilderstone" rather than "Rosencrantz" and "Guildenstern," and the Queen is named "Gertred" (or "Gerterd" [F1v]) and not "Gertrude." In Q2, we find characters called Rosencraus and Gertrard. It is only in F1 that the names assume the general form (with variations in spelling, but the same essential pronunciation) that Jenkins adopts. That he should opt for Rosencrantz and Gertrude in preference to Rosencraus and Gertrard is somewhat odd, given that his stated policy is, for the most part, to follow Q2 as his base text (74–5). In both cases, he suggests that the Q2 names may be misreadings of the originals (163, 423), but it is hard not to feel that the real deciding factor here may simply be the burden of tradition: everyone who knows *Hamlet* knows these characters as Rosencrantz and Gertrude, and to tamper with them would have risked Jenkins embroiling his edition in real controversy – controversy of the kind which was prompted by the editors of the 1986 Oxford University Press *Complete Works* when they changed Falstaff's name to Oldcastle (see David Bevington's and John Drakakis's chapters in this volume).

Moving on from text divisions, stage directions, and character names, we come to the text of the dialogue itself. Here it is useful to cut directly to Hamlet's soliloquy. To begin with the syntactical division of the speech, both Jenkins and F1 break the soliloquy down into six sentences, though their divisions are rather different from each other. Thus, for example, where F1's first sentence runs through seven and a half lines, to end at "That Flesh is heyre too?," Jenkins's first sentence ends in the fifth line, at "by opposing end them." While both begin a sentence at "To die, to sleep," F1 ends this sentence at "Must giue vs pawse," while Jenkins uses a dash here and carries the sentence on to end at "so long life." The contrast with Q2 is even more striking. This text breaks the soliloquy down into just two sentences. The first is a full 27 lines long, terminating at "we know not of." Though quite different from each other in terms of the number of sentences they present, Q2 and F1 share a tendency to moderate the flow of the soliloquy using commas. In six separate places in the speech both Q2 and F1 deploy a comma where Jenkins has no punctuation at all. Oftentimes these commas come at line endings, as in the closing lines of the soliloquy (quoting from Q2):

> And enterprises of great pitch and moment,
> With this regard theyr currents turne awry,
> And loose the name of action.

Both Q2 and F1 have line-end commas here, while in Jenkins the lines run on. The effect, in the early editions, is to slow the tempo of the soliloquy as it comes to a conclusion.

We have seen that the punctuation and syntactical segmenting of the text differ between Jenkins's edition and the texts first published. As the quotations taken directly from the early editions make clear, there are also variations in the words that appear on the page. In some cases, these changes simply mark the difference between modern and Renaissance spelling conventions, with Shakespeare's era lacking formalized rules for "correct" spelling. Jenkins is producing specifically a "modern spelling" edition and so he eliminates Renaissance variations from his text. In most cases, this is simply a matter – as in the instance of the lines from Q2 quoted above – of substituting "their" for "theyr," "turn" for "turne," and so forth. However, it is also the case that Renaissance spelling can often carry a richer sense of meaning than its modern equivalent. Thus "loose" in the above quotation can both signal the sense of "lose" (the meaning which Jenkins chooses for his text) and carry an echo of to let "loose," to release, to let fall. Similarly, in Q2, death is the undiscovered country from which no "trauiler" returns. Jenkins renders this, quite correctly, as "traveller," the logical meaning. But, again, the Renaissance spelling carries within it the notion of "travail," or labor, which is also appropriate to the context.

In modernizing the text, Jenkins is choosing to substitute modern forms for their Renaissance equivalents. But, in some places, the choice to be made is between variations in the actual words being offered by the early editions. As we have seen above, Jenkins opts to accept F1's "Rosencrantz" and "Gertrude" in place of Q2's "Rosencraus" and "Gertrard." In Hamlet's soliloquy, the early texts offer the editor a choice between "theyr currents turne awry" (Q2, G2v) and "their Currants turne away" (F1, TLN 1741). In this instance, Jenkins adopts Q2's "awry," following his base text where, in the case of the character names, he decided to follow F1 instead. This is a simple enough decision, but, elsewhere, the editor of *Hamlet* is faced with more complex problems. For example, Q2 includes some passages which do not appear in F1 and the Folio text also includes material that Q2 lacks. Thus, in the scene where Fortinbras's army marches through Denmark, Q2 alone brings Hamlet on stage to meditate on the soldiers' mission "to gaine a little patch of ground / That hath in it no profit but the name" (K3r). The scene culminates in Hamlet's "How all occasions doe informe against me" soliloquy. Jenkins includes this material in his edition – a predictable enough decision, given, again, that his base text is Q2.

A contrasting instance is provided by the scene where Hamlet, having just returned from England, explains to Horatio what has happened during the course of his voyage. In both Q2 and F1, their conversation is interrupted by the entrance of a courtier (named specifically as "Osricke" in F1), who conveys the king's proposal for the fencing match between Hamlet and Laertes. In Q2, the interruption occurs at the conclusion of Hamlet's

> Dooes it not thinke thee stand me now vppon?
> He that hath kil'd my King, and whor'd my mother,
> Pop't in betweene th'election and my hopes,
> Throwne out his Angle for my proper life,
> And with such cusnage, i'st not perfect conscience?
> (N2r)

The F1 text, however, continues for a further 14 lines before Osricke's entrance and it also makes better sense of "i'st not perfect conscience," ending the phrase with a comma rather than a question mark, and creating, with the next line, a complete question: "is't not perfect conscience, / To quit him with this arme?" (TLN 3571–2). The passage continues, in F1, with Hamlet's expression of regret that "to *Laertes* I forgot my selfe" (TLN 3580). Jenkins decides to include all of these lines in his text, observing in a note that "The absence of these lines from Q2 is difficult to explain except as an accidental omission" (398). Thus Jenkins's general policy is that, where one text provides more material than another, it is best to gather everything together into his own edition.

If we return to Hamlet's soliloquy and turn specifically to the Q1 text of the speech, we are confronted with an even more complex problem. Here is the complete soliloquy, as it appears in Q1:

> To be, or not to be, I there's the point,
> To Die, to sleepe, is that all? I all:
> No, to sleepe, to dreame, I mary there it goes,
> For in that dreame of death, when wee awake,
> And borne before an euerlasting Iudge,
> From whence no passenger euer retur'nd,
> The vndiscouered country, at whose sight
> The happy smile, and the accursed damn'd.
> But for this, the ioyfull hope of this,
> Whol'd beare the scornes and flattery of the world,
> Scorned by the right rich, the rich curssed of the poore?
> The widow being oppressed, the orphan wrongd,
> The taste of hunger, or a tirants raigne,
> And thousand more calamities besides,
> To grunt and sweate vnder this weary life,
> When that he may his full *Quietus* make,
> With a bare bodkin, who would this indure,
> But for a hope of something after death?
> Which pusles the braine, and doth confound the sence,
> Which makes vs rather beare those euilles we haue,
> Than flie to others that we know not of.
> I that, O this conscience makes cowardes of vs all.
>   (D4v–E1r)

This version of the soliloquy, as will be immediately apparent, is radically different from its Q2 and F1 counterparts. Exactly what an editor should do when faced with variation of such a high order is very hard to say. Traditionally, texts like Q1 *Hamlet* have been dismissed as being so anomalous that they do not need to be taken into account when editing Shakespeare. Various narratives have been invoked to try to account for their existence. The theory which found most enduring favor was that the attenuated quartos were the product of "memorial reconstruction" by bit-part actors seeking to make some money by reconstituting the text of a popular play from memory, in order to sell it on to a publisher. This theory made it possible, for almost the whole of the twentieth century, to dismiss the short quartos as wholly irrelevant to the "genuine" text of Shakespeare's plays. However, recent work by Laurie E. Maguire, Paul Werstine, Lukas Erne, and others has radically shaken the certainties of this traditional view. We still do not know exactly what the provenance of these texts is – or, indeed, whether they all share the same kind of history – but, in the present context, it is worth noting that the Q1 version of Hamlet's soliloquy presents us not just with a different set of words from the Q2 and F1 equivalents, but also with a different tone, emphasis, and focus. Where the longer texts of the speech are, broadly speaking, philosophical and abstract, the Q1 version is much more concrete, direct, and political. Where one Hamlet ponders "the proude mans contumely" (Q2, G2r), the other focuses more specifically on "The widow being oppressed, the orphan wrong'd, / The taste of hunger, or a tirants raigne" (Q1, E1r).

Q1 differs from the other early texts of *Hamlet* in many other significant respects. It includes, for instance, a unique scene in which Horatio explicitly outlines Claudius's various acts of treachery to the Queen, leading her to conclude "I perceiue there's treason in his lookes / That seem'd to sugar o're his villanie" (H2v), thus making her a much less ambivalent figure than she is sometimes seen as being, on the basis of her portrayal in the longer texts. In general, Q1 is much more fast-paced and action-oriented than Q2 and F1 and it conforms much more closely to the traditional conventions of the revenge tragedy genre. Dramatically, it might be said to be closer to Zeffirelli's radically cut, accelerated film version of *Hamlet* with Mel Gibson than, for example, the more meditative, stately BBC *Hamlet* featuring Derek Jacobi. Quite where any of this leaves an editor of *Hamlet* is, however, difficult to say.

Over the course of the first half of this introduction, I have focused largely on a single scene from Harold Jenkins's edition of *Hamlet*. I have tried to show how Jenkins's text differs from the original published editions we have inherited from the Renaissance, examining some of his editorial decisions and, in a number of cases, exploring the consequences of these decisions. I have demonstrated how, in many instances, a choice made by Jenkins as editor has served to effect a single particular meaning in the text at the expense of eliminating other meanings or even fruitful textual ambiguities. The purpose of this analysis is not, however, to criticize Jenkins or in any way to belittle his great achievement as an editor. My intention is rather to show what a complex entity the Shakespeare text is and to demonstrate some of the difficulties involved in reducing this complexity to the essentially static format of a print edition.

Our exploration of Jenkins's edition raises a number of fundamental issues about what can and should happen to the Shakespeare text as it is reconfigured for presentation in a modern edition. For instance, what aspects of the text fall entirely within the editor's control? Does the editor have a wholly free hand in modernizing spelling and, if so, what might be lost in eliminating any ambiguities of meaning that inhere in the spelling of the original texts? Is the editor completely at liberty in matters of punctuation and, again, what might follow from this? To what extent should the editor intervene in the presentation of the text in order to make it easier for the reader to find his or her way through it? Should, for example, act and scene divisions be consistently marked as a way of ordering the text on the page? To what extent might such segmenting of the text run against the grain of its being a theatrical document? In the theater, after all, there are no act or scene breaks. Should an editor add or amplify stage directions in order to make the logistics of the action more intelligible to the reader? If this is within the editor's power, then how much information is enough, or too much, or too little? Lengthy, elaborated stage directions were a signature characteristic of John Dover Wilson's Cambridge *New Shakespeare*; in the scene under analysis here he added the direction *"Hamlet, disorderly attired and reading a book, enters the lobby by the door at the back; he hears voices from the chamber and pauses a moment beside one of the curtains, unobserved"* (43). Reading this, it is hard not to feel that Wilson is virtually turning the play into a novel with dialogue, not to mention imposing his own, very specific, reading on the action of the play.

Jenkins, as it happens, explicitly rejects Wilson's suggestion that Hamlet slowly works out that Polonius and the King are spying on him during the course of his exchange with Ophelia. For Wilson, it is this realization – which he reconfirms with a further stage direction that Hamlet *"[remembers the plot]"* (61) – that prompts Hamlet's

9

unexpected question to Ophelia, "Where's your father?" but Jenkins insists that "There is no textual basis for the common assumption that Hamlet's question is prompted by his having just discovered the answer to it" (283). Here, then, Jenkins rejects the reading imposed on the text by one of his predecessors as editor. But elsewhere, as we have seen, he draws quite heavily on the work of other editors in adding to or emending the text. So, for instance, just in the section of the play we have been examining he takes his act and scene division from William D'Avenant's 1676 edition; he follows Nicholas Rowe's 1709 edition in excluding Ophelia from Polonius's and the King's exit; he brings the Queen off stage, following Lewis Theobald's 1733 edition; and he invokes Edward Capell's 1768 text in deleting the "Lords" from the opening stage direction.

All good editors try, as far as they can, to follow their base text wherever they can possibly make sense of it. But, oftentimes, an editor is forced to draw on the extended editorial tradition for help. Thus, for example, in Horatio's description of King Hamlet's battle with the King of Norway, he tells Marcellus and Barnardo that the old king "smot the sleaded pollax on the ice" (Q2, B2r); Q1 also has "sleaded pollax" (B2r) and F1 has "sledded Pollax" (TLN 79). The phrase in its entirety does not make sense: it is certainly possible to imagine King Hamlet smiting the ice with a poleaxe, but it is more difficult to imagine what a "sleaded" poleaxe might be. Jenkins, in common with most editors, solves the problem by adopting the reading of Edmond Malone's 1790 edition: "sledded Polacks." In other words, it is not the ice that King Hamlet smites but, as Jenkins puts it in his note, "Poles borne in sleds" (169). But we should note, of course, that editions published later than the very earliest texts have no real "authority" as such. Malone's solution to this particular textual crux is no more than an elegant guess at a true meaning which most editors feel has been obscured in the earliest editions. So, a question arises as to when it is appropriate for an editor to rely on the work of a predecessor, repeating that predecessor's changes to the text. On what grounds does one accept the emendation of one editor and reject that of another (as Jenkins rejects Wilson's reading of the nunnery scene)?

Returning to the editor's particular role in helping the reader to make sense of the text, we might also ask what level of annotation is appropriate in a modern edition. Whereas the early editions present a text wholly free of commentary, in Jenkins's modern edition, as much as 50 percent (or more) of the page is frequently given over to annotation of one sort or another. At such a great remove from the text's original historical moment this is, of course, inevitable. As long ago as the mid-eighteenth century, Samuel Johnson recognized that the Shakespeare text is replete with topical allusions which quickly become obscure with the passing of time:

> All personal reflections, when names are suppressed, must be in a few years irrecoverably obliterated; and customs, too minute to attract the notice of the law, such as modes of dress, formalities of conversation, rules of visits, disposition of furniture, and practices of ceremony, which naturally find places in familiar dialogue, are so fugitive and insubstantial, that they are not easily retained or recovered. (I, D6r–D6v)

Part of the function of the editor is, precisely, to recover such contextual material and make it available to the reader. But, again, we might ask what the effect is of reading a play when it is heavily freighted with commentary and apparatus. It was, after all, also Samuel Johnson who advised: "Let him, that is yet unacquainted with the powers of *Shakespeare,* and who desires to feel the highest pleasure that the drama can give, read every play from the first scene to the last, with utter negligence of all his commentators" (I, E4r).

The most complicated issue facing an editor is undoubtedly the business of making sense of the relationships among the surviving early texts of any given play. What, for example, lies behind Q2 and F1 *Hamlet?* Or, to put it another way: what was the compositor looking at when he set the text in the printshop? A manuscript in Shakespeare's own handwriting? A copy of the play prepared by a professional scribe? A manuscript that had been used by the King's Men (or their predecessors) for performance? Another printed text? A further question also arises: whatever was in front of the compositor, had it been marked up, amended, annotated, revised, cut, added to, or otherwise changed? And, if so, by whom? By the players, the censor, a professional scribe, or Shakespeare himself? Twentieth-century editors, working within the paradigm of the New Bibliography, had a high level of confidence that they had evolved strategies for answering these questions. R. B. McKerrow proposed some simple tests for establishing whether a play was printed from an authorial manuscript or a playhouse "prompt book," including suggesting that "a play in which the names are irregular was printed from the author's original MS., and . . . one in which they are regular and uniform is more likely to have been printed from some sort of fair copy, perhaps made by a professional scribe" (1935: 464). Likewise, early in the twentieth century, a group of scholars proposed that the "Hand D" that wrote some sections of the manuscript play *Sir Thomas More* was Shakespeare's, thus providing an insight into the characteristics of the playwright's spelling and into idiosyncrasies in his handwriting which might be open to predictable misinterpretation by a compositor (thereby, again, helping in determining whether a printed text was based on an authorial manuscript). Later in the century, another group of scholars proposed that variations in some of the early texts (including *Hamlet*) were an indication that Shakespeare was a revising playwright, who often returned to his texts to update them in one way or another. By the terms of this theory, the omissions/additions that we have logged in comparing Q2 and F1 *Hamlet* have been taken as evidence of Shakespeare's revising hand, cutting and adding to the play some time after its original composition.

The high optimism of the New Bibliographic and, later, Revisionist era faltered as the twentieth century drew to a close. As Paul Werstine has shown, both in his chapter in this volume and elsewhere, it has become increasingly hard over the past decade or so to maintain confidence in the relatively straightforward narratives of textual provenance once so assuredly advanced by editors working within the New Bibliographic (and, latterly, Revisionist) frameworks. Finally, what we are left with is a complex of texts, which often, like so many of Shakespeare's villains, refuse ultimately to account for themselves. As Iago says: "Demand me nothing: what you know, you know: / From this time forth, I neuer will speake word" (F1, TLN 3607–8). It may very well be that, in time, the early texts can be persuaded to speak more about their origins. We may well eventually find a satisfactory narrative that accounts for Q1 *Hamlet* and the other short quartos. We may be able to plot the origins of the longer texts and their interrelationships in a way that is more fully convincing than at present. In the interim, we are stuck with difficult editorial choices and with the interestingly complex textual world that the earliest editions evoke.

What this book seeks to offer, in the main, is an exploration of the parameters and possibilities of this complex world. In the opening chapter of part I Helen Smith provides an insight into the intricacies of bringing a book to print in the Renaissance period, and in chapter 2 Peter Stallybrass and Roger Chartier chart the complex process whereby Shakespeare came to be constituted as an author. Thomas L. Berger and Anthony James West then track the histories of specific Shakespeare texts: the early quartos, in the case of Berger's chapter, and the First Folio in the case of West's.

The second part of the book takes up the issue of the various strategies that have been evolved in an effort to cope with the complexities of the texts we have inherited from the Renaissance. In my own chapter, I trace the attempts that were made in the eighteenth century to map out, for the first time, a systematic and theoretically coherent approach to editing Shakespeare. Paul Werstine analyses the rise of a new, "scientific" mindset within editing as it emerged in the twentieth century and he notes that, while this approach dominated Shakespearean editorial practice for an extended period, ultimately the certainties on which it was founded came to be radically questioned. Leah S. Marcus takes up the issue of how editing has proceeded in the wake of this questioning and, specifically, under the shadow of poststructural interrogations of old textual certainties. Finally, Michael Best indicates how some of the problems mapped out throughout this volume – for example, the existence of multiple, variant texts – can be at least partially solved by deploying the resources of newly emergent digital technologies.

The final part of the volume is dedicated to practical matters. David Bevington takes us through a series of textual cruces in order to demonstrate exactly what the business of editing involves in real terms (with sleeves rolled up and pencil sharpened, so to speak). Sonia Massai helps us to understand what is to be gained by retaining a sense of the separateness of the extended series of individual textual incarnations of a play such as *King Lear*, and the value of cross-reading between them. In the final chapter in this part, Neil Rhodes indicates how new electronic resources can help to shed light on old questions. In a sense, Rhodes brings us full circle here, since the practical exercises he outlines constitute, precisely, an exploration of the world of the material text and its histories that Smith and Chartier and Stallybrass map out in the opening chapters of this volume. John Drakakis rounds off this *Companion* with an overview essay which explores, among other things, the political contexts and ramifications of many of the textual and editorial issues raised in the body of this book.

So: *did* Shakespeare really write the plays? Well, yes, he did, but, as Edward Capell noted in his 1768 edition, "we have nothing of his in writing; . . . the printed copies are all that is left to guide us" (I, 20–1). Capell, himself, imagined that he might "find his way through the wilderness of these early editions into that fair country the Poet's real habitation" (I, 20). He failed; but, then, so has every other editor before and since. George Steevens, characteristically, offered a more realistic assessment of the situation in a prospectus for a new edition, issued in 1766: "there is no single text of Shakespeare that can be depended on; and they are strangely mistaken who talk of restoring it to a state in which it never was" (n.p). Shakespeare's text is, finally, a collaborative venture. He certainly collaborated with fellow playwrights in writing some of his plays (*Henry VIII, Two Noble Kinsmen*, for example). It is highly likely that he collaborated with his acting colleagues in shaping his plays to suit the theatrical and commercial requirements of the Renaissance stage. He had no option but to collaborate with the Master of the Revels' office when it censored the plays by, for example, calling for the removal of oaths or of politically sensitive material from the text. But he has also, perforce, entered into a collaborative relationship with his editors, who have set themselves the task of rendering the plays in a form that makes sense to the audience of their own times. So: Shakespeare wrote the plays, but they are also rewritten in every generation by editors seeking to make sense of them from within a cultural field which shifts from generation to generation. The present volume aims, as best it can, to make sense of Shakespeare's text in the context of our own cultural moment and also of our current, imperfect, knowledge of the textual culture of Shakespeare's time.

Part I

Histories of the Books

Chapter 1

The Publishing Trade in Shakespeare's Time

Helen Smith

While his stage is littered with books and papers, writings and volumes, Shakespeare's plays pay little attention to the technologies which reproduced them for dissemination among a reading public. One of the playwright's few explicit references to the printing press and its associated industries occurs in *2 Henry VI*. Confronting Lord Saye, the rebel Jack Cade complains: "Thou hast most traitorously corrupted the youth of the realm in erecting a grammar school; and whereas before our forefathers had no other books but the score and the tally, thou hast caused printing to be used, and contrary to the King his crown, and dignity, thou hast built a paper-mill" (4.7.29–34).[1] The action of the play takes place during the 1450s, the very decade in which Gutenberg constructed the first hand press, and, crucially, the movable type which made his invention workable: an invention which did not reach English shores until 1475. The first English paper mill was not constructed until 1494, and it took the best part of two centuries to establish a healthy domestic industry for the production of printing or writing paper. The play's rampant anachronism suggests the extent to which Shakespeare's concerns are tied to the conditions of print publication in Elizabethan, rather than Henrician, England. That period is also the focus of this chapter, and the following account will touch on the issues of patronage, literacy, nationalism, and the widespread distribution of print which lurk beneath the rebel Cade's violent judicial rhetoric.

If Shakespeare mentions print only seldom, he mentions publishers even less. A rare exception can be found in *The Rape of Lucrece*, when the poet, lamenting Collatine's description of Lucrece's charms, demands "Or why is Collatine the publisher / Of that rich jewel he should keep unknown, / From thievish ears because it is his own?" (33–5). Collatine's fateful publication is oral and occasional, a far cry from the busy world of the hand press and the bookstall. Bearing in mind the multiple resonances of "publication" for an early modern audience, this chapter will close with a brief exploration of the overlapping modes of publication – print, manuscript, speech, and image – that characterized the era of Shakespeare and his contemporaries. Our own association of publishing and print did not emerge until the later eighteenth century as the boundaries between public and private became more clearly demarcated, and as manuscript reproduction became increasingly associated with the intimate and personal, reinforcing the association of print with the public sphere. The word which Shakespeare would have used to describe a member of the book trades, and which his erstwhile colleagues, Heminge and Condell, employ in the First Folio address "To the great Variety of Readers," is "stationer," a flexible category which includes printers, booksellers, bookbinders, and various other associated or overlapping trades. Although for the sake of clarity, I will occasionally use the term "publisher" in this chapter, it should always be remembered that no member of the early print trade would have used the term to describe himself or herself.

A London Guild of Stationers, whose members were scribes, illuminators, and sellers of manuscript books and writing materials, can be traced back to at least 1403, well before the advent of print. In 1557, with the printing press firmly established in London, the bookmen of the city banded together to form the Stationers' Company, and were granted a royal charter of incorporation by Mary I. In 1559, members received the right to wear their own distinctive livery. The Stationers' Company was no new invention, but the institutional recognition of a network of trades and an artisanal heritage with a long history. Nor did the creation of the Company herald any immediate revolution in the trade. Instead it marked the drive to order and regularize a number of well-established practices, many of which predated the advent of print.

By the time that Shakespeare was writing, some three decades after the incorporation of the Stationers' Company, the London publishing trade was well established. In the year of his birth, 1564, the *English Short Title Catalogue* (*ESTC*) lists 93 printed titles, 86 of which were published in London. By 1592, the year in which Shakespeare was famously attacked as "an upstart crow" in *Greenes Groats-worth of wit*, the figures were 294 and 252 respectively. For 1601, two years after the construction of the Globe theater on London's Bankside, the *ESTC* lists 258 titles, with 222 printed in London, figures that rise to 487 and 416 in 1616, the year of Shakespeare's death, and 566 and 474 in 1623, the year that saw the publication of the First Folio (see Barnard and Bell 2002). At the same time, however, the number of printing houses in existence was strictly controlled, and numbers remained consistent at 22 or 23 until the 1640s, when restrictions established by a Star Chamber decree of 1586 were relaxed.

One reason for the mismatch between a static productive capacity and the growing volume of texts was suggested by D. F. McKenzie, who argued that earlier titles are less likely to survive, with a rapid increase in the rate of loss the further back in time we go. This thesis is supported by the number of entries in the *Stationers' Company Registers* that record titles of which no other trace now remains. Some of these may never have been published, but others almost certainly entered print and have been subsequently lost or destroyed through use. The problem is particularly acute for popular and ephemeral texts such as ballads and almanacs. Margery Trundle, for example, a well-known ballad publisher of the late 1620s, is listed as the publisher of 13 items in the *ESTC*, yet the *Stationers' Company Registers* indicate that at the time of her death she was the owner of at least 30 texts. Similarly, Elizabeth Toye is now associated with only three imprints, yet in 1557, along with John Wallye, she entered 31 ballads in the *Register*. A further explanation for the growing numbers of books apparently issuing from the same number of presses may be that printing houses in the early part of our period were working at a lower proportion of their productive capacity than they were in later years. In 1582, the queen's printer, Christopher Barker, complained that the 22 London printing houses in existence, home to 53 presses, were substantially too many for the market to bear, and that "8. or 10. at the most would suffise for all England, yea and Scotland too" (Arber 1967: I, 144).

Barker's emphasis on the national context may well reflect the Stationers' Company's resentful relationship with the newly established university-based presses of Oxford and Cambridge. With the exception of these two printing houses the Stationers' Company exercised a largely effective monopoly on printing in England. During the first half of the sixteenth century, presses were established in St Albans, Oxford, Cambridge, Tavistock, Abingdon, Ipswich, Worcester, Canterbury, and York, but all of these provincial presses had ceased to operate by 1557. Scotland, governed by its own laws, gained its first press in Edinburgh in 1508, and printing houses in St Andrews and Glasgow followed in the second half of the sixteenth century. The first press in Dublin began to operate in 1551. In England, however, with the exception of Norwich, where Anthony de Solemne operated a printing press from 1568 to 1580, catering to the needs of the Flemish, Dutch, and Walloon "strangers" who made up approximately 40 percent of the city's population, there were no presses outside London until, despite the bitter opposition of the Stationers' Company, a printing house was established in Cambridge in 1583, with another following in Oxford two years later.

Despite strict control of the number of printers and presses allowed in England (most printers were licensed to operate no more than one or two presses), there were always some printers who were prepared to defy the law and risk searches, whether by the pursuivants of the crown, or by officials of the Stationers' Company. Discovery of a secret press could lead to fines, imprisonment, and the defacing of the press, rendering useless some very expensive equipment. Printers who took these risks may have done so in search of profit, as in the complex case of John Wolfe. In a flurry of printing activity, Wolfe appears to have infringed over half the printing privileges owned by members of the Company, or by courtiers who had received a patent from the queen allowing them the sole right to print certain classes of books. When questioned by officials of the Stationers' Company in 1582, Wolfe justified his repeated infractions with the defiant answer that he printed "Because I will live," and a search of his premises in the summer of 1583 revealed five presses, two "in a secret Vau[l]t" (Arber 1967: II, 780; I, 248). Wolfe was, eventually, reconciled with the Company and translated from the Fishmongers' to the Stationers' Company on July 1, 1583. Although this did not entirely prevent his vigorous attempts on other people's patents, Wolfe became an active member of the Company, and, ironically, was particularly active in discovering and prosecuting illicit printers.

Those whom Wolfe pursued might, like him, be looking to increase the often precarious income of a stationer, or they might be driven by religious or political commitment. Perhaps most often, their motives were a combination of principle and profit. What is now probably the best-known of the secret presses of early modern England is that on which Robert Waldegrave printed the Martin Marprelate tracts, moving around the country from the house of one patron to another, at East Molesey, Fawsley, and Coventry. One of his tracts, *Oh Read*

Over D. John Bridges, for it is a Worthy Worke (1588), attacks John Wolfe for his relentless pursuit of Waldegrave, describing him as "alias Machivill . . . [a] most tormenting executioner" (sig. D1r). Having been pursued relentlessly by both the crown and the Stationers' Company, Waldegrave ended his association with the Marprelate tracts, moving to Edinburgh in 1590 and quickly gaining the position of king's printer to James VI. In this role, he enjoyed a long and successful career, though his royal elevation did not prevent new skirmishes with the English authorities, who disliked his continuing Puritan sympathies, and with the Stationers' Company, who saw his Scottish editions of various texts as attempts at piracy. What the overlapping careers of John Wolfe and Robert Waldegrave remind us is that the line between licit and illicit printing was a fine one in early modern England. Printers could move with relative ease from the right to the wrong side of the law, and back again.

The 97 founding members of the Stationers' Company, those who set many of its regulations in place, were, for the most part, printer-publishers, following in the tradition established by William Caxton, the first English printer. Even at the moment of the Company's incorporation, however, the organization of the trade was shifting into new and distinct forms, as the physical labor of printing became separated from the business of finding new texts and financing their production. Slowly the balance of power in the trade moved from those who manufactured books to those who paid for them and held the rights to the copy that was reproduced. Where, in the first part of our period, some power might still lie with the printers, who had an intimate relationship with the means and mechanisms of production, by the end, it had largely shifted to those stationers who controlled what we would now describe as the intellectual property of the trade, as well as the flow of investment capital. As early as 1582, the queen's printer Christopher Barker, who was, it must be noted, a somewhat biased observer, complained that booksellers were able to drive such fierce bargains that the printer made little if any profit on most editions. The precise relationship between printer and publisher can perhaps be best described by examining a typical imprint of the period.

The first quarto of *The Tragedie of King Richard the second* (1597) declares its place of publication as "LONDON / Printed by Valentine Simmes for Androw Wise, and / are to be sold at his shop in Paules church yard at / the signe of the Angel. / 1597." In this instance, Valentine Simmes was the printer: the person who owned the manufacturing equipment and who, along with his workmen, produced the book. The master printer oversaw a complex set of processes, from the casting off of the text (working out how many words would fit in each line, and how many lines on a page) to the setting of type in formes, the operation of the presses, the checking and correction of the text during production, and the drying and storage of completed sheets in the correct order. He or she (a small but substantial number of early modern stationers were women, almost all widows who had inherited the business from their husbands) often had to keep careful track of work on several presses on which a number of different books, along with smaller ephemeral texts and pieces of jobbing work, were being printed concurrently. To print only one book at a time would occupy too high a proportion of a printer's valuable resources. Larger texts were not infrequently split between several printing houses, spreading the financial burden between a number of workers and presses. This was also a useful technique for the production of illicit or potentially subversive texts, allowing printers and pressmen to deny any knowledge of the nature of a book of which they had printed only one small part.

As was the case for *Richard II*, the majority of printers manufactured books on behalf of another agent, in this case Andrew Wise. It is Wise whom we would now describe as the publisher, responsible for purchasing sufficient paper stocks, paying the printer, compositor (who set the type for printing), and corrector, and also paying for presswork. Pressmen, known by their colleagues, who would sometimes taunt them with wisps of hay or straw, as "horses" because of the sheer physical labor involved in their work, were usually paid a piece rate. The publisher was usually also the primary retail agent, and the imprint gives full details of where the text can be bought. To purchase copies of *Richard II*, the customer or client would visit the many bookshops of St Paul's Churchyard, looking for Wise's shop sign, painted with an angel. This detailed information as to location was primarily for the benefit of others in the trade rather than the casual customer. As Peter Blayney points out, although the public could purchase books at these sites, the imprints effectively identify the wholesale retailers of the text: the distributors from whom other members of the trade could purchase or exchange books to sell on to their own customers (1997: 390).

Illicit, subversive, or satirical books often exploited the conventions of the imprint, both disguising their origins and declaring their comic or irreverent intent. The first Marprelate tract, *Oh Read Over*, also known as *The epistle to the terrible priests* (1588), which Robert Waldegrave printed at East Molesey, declared itself to be "printed oversea, in Europe, within two furlongs of a bounsing priest, at the cost and charges of M Marprelate, gentleman." As Patrick Collinson points out, Waldegrave's mocking imprint at once described and denied the geography of early modern London. "Europe" referred to the house from which the tract was published, and which stood a little over two furlongs away from Hampton Court Palace where John Whitgift, Martin's "bouncing priest," met with his fellow divines to determine church policy (Collinson 1967: 391).

While printing itself was carefully regulated, even if, as we have seen, that regulation was not always effective, involvement in the early modern publishing trade was not restricted to members of the Stationers' Company. Noble or aristocratic patrons might sponsor the publication of a text they considered particularly important. In 1592, for example, the antiquary Sir Edward Stradling financed the publication of 1,250 copies of Siôn Dafydd Rhys's *Cambrobrytannicae . . . linguae institutiones*, a Welsh grammar in Latin, declaring "I do give fifty of them ready bound to my friend Mr. Doctor Davys, the author of them; and my will is, that the rest of them shall be given and bestowed from time to time by my cousin, Sir John Stradling, upon such gentlemen and others as he shall think fit" (Williams 1948: 195–6). Many authors took on the role of publisher themselves: paying for the production and distribution of their own texts. This is another convention invoked in the false imprint to *The epistle to the terrible priests*, which declares itself to be published at Marprelate's own "cost and charges," at the same time mocking those members of the community of print who insisted on their social elevation, describing themselves as "gentlemen" on title-pages and in prefaces and dedications. Some authors sold on their printed texts, most often the case if they ran a related business, teaching handwriting or languages, for example, or selling instruments, whether musical or nautical. Some gained financial or political rewards from dedications to a patron. Yet others distributed their books free of charge. This was especially the case for several church ministers who paid handsomely to spread the word of God to their parishioners in printed as well as spoken form.

It was not only authors, however, who might look to the intercession of a patron for financial aid, for political support, or to secure some favor, privilege, or position. Stationers too sometimes developed clear links with a noble or aristocratic patron, who might, in turn, exercise some say in the nature and complexion of the texts emerging from his or her client's presses. England's first printer, William Caxton, identified himself in colophons and dedications as the servant of Margaret, duchess of Burgundy. In the early 1580s, John Charlewood, like John Wolfe a persistent printer of other men's privileged copies, identified himself as servant to the Catholic Philip Howard, earl of Arundel. Where Charlewood's business prospered, Arundel, who, with his wife, also sponsored manuscript publication from their house in Spitalfields, died in the Tower in October 1595, amid rumors that he had been poisoned by his cook. Within the confines of the established church, John Day, one of the finer printers of the period, enjoyed the protection of Archbishop Parker. In 1566, Day commissioned a special set of Anglo-Saxon typefaces in order to print Aelfric's *Testimonie of antiquitie*, which was edited by the archbishop. The text was both religiously and politically significant, establishing a series of ancient precedents to oppose to the practices of the Catholic church. In recognition of his efforts, Day was granted a patent giving him sole right to print Alexander Nowell's popular *Catechism* in 1570, a patent which was later extended to include all of Nowell's writings. Christopher Barker, as well as enjoying royal support, marked his texts with a printer's device that featured the tiger's head from his patron Sir Francis Walsingham's crest, and, in 1576, established a second shop in Paternoster Row (an area heavily associated with religious printing) marked by the sign of the tiger's head.

However he or she was financed, or whoever took on the role, the first step for the early modern publisher was to secure the rights to the relevant copy, often through a one-off payment to the author. We have little evidence, however, to tell us how much authors might expect to receive for their handiwork. Those authors who name a price usually do so in the context of a complaint, humorous or otherwise. John Stephens, in the "Epistle Popular" to his 1613 play, *Cinthia's Revenge*, derides the manner in which "our pie-bald Naturalists, depend upon poore wages, gape after the drunken harvest of forty shillings, and shame the worthy benefactors of Hellicon" (sig. A2v), while in the anonymous play *The Second Part of the Return from Parnassus* (c. 1601), the printer John Danter is seen explaining to Ingenioso (a figure for Thomas Nashe) that "good fayth, M. Ingenioso, I lost by your last booke; and you know there is many a one that pays me largely for the printing of their inventions, but for all this you shall have 40 shillings and an odde pottle of wine" (Leishman 1949: 247–8). This evidence, however, is inconclusive. Not only does Danter eventually up his price, declaring he will have Ingenioso's "Chronicle of Cambridge Cuckolds" "whatsoever it cost," it also seems that "40 shillings" was a colloquial term to describe any insignificant sum of money. In court records from the period, defendants or plaintiffs who describe themselves as being "worth little or nothing" will often estimate their wealth at 40 shillings. Somewhat paradoxically, the repeated invocation of this precise sum in complaints at stingy patrons, swipes at booksellers, and declarations of poverty serves to under-mine its reliability as a historical source.

Publishers could, however, provide both economic and intellectual support beyond a simple one-off payment. While few English stationers had the skills, the humanist learning, or the literate acquaintance of the continental master printers, their shops and offices were nonethe-less depositories of learning, and often better stocked than an author's private library. In the course of a 1616 dispute over his proprietary rights in the Protestant divine William Fulke's *Confutation of the Rhemish Testament* (first edition 1589), the stationer John Bill recounted the history of the text's production:

> Doctor Fulke being not sufficiently stored with bookes to performe it cam[e] to London to master Bishop a stationer where he and two of his men with their horses were mayntained by Bishop for 3. quarters of a yeares space and of Bishop he had such bookes for ye making of the treatise as he wanted. When it was finished Bishop in consideracon of his former charge and for ye diett Doctor Fulkes fri[e]nds likewise had of Bishop when they cam[e] to visit Doctor Fulke as also for 40[li] which Bishop gaue to Doctor Fulke and for diuers bookes giuen him he had ye printing of yat copie to him and his Assignes. and this appears by witnesses as also by ye Registry of ye Stationers hall where this was entred before ye master and wardens of ye Stationers at a Court the[n] holden as all copies which are bought by Stationers are. (Arber 1967: III, 39)

If John Bill, one of Bishop's three assigns, is to be believed, his col-league's support for Fulke's mammoth project included a payment of £40, the loan and gift of several books, paying for the maintenance of Fulke, two servants, and their horses, and entertaining the divine's friends. Little wonder that Bishop and Bill felt they had a clear right to print and profit from subsequent editions of the *Confutation*.

What is certain is that modern notions of copyright and intellectual property are largely an invention of the eighteenth century, and do little to illuminate our understanding of early modern authorship or the Renaissance publishing trades. Just as the playwright of Shakespeare's time gave up all rights in his play once he had received payment from the theater owner, so the scribbling author handed over his or her proprietary rights along with the manuscript copy. And if somebody else, whether friend or thief, handed over that copy instead, the rights of the authors were similarly overridden; their only real redress was to attempt to persuade another publisher to issue a different, or corrected, edition. As George Wither, another consistent complainer, grumbled in *The Schollers Purgatory* (1624): "by the lawes of their Corporation, they [the Stationers' Company] can and do setle vpon the particular members thereof p[e]rpetuall interest in such Bookes as are Registred by them at their Hall . . . notwithstanding their first Coppies were purloyned from the true owner, or imprinted without his leaue" (sigs. B6v–7r). In practice, the situation was more complex than this. Some authors (the most-trumpeted instance being Ben Jonson) took a detailed and ongoing interest in the production of their works, while others (traditionally Shakespeare, though this orthodoxy is now being challenged) were little concerned with the fate of their texts after they were consigned to the press, or, earlier, to the acting companies.

Church authorities, however, took a continuing interest, officially at least, in printed texts. Just as, from 1581, all plays had to be approved by the Master of the Revels before they could be acted, all printed texts, following the Star Chamber decree of 1586, had to be licensed by the Church Court of High Commission. In practice, this responsibility was often devolved to a panel of junior clerics. In the later part of our period, Sir George Buc, who was Master of the Revels from 1610 until he was declared insane in 1621, was, from 1607 onwards, responsible for licensing plays for the press as well as for the stage. This move away from the Church Courts reflects a gradual shift from religious to secular oversight of the press as we move from the Elizabethan to the Jacobean period. The requirement for ecclesiastical or other authority should not, however, be used to paint a picture of blanket censorship and rigorous control over artistic, religious, or political expression. Many texts appeared without an ecclesiastical license, and few of them were pursued or prosecuted unless they seemed to threaten disorder in the state. Elizabethan and Jacobean England was a political culture well aware of its own vulnerabilities, and of the potent power of the written and circulating word. It was not, however, as many earlier commentators held, a culture of systematic and retributive censorship and oppression. As John Barnard reminds us:

> The continuing attempts throughout the period to control the output of
> the London presses and the circulation of manuscripts and of unlicensed,
> pirated or subversive books or pamphlets, whether through licensing,
> the Stationers' Company, the Star Chamber, Parliamentary acts or, after
> the Restoration, through Sir Roger L'Estrange's appointment as Surveyor
> of the Press, were only intermittently successful. (Barnard 2002: 3)

The Company's own regulations and procedures were, as a rule,
pragmatic rather than ideological. The charter granted by Mary I in
1557 declared that no new book should be published without the
Company's consent, which could be obtained for a small fee, assuming no objections were raised. The Company might protect itself and
its members by refusing to allow a book to be licensed until it had
been reviewed by the ecclesiastical authorities. More often, however,
the reason for refusing a license would be that prior rights to the text
were held by another member of the Stationers' Company. The Company's overriding concern was to make sure that stationers' rights
to copy were not infringed. This was particularly important given that
the early modern concept of copy was much more elastic than our
modern notion of copyright. Once a title was registered, a stationer
held rights not just to the text in question but to other books on the
same topic and to different versions of the same story.

Once they had received the appropriate external authority and a
license from the Stationers' Company, printers and booksellers sometimes chose to record their proprietary rights in the Company *Registers*.
As Peter Blayney has decisively shown, however, registration was not
a legal requirement, nor was it insisted upon by the Company. It was
simply the most convincing mechanism by which the stationer could
establish ownership of a text or title, and the clearest safeguard against
other publishers attempting to profit from the same, or a similar,
work (Blayney 1997: 400–4). As John Bill put it in his letter to the
Bishop of London, "And this entry in ye hall booke is the commun
and strongest assurance yat Stationers haue, for all their copies, which
is the greatest part of their Estates" (Arber 1967: III, 39). In 1622, six
years after Shakespeare's death, some moves were made to regularize
this *ad hoc* procedure and insist on registration, but these were rarely
enforced, and it was not until 1637 that the Star Chamber issued a
decree stating that every book should "be first lawfully licenced and
authorized . . . and shall be also first entred into the Registers Booke
of the Company of Stationers" (Arber 1967: IV, 530).

To return to our brief case study, on August 29, 1597, Andrew
Wise both licensed and registered his copy of *Richard II*, paying the

standard sum of 6d. for a license, and an additional 4d. to the clerk for registration. Wise may have been optimistically hoping for a bestseller which others would be quick to print if he did not establish his rights. Certainly his was an unusually successful venture in play-book publication, with one edition in 1597, and two new printings following in 1598. As a rule, however, printed drama was a gamble for any publisher. The consistent bestsellers of early modern England were religious texts, school books, and ephemeral products, such as almanacs and ballads. When we bear in mind the fact that, with the exception of items of jobbing printing such as advertisements, anonym-ous proclamations, and mortality bills, over half of all texts printed during our period were religious in content, and that even those that were not explicitly theological often invoked the presence of an all-powerful God, we are reminded of the historical and textual contexts in which the works of Shakespeare must be read: a context that is too easily ignored if the plays are read only alongside other dramatic texts, or selections of lyric verse.

With an eye on the financial risks of overproduction, Peter Blayney has estimated that a first edition of a playbook might consist of some-where between 800 and 1,200 copies (1997: 405–10). A larger edition would, of course, make a greater profit if it sold out reasonably quickly, but it also risked much greater losses if, or often when, it did not. If the first edition did sell out, establishing a demand for the book, the publisher might risk a larger second edition, particularly as the over-heads for copy and licensing were already covered. The trade as a whole was heavily dependent on reprints, and guaranteed sellers were as popular with stationers as they were with readers. Books which were protected by a privilege or patent, and were guaranteed to be in demand either because they were consistently popular (ABCs and almanacs), or because they were to be purchased for churches by order of the crown (certain Bibles, the *Book of Common Prayer*, and Fulke's *Rhemish Testament* in later editions), might run to as many as 2,000 copies. Where books were not printed for profit, but for personal distribution to friends or patrons, numbers might be much lower. In 1577 John Dee had 100 copies of his *General and Rare Memorials* printed by John Day. The first edition of King James's *Basilicon Doron*, printed by Robert Waldegrave in Edinburgh in 1598, ran to only seven copies, two of which still survive.

In the early modern period, as now, stationers had an array of tactics to persuade the customer to part with his or her money. These included furnishing the book with an intriguing title, fronting it with a dramatic woodcut illustration that might have little connection with the subsequent contents, and including a dedication to a noble patron, a practice that seems to have been as often a marketing ploy as a genuine quest for aristocratic favor. Publishers and authors gathered together commendatory verses from friends, acquaintances, and hack writers, and prefaced even unaltered editions with the words "newly corrected." Even the standard trope of unauthorized publication might work to draw in a potential reader, offering the frisson of access to a forbidden text. Stationers paid for the printing of additional copies of title-pages and nailed them to posts or walls.

Not all authors enjoyed this public exposure, at least according to Ben Jonson, who in a verse address to his bookseller begged that his book should not be

> offer'd, as it made sute to be bought;
> Nor have my title-leafe on posts, or walls,
>   Or in cleft-sticks, advanced to make calls
> For termers, or some clerck-like serving-man,
>   Who scarce can spell th'hard names: whose Knight lesse can.
> ("To my bookseller," ll. 6–10)

Here Jonson is repeating the common lament that members of the nobility were more interested in hunting and hawking than in reading, and it is their servants he expects to eye his overexposed texts, even if they are liable to stumble over the most difficult words. But what might Jonson's clerk or trainee lawyer expect to pay for his book, assuming he could both find and read it? In 1598, the Court of Assistants of the Stationers' Company issued an order limiting the price of new books. Books without illustrations should be sold for no more than a penny for two sheets if they were set in pica or English type, and no more than one penny for one-and-a-half sheets if they were set in the smaller brevier or long primer fonts. Peter Blayney has, however, pointed out that these were wholesale prices, which could sometimes be reduced further thanks to trade discounts, and that the ordinary customer could expect to pay approximately 50 percent more before binding (1997: 410). Most play quartos cost around 6d., while the actor Ned Alleyn paid 5d. for a copy of Shakespeare's sonnets in June 1609. A contemporary diarist and courtier, Richard Stonley, paid 12d. for a copy of *Venus and Adonis* 16 years earlier in 1593 (Schoenbaum 1977: 175–6). These prices can be placed in some kind of context if it is remembered that £5 or £6 (somewhere between 200 and 240 quarto playbooks) was a typical annual income for many in the period.

Readers could buy their books from a broad range of outlets. The center of the London, and indeed the national, book trade was St Paul's Churchyard, described by Thomas Nashe as "the peruser of euerie mans works and Exchange of all Authors" (1592, sig. D3r). Other important sites for the early book trade included the area around Westminster Hall, the main concourse leading from Cheapside to Cornhill, and the notorious areas of Little Britain and Smithfield, associated with the production and sale of ballads and other forms of cheap print. Booksellers ranged from those possessing substantial commercial properties, at least two stories high, to street peddlers and mercuries (hawkers or distributors of pamphlets) like the "Termers and Cuntrie chapmen" described by Thomas Middleton in his preface to *The Familie of Loue* (1608). Unlike printing, bookselling was never confined to London. Itinerant peddlers would purchase stocks from the shops that lined London Bridge or Smithfield Market, close to the major routes out of London. Provincial booksellers could also replenish their stock at a series of major book fairs in cities and towns including Oxford, Salisbury, Bristol, Ely, Nottingham, Coventry, and Sturbridge, near Cambridge.

Substantial cities usually boasted at least one bookshop, while other traders both in cities and in smaller towns might carry a few books alongside their usual stock-in-trade. The City of York had its own Company of Stationers and Booksellers, whose regulations were confirmed by the Corporation in 1554. Booksellers in provincial towns sometimes developed strong trading links with London printers, and commissioned texts themselves, stepping into the role of publisher. The London printer Anne Griffin, for example, was at the center of a purchasing and distribution network that covered much of the south of England. Griffin printed one edition of Niccolo Balbani's *The Italian Convert* (1635) with variant issues sold by "H. Hammond of Salisbury," "W. Browne of Dorchester," "J. Cartwrit of Coventry," "E. Dight of Exeter," "P. Whaly of Northampton," "M. Sparke," and "A. More," presumably in London. Another text manufactured by Griffin, *A true and certaine relation of a strange-birth, which was borne at Stone-house in the Parish of Plinmouth* (1635), was produced in two variant issues, one sold by her long-term associate Anne Boler in London and another intended for the local audience catered for by "W. Russell in Plinmouth."

The book trade also crossed national boundaries. Within what is now the United Kingdom, stationers traveled between Edinburgh,

Glasgow, and London to sell or purchase new books. Strong overseas links were maintained with Jesuit centers, such as St Omer and Douai in the Spanish Netherlands, from whence illicit Catholic texts were smuggled into the country. Records suggest that the vast majority of Catholic texts circulating in this period were printed abroad. Individual purchasers and stationers also traveled to some of the major European book fairs, particularly that at Frankfurt, to maintain their libraries or purchase the latest works of humanist learning. The demand for Latin texts was largely met through a tight network of stationers, many of European origin, who maintained strong trading links with the continent, importing large numbers of small-format classics, and smaller numbers of learned texts in folio. Foreign involvement in the Latin trade, always viewed with some suspicion by a protectionist domestic industry, diminished gradually during the period. The crown made a number of attempts to safeguard or create English jobs, particularly through repeated prohibitions on the importation of bound books, as well as limitations on the importation of paper.

Though English presses could not, as a rule, produce the quality or volume of Latin works that their customers demanded, English binders could still stitch and cover them. Despite this, many members of the nobility preferred to take or send their books back to the continent to have them bound by famous craftsmen, although the earl of Leicester showed his support for the domestic trade by employing only English binders to produce his simple brown calf bindings, stamped with his crest, the bear and ragged staff. Until the later part of the period, however, the paper in even a native book had usually to come from the continent, particularly the paper mills of Holland, France, and Italy. Paying attention to the industries of papermaking and bookbinding, and their connection to the politics and economics of publication, brings us finally to call into question the title of this chapter. While it is certainly possible to speak of the publishing trade in Shakespeare's time, it is perhaps more accurate to speak of numerous related publishing trades.

At the beginning of Shakespeare's *King Lear*, in a moment of potent dramatic irony, the aging monarch declares to his assembled court: "We have this hour a constant will to publish / Our daughters' several dowers, that future strife / May be prevented now" (1.1.42–4). As any reader will be quick to realize, Lear, like the narrator of *Lucrece*, is using the term "publish" not in its most usual modern sense, "to place before or offer to the public, now *spec.* by the medium of a book, journal or the like," but in its older sense, "to announce in a formal or official manner; to pronounce (a judicial sentence), to promulgate (a law or edict); to proclaim" (*OED*, defs. 4.b; 2.a). In early modern England, publication did not necessarily imply the reproduction of printed copies. It could mean the act of writing, as when a courtier "published" ("to tell or noise abroad" [*OED*, 1.1.a]) the most recent court gossip in a private letter to his or her friend in the country. It could also, as in *Lear*, mean the act of speaking with the intention of making information, whether news, legal and political proclamations, or scandal, more widely known. Lear's avowed intention is to make public his divisions of the kingdoms; the act of speaking *is* here the act of publishing.

In the world of ballad singers, or itinerant salesmen, like Autolycus in *The Winter's Tale*, the realms of print and oral publication overlapped, as they did too in taverns, coffee houses, and religious meetings of various kinds. Printed texts were made public and disseminated through speech and song, as well as private reading. And, as much recent scholarship has made increasingly clear, it was not just print and orality that overlapped to make up the complex web of publication and communication in early modern England. The manuscript reproduction of texts was still a vital industry. Provincial towns in particular must have been heavily reliant on the work of scriveners to circulate information in multiple copies. Manuscript production continued to thrive well into the late seventeenth century, and texts could be published either through their multiple reproduction in scriptoria or through the gradual dissemination of a copied and recopied text: the primary mode, for example, by which John Donne's poems were published prior to his death. Surviving commonplace books of the period illustrate the diversity of verses, satires, jokes, and recipes that were published to an ever-expanding audience as they passed from hand to hand.

Manuscript circulation did not always imply a restricted readership. Where many authors blamed their unwilling decision to publish on the prior circulation of an illegitimate or faulty copy, Thomas Nashe, in an unusual twist on the standard dedicatory trope of a pirated text, informed his dedicatee, Lady Elizabeth Carey, that

> the vrgent importunitie of a kinde friend of mine (to whom I was sundrie waies beholding) wrested a Coppie from me. That Coppie progressed from one scriueners shop to another, & at length grew so common, that it was readie to bee hung out for one of their signes, like a paire of indentures. (1594: Aijv–r)

Manuscript publication, according to Nashe, has been as effective and pervasive as print. Ben Jonson's 1626 comedy, *The Staple of Newes*, reminds us of the flourishing early modern trade in scribal separates and newsletters, offering an intriguing picture of the dynamics of an early news office, publishing social and political gossip for a wide range of readers.

Many religious books, particularly Catholic texts, circulated widely in manuscript. Even texts which were printed, such as the anonymous *Leicester's Commonwealth* (1584) and Father Robert Persons's *A Conference About the Next Succession* (1594), were often hand copied by would-be owners who did not wish either to purchase or to possess illegal printed texts. At the same time, the act of copying was understood to construct an intimate relationship with the divinely inspired word, and to demonstrate a devout attention to the religious text. In these instances, manuscript and print were not exclusive choices. Texts could, and often did, circulate in both media, as well as through the spoken word.

The very notion of a publishing trade threatens to restrict our understanding of the multiplicity of mechanisms through which texts could be made public, or sent abroad, in early modern England. It also serves to disguise the sheer variety of the industries and processes which came together to produce the early modern book. As D. F. McKenzie reminds us: "Almost all texts of any consequence are the product of the concurrent inter-action of ideologies and institutions, of writers, publishers, printers, binders, wholesalers, travellers, retailers, as well as of the material sources (and their makers and suppliers) of type, paper, cord, and all the appurtenances of a printing house" (1992: 128). The publishing trades of early modern England relied upon such diverse industries as papermaking, metalwork, engraving and woodcut production, the fabric and clothing industries (the eventual source of the rags which made the paper), leatherwork, carpentry, and transport services. An attention to the material detail of the book does not only illuminate our understanding of literary production and ownership, of how and where books were bought and sold, and of the mechanics of printing. It also brings into focus, if just for a moment, the many and varied human transactions and relationships that underlie the act of publication, and the numerous labors that come together to make possible the existence of any circulating text.

Note

1 All references to the works of Shakespeare are from Richard Proudfoot, Ann Thompson, and David Scott Kastan (eds.), *The Arden Shakespeare: Complete Works* (London: Thomson Learning, 2001).

Chapter 2

Reading and Authorship: The Circulation of Shakespeare 1590–1619

Peter Stallybrass and Roger Chartier

In 1991, Paul Bertram and Bernice Kliman edited a *Three-Text Hamlet*, in which they printed the First Quarto, the Second Quarto, and the First Folio of *Hamlet* side by side. The most striking difference between the three texts is between the First Quarto and the other two texts, since it is little more than half their length. In other words, a lot of the First Quarto in this edition is blank space. Few people apart from scholars read the First Quarto today. So why publish it? The first reason is historical. When modern editors publish a "best" text, whether supposedly corresponding to what Shakespeare first wrote or to the theatrical version that was first staged, they are creating something that had no previous existence. Any historical work that takes such a text as its starting point is a form of science fiction, in which the modern edition travels back in time to take its place beside Renaissance manuscript records and printed books, as if the "best" Shakespeare that the editor has just produced was already exerting its influence four hundred years earlier. There are, of course, many reasons for modern editions, two of the most important being for modern stagings of Shakespeare and for various kinds of educational use from primary schools to universities. But a modern edition is just that: an artifact of our own culture (see de Grazia 1991a).

Reading the early printed texts reminds us that the "Shakespeare" that we now treat in the singular has been composed by multiple historical agents (theater companies, actors, publishers, compositors, editors) who have produced the plural Shakespeares that continue to multiply. But the questions of what *Hamlet* we read and how it has been edited are much more than "historical" ones, in the limiting sense of that term. As David Scott Kastan writes, "literature exists . . . only and always in its materializations," which are "the conditions of its meaning rather than merely the containers of it" (Kastan 2001: 4). Even if we could recreate a Shakespearean manuscript, it would be unprintable. It was the responsibility of Renaissance printers to transform writer's scripts into readable texts. In the *Art of Printing*, Joseph Moxon wrote that "a *Compositor* is strictly to follow his *Copy*," but he immediately retracts this by noting that "the carelessness of some good Authors, and the ignorance of other Authors, has forc'd *Printers* to introduce a Custom, which among them is look'd upon as a task and duty incumbent on the *Compositor*, viz. to discern and amend the bad *Spelling* and *Pointing* of his *Copy*, if it be English" (Moxon 1958: 191–2).

The need for the compositor's intervention is revealed by the one piece of a play manuscript that may be in the hand of Shakespeare. If so, it reveals Shakespeare not as "author" but as one of several revisers of a play called *The Book of Sir Thomas More*. Here are two passages as they appear in a modern transcription of the manuscript:

all Shreiue moor moor more Shreue moore
moor *graunt them remoued and graunt that this yo[u]r noyce*
   hath Chidd downe all the matie of Ingland
   ymagin that you see the wretched straingers
   their babyes at their backes, ["and" del.] *w[i]t[h] their poor lugage*
   plodding tooth portes and costes for transportacion
   (Greg 1961: 75–6)

Even though spelling and punctuation were not standardized in Renaissance England, no printing house would put out a play that looked anything like this. In the first example, neither the speech prefix nor the proper name of Sir Thomas More begins with a capital, and the two words that compose the line are spelt five different ways. Moreover, they are entirely unpunctuated. Without the context, it would be impossible to know whether "Sheriff" and "More" are one and the same person or whether "more" is a proper, not a common, noun. There was a reason why Shakespeare (or whoever wrote the manuscript) did not worry too much about such things. Professional dramatists wrote for professional orators [actors], whose job was to translate scripts into performances according to their own exacting standards. Compositors, on the other hand, and sometimes scribes as intermediaries, had to take performance scripts and turn them into readable texts.

"Underpunctuated" scripts *required* collaboration – of the professional actor to phrase the words and, if printed, of the compositor to "point" them (Hammond 1994). The instability of the text, while increasingly emphasized by modern theoretical and editorial practices, is the material result of the multiple agents in the theaters and printing houses, all *readers* of the text, in the making of the performances and books through which spectators and readers encountered specific versions of the script/text. There is no single "original" text that we can find behind the various materializations of *Hamlet*. In all three early editions of *Hamlet*, Horatio responds with fear to the Ghost. But his fear takes different forms: "it horrors mee" (Q1); "it horrowes me" (Q2); "It harrowes me" (F1).[1] As compositors reset the letters, they recomposed the text. Their readings are the material precondition of all later readings.

Acquiring Shakespeare

How did Shakespeare become a printed text in the first place? By 1600, Shakespeare was already a very successful writer. Just how successful is hard to gauge. But his name must have been widely known among London book-readers. In 1593, a poem called *Venus and Adonis* had been printed by Richard Field, one of the best printers in London. A Latin quotation on the title-page put as much distance as possible between Shakespeare, the professional writer for the stage, and Shakespeare the poet:

> *Vilia miretur vulgus: mihi flauus Apollo*
> *Pocula Castalia plena ministret aqua.*

("Let the common herd be amazed by worthless things; but for me let the golden Apollo provide cups full of the water of the Muses." Ovid, *Amores* 1.15.35–6)
   (Shakespeare 1593, title-page)

Although there is no mention of the author on the title-page, this is not an anonymous poem. At the beginning of the pamphlet, there is a dedication "To the Right Honorable Henry Wriothsley, Earle of Southampton, and Baron of Titchfield," signed by a writer who had never claimed authorship in print before: "William Shakespeare."

The assertion that *Venus and Adonis* contained the water of Apollo did not mean that it was only marketed for the elite. On the contrary, it was a cheap pamphlet that would usually be sold unbound for a few pennies. And it made Shakespeare's fame. New editions were printed in 1594, 1595, 1596, and two new editions in 1599. Four new editions of *Venus and Adonis* were published according to their title-pages in 1602 for the bookseller William Leake, who owned the copy, but only one of those editions was definitely printed by him. The other three editions were probably printed by Robert Raworth in about 1607, Henry Lownes in about 1608, and an unknown printer in about 1610. Robert Raworth, the printer of the c. 1607 edition, had no right to the copy. But he clearly thought the poem was so popular and profitable that it was worth taking the risk. It was a miscalculation. In the *Stationers' Company Registers*, the following note was made some time in the 1630s: "Robert Raworth supprest for printing anothers Copy." An earlier note helps clarify the reason for Raworth's suppression: "Master Adam Islip: sold his printing house to Robert Raworth and John Monger (is a compositor) about 26 yeeres since for 140 li. they held it about a yeere and then were supprest (for printing *Venus and Adonis*)" (Jackson 1957: 703, 711). It is the subject of present debate just how popular Shakespeare's plays were at this time, but there was probably no play for which a printer would have been tempted to risk his livelihood in 1607. By 1636, there had been 16 editions of *Venus and Adonis*. That the copies were not only bought but also read is suggested by how few have survived and the bad condition of many of those copies.

The relative impact of Shakespeare's published poems as compared to his published plays during his lifetime is confirmed by the few surviving records of buyers and collectors. The Bodleian Library notoriously excluded vernacular plays and other "baggage books," but when Robert Burton donated his books to Oxford, he included Shakespeare's two narrative poems, both carefully recorded by the Bodleian's librarian, John Rous: "Venus and Adonis by Wm Shakespear Lond." and "The rape of Lucrece by Wm Shakespear Imperfect." Rous recorded not only the title of each book but also the name of the author. After Shakespeare's death, Leonard Digges would write commemorative poems in celebration of Shakespeare's plays both for the 1623 First Folio and for the 1640 *Poems*, in the latter of which he incongruously eulogized the dramatist as opposed to the poet. But while Shakespeare was alive, Digges's only recorded views are of Shakespeare's poems, when he compared Lope de Vega's sonnets to those of "our Will

Shakespeare." The famous actor and theatrical entrepreneur Edward Alleyn left no record of buying any of Shakespeare's plays. But he did purchase *Shake-speares Sonnets* in 1609, the year of the book's publication. And the first record that we have of Shakespeare as an author is Richard Stonley's purchase of "Venus & Adhonay per Shakespeare" on July 12, 1594 (Nelson 2005).

In another early record, Gabriel Harvey wrote in the margins of a book: "The younger sort takes much delight in Shakespeares Venus, & Adonis: but his Lucrece, & his tragedie of Hamlet, Prince of Denmarke, haue it in them, to please the wiser sort" (Nelson 2005: 54). We now assume that Harvey is elevating the reputation of *Lucrece* by coupling it with *Hamlet*. But we should surely read the lines of influence the other way round. A play like *Hamlet* could be rescued from oblivion because it had the virtues of a poem like *Lucrece*. Before 1623, the name of Shakespeare as a published writer was above all connected to the two narrative poems that he had written in the 1590s, probably during a period when the theaters were closed because of the plague.

Much attention has recently been paid to the use of Shakespeare's name on the title-pages of plays in the seventeenth century. And there can be no question that his name did indeed help to sell plays. But to what extent was this an attempt to associate the plays with what was *still* Shakespare's bestselling work: *Venus and Adonis*? If one looks at the few traces left by readers of Shakespeare during his lifetime, there is little evidence that his name was important as a playwright, however popular the plays themselves. William Drummond of Hawthornden drew up a list of the books that he had read in 1606. The books included "Romeo and Iulieta Tragedie"; "loues labors lost comedie"; "The passionate pilgrime"; "The rape of Lucrece"; "A midsommers nights Dream comedie"; "The Tragedie of Locrine" (attributed to Shakespeare on its title-page). But Drummond does not name the writer of any of these books. And there is no trace of Shakespeare in his later reading, suggesting that he thought that *all* the poet-dramatist's work was more suitable for the younger, rather than the wiser, sort. Nevertheless, when Drummond catalogued his books, he implicitly distinguished between the plays and the poems. Scattered among his collection of books in English were "*the tragedie of Romeo & Iulieta*" (no. 30) and "*a midsumer night dreame*" (no. 48). But the two narrative poems were catalogued together: "*Venus & Adon. by Schaksp.*" (no. 18) and "*the rap of Lucrece idem*" (no. 19) (Macdonald 1971: 200). The "authorial" Shakespeare was above all Shakespeare the poet, not Shakespeare the dramatist.

Shakespeare Unbound and Bound

But is "author" the right name for the writer of such popular successes as *Venus and Adonis* and *Lucrece*? If these poems were "the water of the Muses," as the title-page of *Venus and Adonis* claimed, they were certainly not contained within the cups of the golden Apollo. Dedicating *Lucrece* to the earl of Southampton, Shakespeare wrote: "The love I dedicate to your Lordship is without end: wherof this Pamphlet without beginning is but a superfluous Moity." Shakespeare's love is "without end"; his "Pamphlet" is not, as the fate of most of the copies (and perhaps of whole editions) shows. The fact that the quartos of the poems and plays alike were mainly sold unbound is shown both by the loss of all but a few copies and by the fact that many of those remaining copies are missing title-pages, final leaves, or whole gatherings. An unbound pamphlet may be a runaway success, but it is still a form of ephemera.

It was perhaps to avoid the ephemeral status of the quarto that John Harrison the elder, who had published the first edition of *Lucrece* in quarto, reprinted the poem as an octavo in 1598, having already reprinted *Venus and Adonis* as an octavo in 1595 or 1596. The smaller format of the octavo usually carried greater prestige, having been made famous for high-quality, pocket-sized classics by Aldus Manutius at the beginning of the sixteenth century. All the later editions of the two poems up to 1630 were also published as octavos, so it would certainly have been possible to bind the later editions of all three volumes of Shakespeare's poetry (including the 1599 octavo *The Passionate Pilgrim*, attributed to Shakespeare, although the majority of poems are by other hands) together. In fact, an early reader created a quasi-Shakespearean collection of the poetry by binding a 1599 *Venus and Adonis*, a 1600 *Lucrece*, and *The Passionate Pilgrim* (made up from two different 1599 [?] editions) together with a 1600 copy of Thomas Middleton's *The Ghost of Lucrece* and a 1595 copy of *Emaricdulfe. Sonnets written by E.C. Esquier*.[2] It was only through a few such bound miscellanies that most of the few surviving copies of the poems were preserved.

If Shakespeare's poems, his most popular publications, were largely read to death, the same is true of his plays, given their unbound format. From the perspective of 1623, it seems inevitable that Shakespeare-the-dramatist is "not of an age, but for all time." It is, after all, materially true. The Folger Library alone has more than 80 copies of the First Folio. Not surprisingly, given how many copies survive, the First

Folio (and the millions of copies of the "works" that have succeeded it) conditions how we think about Shakespeare as an author. By contrast, the first edition of *Venus and Adonis* survives in a single copy in the Bodleian Library and the first edition of *The Passionate Pilgrim* only survives as a fragment, without a title-page, "completed" with leaves from the second edition, and bound up with the miscellany above. Unbound pamphlets are not the materials of immortality, whatever claims a writer may make about the immortality of verse.

The texts that Shakespeare wrote were published as pamphlets, not bound books. This was true both of the poems that made Shakespeare a famous author and of the plays that, from 1598, capitalized on Shakespeare's name. Only when bound could such ephemera survive. Sir John Harington amassed a collection of 135 printed plays. Most of these plays he bound up into 11 volumes, each volume containing between 9 and 13 plays. Several of these plays are by Shakespeare: *The Merchant of Venice*, *1* and *2 Henry IV*, *Henry V*, *Richard II*, *Richard III*, *Romeo and Juliet*, *The Taming of a Shrew* (if we accept that as canonical), *Much Ado About Nothing*, *Love's Labour's Lost*, *Midsummer Night's Dream*, *Merry Wives of Windsor*, *Henry VIII*, *Hamlet*, *King Lear*, *Pericles*. That Harington bound the books at all shows that he wanted to preserve them as part of his library. And he clearly had the makings of "Shakespeare's Works." But he did not categorize the plays by author. Shakespeare's plays are bound in 6 of the 11 volumes. The first volume, composed of 13 plays, comes closest to an "authorial" anthology, containing Shakespeare's *The Merchant of Venice*, *1* and *2 Henry IV*, *Richard III*, and *Hamlet*, together with *The London Prodigal* and *Locrine*, both of which had been attributed to Shakespeare on their title-pages. But the volume also contains "King Leire.: old:," so called to distinguish it from "King Leyr. W. Sh.," three plays by or partly by Ben Jonson, George Chapman's *Monsieur d'Olive*, and the anonymous *Trial of Chivalry*. And Harington did not record the names of any of the playwrights in this volume with the single exception of "Ben: Iohnson" as the author of *Sejanus*.

Of the 130 plays that Harington bound, only 17 are attributed to an author. Harington, one of the most knowledgeable courtiers in literary matters and a well-known writer, names Shakespeare as the author of only four plays – *King Lear*, *The Merry Wives*, *A Yorkshire Tragedy*, and *A Puritan Widow* – two of which are now generally believed to be apocryphal. Yet Harington's binding of playbooks also reveals that authorship played no role in the organization of his collection. All 11 of his volumes of playbooks are miscellanies, in which playwrights like Ben Jonson and Shakespeare rub sides with Edward Sharpham, Barnabe Barnes, and a great majority of anonymous plays (a category which includes most of the plays now attributed to famous authors) (Greg 1957: 1306–13).

It is worth dwelling on Harington's library in such detail because it suggests that what playwrights shared was more interesting than what differentiated them. The material basis for the creation of the individual author's works is the practice of binding his or her texts together with each other. So elementary is this observation that it normally passes unnoticed. But when play-pamphlets from the Renaissance have survived, it is usually because collectors treated them *as plays* rather than as authored texts and bound them together as miscellanies.

The 1623 First Folio of Shakespeare's plays has had such a powerful impact upon the construction of Shakespeare's authorship because it marketed Shakespeare in bound volumes in which he was *bound with himself*. But the First Folio was preceded in 1619 by 10 "Shakespeare" quartos published by Thomas Pavier and printed by William Jaggard. Even though each play had a separate title-page (most of them with false information about printing and date of publication), the first three plays were printed with continuous signatures, and it is clear that Pavier intended to sell all 10 plays bound together (see Murphy 2003: 255–8). If we refrain from looking back at Pavier's project from the canonical perspective of 1623, we can see that it was in sharp contrast with Harington's method of binding miscellaneous playbooks together. Pavier imagined a collection of plays that, like the First Folio, had as its organizing principle a single author: the professional playwright, William Shakespeare. But Pavier's canon had more in common with Harington's "Shakespeare" plays than with the canon of 1623. To six plays that were reprinted in the First Folio (three in very different forms), Pavier added *Pericles* (not published in F1 but now at least semi-canonical) and two plays that are now considered apocryphal: *A Yorkshire Tragedy* (named on the title-page as *"Written by* W. Shakspeare" in the 1608 Quarto and initialed with "W. S." by Harington on his list) and *The First Part of the True and Honorable History of the Life of Sir Iohn Old-Castle* (first published by Thomas Pavier with no named author in 1600). Pavier thus printed variant texts of four of the plays that are part of the F1 canon and three plays excluded from its canon. But his project was the first serious attempt to materialize Shakespeare as a dramatic author in the form of a bound book. Prior to Pavier, Shakespeare's complete texts appeared only in the perishable and disposable form of pamphlets.

Commonplacing Shakespeare

If Shakespeare's individual poems and plays were only published in perishable form, fragments of them began to circulate in printed commonplace books in the same period that Shakespeare's name was beginning to appear on the title-pages of plays. These commonplace books of "English poesy" were part of a larger project under the patronage of John Bodenham, a member of the London Grocers' Company, who, with the help of others, decided to transform his own extensive reading notes into printed commonplace books. In 1597, the publisher and bookseller Nicholas Ling organized Bodenham's reading of classical and Christian "authorities" into *Politeuphuia. Wits Common Wealth*, a "methodicall collection of the most choice and select admonitions and sentences, compendiously drawne from infinite varietie, diuine, historicall, poeticall, politique, morrall, and humane" (Ling and Bodenham 1597: sig. A2–A2v). *Politeuphuia* provided the explicit model for Francis Meres's *Palladis Tamia. Wits Treasury*, published the following year, which, as the title-pages announced, constituted *"the Second Part of Wits Common Wealth."* Meres's commonplace book was, he claimed, a "stalke of the same stemme" as *Politeuphuia* (Meres 1598: sig. A3v). But Meres goes further than Ling in explicitly putting modern vernacular poets on a par with the Greek and Roman classics.

It has taken a historian of Latin commonplace books to recognize how radical a departure this was. In *Printed Commonplace-Books and the Structuring of Renaissance Thought*, Ann Moss writes:

> Before the final years of the sixteenth century there is little evidence that vernacular literature (as distinct from vernacular translations, proverbs, and the sayings of important historical figures) had acquired sufficient status to be excerpted for commonplace-books, at least in print. Linguistically, the exclusively Latin (and Greek) culture of the schoolroom was radically different from the culture outside, and the tool for probing, analysing, storing, indexing, and memorizing school culture was the Latin commonplace-book. (Moss 1996: 209)

But for Meres, "our English Poets" are directly comparable to "the Greek, Latine, and Italian Poets." Beginning with Chaucer, Gower, and Lydgate, by way of "our rarest Poet," Sir Philip Sidney, and the "most exquisit wit" of "so diuine a Poet" as Edmund Spenser, Meres arrives at Shakespeare:

> As *Euripedes* is the most sententious among the Greeke Poets: so is *Warner* among our English Poets.
>
> As the soule of *Euphorbus* was thought to liue in *Pythagoras*: so the sweete wittie soule of *Ouid* liues in mellifluous & hony-tongued *Shakespeare*, witnesse his *Venus* and *Adonis*, his *Lucrece*, his sugred Sonnets among his priuate friends, &c.
>
> As *Platus* and *Seneca* are accounted the best for Comedy and Tragedy among the Latines: so *Shakespeare* among ye English is the most excellent in both kinds for the stage; for Comedy, witnes his *Gentlemen of Verona*, his *Errors*, his *Loue labors lost*, his *Loue labours wonne*, his *Midsummers night dreame*, & his *Merchant of Venice*: for Tragedy his *Richard the 2. Richard the 3. Henry the 4. King Iohn, Titus Andronicus* and his *Romeo and Iuliet*.
>
> As *Epius Stolo* said, that the Muses would speake with *Plautus* tongue, if they would speake Latin: so I say that the Muses would speake with *Shakespeares* fine filed phrase, if they would speake English. (Meres 1598: sig. Nn7, Oo1v–Oo2)

Meres praises Shakespeare not only as the "mellifluous & honytongued" author of the narrative poems and the as yet unprinted "sugred Sonnets," circulating "among his priuate friends," but also as a dramatist (see Erne 2003: 65–70).

Meres's praise, however, was not aimed at elevating the status of professional playwrights but at establishing a canon of English poetry. To do that, it was necessary to detach Shakespeare's scripts from the theater and, indeed, from dramatic action altogether and to establish Shakespeare himself as an "authority" on a par with the classical authorities: in other words, to show that Shakespeare belonged with Cicero and Aristotle. The derivativeness of Meres's criticism has obscured what was radical about the whole program that Bodenham set in motion: namely, to use popular, contemporary writers as suitable materials for commonplacing, a practice that had been based exclusively on Christian and classical "authorities."

In fact, Meres's volume pales beside Bodenham's larger project. In 1600, A. M. (Anthony Munday) edited the notes that Bodenham had gathered from his reading of English poets to create a commonplace book drawn entirely from contemporary vernacular writers. The book, published as *Bel-vedére, or, The Garden of the Muses*, gave a particular significance to what had already become a commonplace about Shakespeare: that he was "Honie-tong'd *Shakespeare*" (John Weever, 1595), "Sweet Shakspeare" (William Covell, 1595), "mellifluous and honytongued" (Meres, 1598), "Sweete Mr. Shakespeare" (1600) (Ingleby et al. 1932: I, 24, 23, 67). Shakespeare was sweet and honey-tongued because, like Bodenham, he knew how to suck the nectar out of other people's books. The bee, gathering the nectar of other people's flowers, was the model for reader and writer alike. Munday praised "his louing and approoued good Friend, *M. Iohn Bodenham*," who, never having been to university (like Shakespeare), was nevertheless "First causer and collectour of these floures":

> Like to the Bee, thou euery where didst rome,
> Spending thy spirits in laborious care:
> And nightly brought'st thy gather'd hony home. . . .

Or, as William Rankins writes, "the Muses Garden" is a

> planted Eden of collected sweets,
> Cropt from the bosome of the fertile ground,
> Where Science with her honey-current greets
> The sacred Sisters.

And Richard Hathway in the final laudatory poem claims that "this Volume" is "The hiue where many Bees their honey bring" (Bodenham and Munday 1600: sig. A7, A8).

The analogy between the reader and the bee is, in the positive sense that the Renaissance reserved for the term, the commonplace of commonplacing. The bee requires materials from which to manufacture sweetness, and it works in three stages: first, it selects from all the flowers that it visits only the best; then it returns to the hive and sorts the nectar into different, discrete cells; and finally, it transforms the nectar into honey. The three practices of the bee provided the necessary model for the relation between reading and writing. Like the bee, the reader selected from the flowers of his of her reading, noting down the important passages in the margins of the books being read and/or in a "waste book," in which the passages were written down as they were encountered. But once the "best things" had been selected, they should then be transferred into a commonplace book, organized under topical headings either alphabetically or with an index to make specific passages easily retrievable. Only then, when one's reading had been inventoried, did one have the materials of invention. For Bodenham, the organization of his reading notes into printed books was itself the work of invention.

But there were multiple different ways of inventorying one's reading. The *Bel-vedére, or, The Garden of the Muses* is itself a formal exercise in the productiveness of constraints: every heading in *Bel-vedére* is divided into three parts (definitions, similes ["As . . . so . . ."], examples ["*Aristides* so loued Equitie . . ."; "*Catilines* wicked life . . ."]); no "sentence" is of more than two lines (and most are of one); and every line is composed of 10 syllables. Although all the quotations are anonymous, the authors from whom they are drawn are named in the epistle and compose a canon of modern English writing drawn from the published works of "Thomas, Earl of Surrey, The Lord Marquis of Winchester, Mary, Countess of Pembroke, Sir Philip Sidney," the "priuate labours and translations" as well as the published work of other writers, and the works of "Moderne and extant Poets." It is here that "William Shakspeare" appears, below Spenser, Constable, Daniel, Lodge, Watson, Drayton, Davies, Thomas Hudson, Henry Locke "Esquier," Marston, Marlowe, and Jonson, and above Churchyard, Nashe, Kyd, Peele, Greene, Sylvester, Breton, Markham, Thomas Storer, Robert Wilmot, Middleton, and Barnefield (Bodenham and Munday 1600: sig. A3v–A5v).

Shakespeare thus emerges as a canonical English poet in a bound volume neither through poems nor through his plays but rather through individual "sentences" (of 10 or 20 syllables) extracted from his works and organized under topical headings. There is an important feature of *Bel-vedére*, though, that materially links it back to the 1594 publication of *Lucrece* (and to its subsequent reprintings in the sixteenth century). *Lucrece* was printed with quotation marks in the margins beside specific passages, thus emphasizing them as suitable for memorization and/or collection in a commonplace book. As Ann Moss notes,

> Very specifically related to commonplace-books since their inception were the marginal markers, usually some form of "quotation mark," used to signal lines worth noting, memorizing, and extracting for insertion in the reader's commonplace-book. . . . "Quotation marks" used in this way proliferated in both Latin and vernacular literary texts printed in the late sixteenth and early part of the seventeenth century, and did so for the very sound commercial reason that they served the habit of looking for exceptional material. They are the printed equivalent of the manuscript marginal pointers and underlinings so frequently made in printed books at the same time for the same purpose. (Moss 1996: 210–11)

Lucrece, already marked up for commonplacing, was by far Bodenham's most important source for the quotations he took from Shakespeare in

Bel-vedére. He took 88 quotations from Shakespeare's plays but he took 91 from *Lucrece* alone (see Crawford 1932b). The typographic device that signaled the commonplaces in *Lucrece* made it explicit that this poem, even if it only appeared as a "Pamphlet," contained the nectar for a bee like Bodenham to collect, reorganize, and disseminate. We can now give new meaning to Gabriel Harvey's claim that "The younger sort takes much delight in Shakespeares Venus, & Adonis: but his Lucrece, & his tragedie of Hamlet, Prince of Denmarke, haue it in them, to please the wiser sort." Harvey was one of the greatest commonplacers of his day and he recognized in both *Lucrece* and *Hamlet* suitable material for the commonplace books of the "wiser sort."[3] And *Lucrece* had been printed to *mark* its suitability for serious reading.

Even though the marking device for commonplaces is typographically the same as what we now call "quotation marks," it serves exactly the opposite function, as Margreta de Grazia has brilliantly shown. Modern quotation marks serve to fence off speech as private property (what *you* say as opposed to what *I* say), whereas Renaissance "quotation marks" (which we will from now on call "commonplace markers") note the passages that can and should be noted down by readers for their own reuse. In other words, commonplace markers materialize the *opposite* of intellectual ownership, emphasizing language as communal property (see de Grazia 1991a, 1991b). When that language was Latin, the "community" was restrictively defined by access to schooling. Commonplaces, in other words, had not originally meant proverbial wisdom but rather the cultivated knowledge of the "literate" (meaning, those who knew Latin). By printing *Lucrece* with commonplace markers in 1594, Richard Field produced a book that drew attention to the fact that it had already been read as a canonical text.

By whom had it been read and marked up? We do not know. But we can show that this "already-read" *Lucrece* had a direct impact upon Bodenham in his own reading of the poem.[4] Here are three stanzas from Field's 1594 edition of Shakespeare's *Lucrece* that had been heavily annotated with printed commonplace markers.

> The little birds that tune their mornings ioy,
> Make her mones mad, with their sweet melodie,
> "For mirth doth search the bottome of annoy,
> "Sad soules are slaine in merrie companie,
> "Griefe best is pleas'd with griefes societie;
>   "True sorrow then is feelinglie suffiz'd,
>   "When with like semblance it is simpathiz'd.

"Tis double death to drowne in ken of shore,
"He ten times pines, that pines beholding food,
"To see the salue doth make the wound ake more:
"Great griefe greeues most at that wold do it good;
"Deepe woes rowle forward like a gentle flood,
   Who being stopt, the bou[n]ding banks oreflowes,
   Griefe dallied with, nor law, nor limit knowes.

You mocking Birds (quoth she) your tunes intombe
Within your hollow swelling feathered breasts,
And in my hearing be you mute and dumbe,
My restlesse discord loues no stops nor rests:
"A woefull Hostesse brookes not merrie guests.
   Ralish your nimble notes to pleasing eares,
   "Distres likes du[m]ps whe[n] time is kept with teares.
   (Shakespeare 1594, sig. H3v, ll. 1107–27)

From these three stanzas, Bodenham selected no fewer than 11 different "sentences," including all but two of the marked lines, and distributed them under three different headings: "Of Pleasure" ("For mirth doth search the bottome of annoy"); "Of Death" ("Tis double death to drowne in ken of shore"); "Of Griefe" (for all the other selections) (Bodenham and Munday 1600: 203, 142, 232). Even the several lines from the three stanzas that Bodenham commonplaced under "Griefe" were organized discontinuously into one- and two-line units, interspersed with other quotations, drawn from other parts of *Lucrece* and *Richard II*, and from other writers.

Although the "authorities" are listed at the beginning of *Bel-vedére*, the radical fragmentation of the sentences, together with their anonymity, worked against authorship as a relevant category, since it broke poems and plays down into the commonplaces out of which they had been constructed in the first place. Nevertheless, *Bel-vedére* established a novel conception of commonplacing, no longer comparing living writers to the classics, as Meres had done in 1598, but taking "Moderne and extant Poets," who wrote in the culturally and geographically marginal vernacular of English, as suitable authorities on which to base an entire commonplace book.

In the same year that Ling published *Bel-vedére*, he also published Robert Allott's *Englands Parnassus: or the Choysest Flowers of our Moderne Poets*. In *Englands Parnassus*, as in *Bel-vedére*, Shakespeare is one of a whole canon of modern English poets (with Spenser particularly prominent) but he is well represented, with 13 quotations from *Romeo and Juliet*, seven from *Richard II*, five from *Richard III*, three from *Love's Labour's Lost*, and two from *1 Henry IV*. The main emphasis, however, falls upon the narrative poems, with 26 quotations from *Venus and Adonis* and 39 from *Lucrece*, again by far the most popular text. As in *Bel-vedére*, the poems heavily outweigh the plays (65 to 30), the more so since some of the passages from *Lucrece* are longer than anything from the plays. But there are two major differences between *Englands Parnassus* and *Bel-vedére*. In *Bel-vedére*, Bodenham and Munday literalized the connection between "sentence" as commonplace and "sentence" as grammatical unit by making the two coincide; in *Englands Parnassus*, Allott breaks that connection much of the time, occasionally quoting so much that the passages tend to lose their function *as* commonplaces on specific topics. Second, the great majority of passages in Allott's *Parnassus*, however short, are followed by the poet's name.

It is perhaps the passages from the plays that give the clearest idea of what was involved in Allott's commonplacing. In Q1 *Richard III*, there is the following exchange between the Duchess of York and Queen Elizabeth:

Du.   Why should calamitie be ful of words?
Qu.   Windie atturnies to your Client woes,
      Aerie succeeders of intestate ioies,
      Poore breathing Orators of miseries,
      Let them haue scope, though what they do impart,
      Helpe not at al, yet do they ease the hart.
      (Shakespeare 1597a: sig. I4v, 4.4.126–31)

This becomes in *Englands Parnassus*:

                    — Words
          Windie atturnies of our clyent woes,
          Ayery succeeders of intestate ioyes
          Poore breathing Orators of miseries,
          Let them haue scope, though what it do impart,
          Helpe not at all, yet doth it ease the heart.
                    W. Sh.
          (Allott 1600: 307)

Placed under the topic heading "Words," the aim of this selection is antithetical to a literary or dramatic reading that would seek to recall character and context. It is the *perspective*, not the *speaker*, that matters, a perspective that can now be appropriated for a range of uses that have no connection to Queen Elizabeth's interactions with the Duchess of York. This change of function is signaled both by the transformation of the words of the two dramatic characters into a single speech and by the change of "*your* Client woes" to "*our* clyent woes." The perspective needs to be generalized not because it is exhaustive. On the contrary, the sheer copiousness of *Englands Parnassus*, as of most commonplace books, makes a virtue of the multiplication of contrasting and conflicting perspectives on a single topic.

The turning of selected passages into a commonplace book is the work of Allott as reader, note-taker, and compiler. The *re*attachment of commonplaces is the work of the reader, whether for eloquent speech, composition of a letter or poem, meditation or consolation, or any other unforeseeable use, which Allot has partially foreseen to the extent that he has worked precisely to make such reattachments possible (see Roberts 2003: 130–1). Sententiae do not belong to Hamlet, or Polonius, or Gertrude (any more than they belong to Shakespeare, except in so far as Allott himself and the reader, if he or she pleases, forge such a connection). But Allott undoubtedly encourages the reader to say (and note), "As Shakespeare says . . . ," not only by his repeated naming of sources but also by the greater length of some of the quotations that take the speech or stanza(s) as the relevant units rather than the sentence.

One can see the different strategies of the two collections by comparing the same line as it appears in each of them. Both books use the line "Tis double death to drowne in ken of shore" from *Lucrece*. Here is how it appears in the 1594 edition of Shakespeare's poem:

> "Tis double death to drowne in ken of shore,
> "He ten times pines, that pines beholding food,
> "To see the salue doth make the wound ake more:
> "Great griefe greeues most at that wold do it good;
> "Deepe woes rowle forward like a gentle flood,
>   Who being stopt, the bounding banks oreflowes,
>   Griefe dallied with, nor law, nor limit knowes.
>   (Shakespeare 1594: sig. H3v, ll. 1114–20)

Bodenham extracted the single line, "Tis double death to drowne in ken of shore," placing it under the heading "Of Griefe" as a discrete sentence. The quotation immediately before it has been extracted from Samuel Daniel's *The Tragedie of Cleopatra* (Daniel 1594: sig. L8):

Neere death he stands, that stands too neere a crowne.
It's double death to drowne in ken of shoare.
(Bodenham and Munday 1600: 232)

To emphasize the line from *Lucrece* as a free-standing sentence, Bodenham changes the end-of-line comma of *Lucrece* to a period and changes
"Tis" to "It's." Allott selects the same line under the heading of "Woe":

Tis double death to drowne in ken of shore,
He ten times pines, that pines beholding food:
To see the salue doth make the wound ake more,
Great griefe greeue most at that would doe it good,
Deere woes rowle forwarde like a gentle flood:
Who being stopt, the bounden bankes ore flowes,
Greefe dallied with, nor law nor limmit knowes.
Idem. [referring to "*W. Shakespeare*" two passages above, the second
passage also being marked *Idem*]
(Allott 1600: 306)

Allott, unlike Bodenham, quotes the whole stanza, not just the single
line about "double death," and he assigns the author. Like *Bel-vedére*,
however, *Englands Parnassus* deletes all of *Lucrece*'s commonplace
markers, for the obvious reason that the extraction of the passage has
already fulfilled the markers' function.

Bodenham, Ling, Munday, Allott, and the printers they worked
with formed, reformed, and disseminated Shakespeare. The author
that they constructed, however, bears little relation to Shakespeare's
modern canonical identity as playwright and poet. If the Shakespeare
of the commonplace books is "not of an age, but for all time," it is
because he can be transformed into reusable fragments. These books
collect "the Choysest Flowers of our Modern Poets" and organize
selections for the appropriation of readers. Such books were by no
means antithetical to the reading and writing of whole works. Nicholas
Ling, who played such a central role in the organization and publication of Bodenham's reading notes, was also the publisher of both Q1
and Q2 *Hamlet*. By 1607, he also owned the copy to *Romeo and Juliet*,
Love's Labour's Lost, "the taming of A Shrew," works by Greene, Lodge,
Nashe, and Munday, and 11 separate titles by Michael Drayton that
he gathered together and entered in the *Stationers' Register* as "Mr
Draytons poemes" (Arber 1967: III, 147, 161). As this latter project
shows, Ling was involved, if on a much smaller scale, in the same
kind of project as the compilers and publishers of the First Folio,

bringing the smaller pieces of Drayton's "scattered limbs" into a single octavo volume that would bind an author with no one but himself.

But the commonplace books that Ling also published give us an extraordinary insight into how poems, plays, and "works" were *read* in early modern England. They were read above all for reuse in the form of fragments. *Hamlet* was a very successful play in the seventeenth century but it was massively outsold by Ling's single most popular publication: *Politeuphuia*, the commonplace book that Ling himself had helped to compile from Bodenham's reading notes. And when Q1 and Q2 *Hamlet* were published by Ling in 1603 and 1604–5 respectively, their relation to the new practice of commonplacing vernacular poetry that Bodenham had done so much to promote was materialized in the traces of two separate readings of the plays (by actors, scribes, compositors, correctors, publishers, compilers, whomever). The traces are the commonplace markers besides specific passages, markers that encourage the extraction of the lines from their existing context and their storage for later reuse.

Q1 (Corambis [transformed into Polonius in Q2] and Ofelia]):

Cor. "Be thou familiar, but by no meanes vulgare;
        "Those friends thou hast, and their adoptions tried,
        "Graple them to thee with a hoope of steele . . .
        (Shakespeare 1603: sig. C2, 1.3.61–78)

Q2 (Laertes):

        "The chariest maide is prodigall inough
        If she vnmaske her butie to the Moone
        "Vertue it selfe scapes not calumnious strokes
        "The canker gaules the infants of the spring . . .
        (Shakespeare 1604: sig. C3v, 1.3.36–9)

Q2 (Gertrude):

Quee. "To my sicke soule, as sinnes true nature is,
        "Each toy seemes prologue to some great amisse,
        "So full of artlesse iealousie is guilt,
        "It spills it selfe, in fearing to be spylt.
        (Shakespeare 1604: sig. K4, 4.5.17–20)

It is striking that none of Hamlet's lines is marked up in either Q1 or Q2. In the commonplace tradition, Hamlet would long be over-shadowed by Polonius, or rather by Polonius's language, since the dramatic character is displaced in the appropriation of the lines by the reader. The later emphasis upon character has effaced the way in which Shakespeare was transformed into an "authority": as that author of fragments, "the Choysest Flowers" of the "mellifluous and hony-tongued," "Sweete Mr. Shakespeare."

The Bodenham–Meres–Ling–Munday–Allott project had astonish-ingly rapid effects upon the publication of "reading" texts of plays that had been written for the professional theater. Prior to 1600, no such play had ever been printed with commonplace markers, although it is notable that the first vernacular text to be so marked was indeed a play (*Gorboduc*), written by two young lawyers for performance at the Christmas revels of the Inner Temple in 1561–2. During the rest of the sixteenth century, other plays written by amateurs or by profes-sionals but not for public performance were also printed with com-monplace markers. In the 1580s and 1590s, such markers began to be used increasingly for vernacular poetry and, for the first time, for a vernacular prose work (Sir Philip Sidney's 1590 *The Countesse of Pembrokes Arcadia*). Before 1600, G. K. Hunter (1951–2) records 20 separate titles printed with commonplace markers, none of which was a play written for the professional theater.[5]

But between 1600 and 1610, there was a remarkable transforma-tion: of 40 titles printed with commonplace markers, 29 were plays written by professional dramatists, mostly for the children's compan-ies but also for the Chamberlain's Men/King's Men. The first such play was Ben Jonson's *Euery Man Ovt of his Hvmovr*, which was pub-lished in 1600 in three separate editions, one of which was by Nicholas Ling. By the time that Q1 *Hamlet* was published in 1603, seven other professional plays had been printed with commonplace markers. It is worth stressing that such markers indicate that the plays were published *preread*, and it is indeed probable that the circle round Bodenham, who had access to some texts *prior to publication*, was one of the sources for the printers' copies of these plays.[6] It should equally be stressed that Ling himself was the publisher of only one of the commonplaced plays apart from *Hamlet*. In fact, a minimum of 13 printers and 24 booksellers were involved in their publication, to judge from their title-pages and the ascriptions in the *ESTC*. When the students of St John's College, Cambridge, mocked not only the pro-fessional dramatists but above all John Bodenham in their *Parnassus* plays, they were responding to the beginnings of a direct challenge to the primacy of a Latin commonplace tradition and its promoters and guardians, the universities (Anon. 1606: sig. B).

In 1600, Bodenham, a grocer who had never been to university, had enlisted publishers, writers, and compliers to establish a canon of vernacular poets that included professional dramatists, even if Shakespeare continued to be represented primarily through his narrative poems, and above all *Lucrece*. In the next 10 years, however, it was to be above all plays for the professional theater that were marked up as the sources of reusable "sentences." And when in 1655 John Cotgrave published *The English Treasury of Wit and Language*, the contents were gathered "[o]ut of the most and best, of our English Drammatick Poems; Methodically digested into Common Places for Generall Use." Shakespeare is well represented, the quotations now taken from the folio of his gathered plays. The poems no longer find a place in Cotgrave's collection, any more than they did in the folios. But under "Of Chastity, Continence," one finds Laertes's speech to Ophelia, which had been noted with printed commonplace markers in Q2 *Hamlet* (Cotgrave 1655: 42). And although the "digested" passages from the plays are printed without attribution, a contemporary reader has written in attributions to many of the sententiae: "Shakespears Timon"; "Shakespear's Julius Caesar"; "Richard Second Shakespear's." But despite Cotgrave's heavy use of it, the folio does not yet define the canon of Shakespeare's plays. The reader has marked not only four references to "Shakespear's Pericles" but also seven references to "Shakespears Puritan" (*A Puritan Widow*, attributed to Shakespeare in Pavier's "collected works"): seven passages from *The Puritan Widow* compared to four passages from *King Lear* (only three of which have been attributed to the play by the reader) (Ingleby et al. 1932: II, 47–53). By 1655, Shakespeare's plays provided authoritative sources for sententiae, but what constituted the canon of his plays was still radically unsettled.

Whatever the canon, it was increasingly the plays attributed to Shakespeare rather than the poems that were quoted. And specific characters from the plays began to take on separate lives. In the *Shakespeare Allusion-Book*, there is an appendix that lists the plays and poems in order of the number of allusions to each during the seventeenth century. "For the purposes of this Index," a headnote reads, "Falstaff is treated as a work." As a "work," "Falstaff" ranks second only to *Hamlet* (Ingleby et al. 1932: II, 536). "Character," in other words, had begun to assume a dominant place in the reception of Shakespeare's plays. In his 1728 edition of Shakespeare, Alexander

Pope reaffirmed the centrality of "character" to Shakespeare's genius, claiming that "every single character in *Shakespear* is as much an Individual, as those in Life itself." But he also suggested a quite different way of reading Shakespeare, one that had been marked out in Nicholas Ling's Q1 and Q2 *Hamlet*: "Some of the most shining passages are distinguish'd by comma's in the margin; and where the beauty lay not in particulars but in the whole, a star is prefix'd to the scene" (I, xxiv).

Like Q1, Pope used quotation marks beside Polonius's advice to Laertes to note a "shining" passage, worthy of particular attention. Hanmer and Warburton followed Pope's example in marking the most quotable passages in Shakespeare – passages that were quotable not because they "belonged" to a specific character and context but, on the contrary, because they were extractable and could be "Methodically digested into Common Places for Generall Use," as Cotgrave put it (see de Grazia 1991a: 215–16). In 1724, another commonplace book of dramatic fragments, organized by topic, was printed in London as a *Thesaurus Dramaticus*, "containing all the celebrated passages, soliloquies, similies, descriptions, and other poetical beauties in the body of English plays, . . . digested under proper topics" (Anon. 1724). Even as the Shakespearean folios and subsequent *Works* began to constitute a bound, canonical author, the commonplace books that Bodenham and his collaborators published in 1600 initiated the dissemination of Shakespeare as fragmentary quotations scattered under topical headings, quotations that oscillated between defining the genius of Shakespeare and being an unattributable part of the "Generall Use" of English.

Notes

1 *The Three-Text Hamlet*, TLN 56, 1.1.44. All quotations from Shakespeare are keyed by act, scene, and line numbers to *The Riverside Shakespeare*, ed. G. Blakemore Evans (Boston: Houghton Mifflin, 1974, second edition 1997).
2 Folger Shakespeare Library, STC 22341.8/22342, 22347, 17885.5, 4268, 22358a (in order of binding).
3 On Harvey's commonplacing, see Stern (1979); Jardine and Grafton (1990). On the commonplace tradition more generally, see particularly de Grazia (1991a, 1991b, 1994). The criticisms of de Grazia by King (2004) suggest some revisions to de Grazia's argument but they do not satisfactorily address her central points. See also William Sherman's important analysis of the tradition (forthcoming).

4 For an analysis of the shift from commonplacing to narrative readings of
   Lucrece, implied by the 1616 and 1655 editions, see Roberts (2003: 113–
   29).
5 We are indebted to Hunter's article throughout.
6 In *Bel-vedére*, Bodenham specifically claims that he has drawn upon "priuat"
   manuscripts, "according as they could be obtained by sight, or fauour of
   copying" (Bodenham and Munday 1600: sig. A4v). These include lines
   from some poems that have been preserved in the Harleian and Egerton
   mss. And Allott's *Englands Parnassus* includes extracts from Ben Jonson's
   then unpublished poems and plays *Euery Man in his Hvmovr*, as well as
   from at least one other play that was never printed. See Allott (1600:
   xxix–xxxiii).

Chapter 3

Shakespeare Writ Small: Early Single Editions of Shakespeare's Plays

Thomas L. Berger

The world is obliged to nod approvingly at, if not kneel to, Shake-speare's folios, those collections of 36 plays first printed in 1623, then again in 1632, 1663–4,[1] and 1685. Shakespeare's earliest dramatic publications, with or without his approval, with or without his active interest, were printed individually in a quarto format (half the size of a folio), a sheet of paper printed on both sides, folded twice to yield four leaves (or eight pages). These quartos were by our standards large books, the quarto leaf (yielding two pages) being about the size of a modern magazine or, perhaps more appropriately, a newsstand comic book. The shortest of Shakespeare's plays, *The Comedy of Errors*, occupies a little over 15 double-columned pages in the First Folio. The longest, the second quarto of *Hamlet*, occupies 64 quarto pages in its short version of 1603, 104 quarto pages in the longer version of 1604, and just over 28 pages in the First Folio. Between these extremes lie the lengths of the rest of his published dramatic output.

The origins of many of these quarto editions are often difficult to determine. Textual historians, no less paranoid than the average citizen, are quick to sniff out corruption and foul play. The usual process of publication, a process that admits for many variations, legal and illegal, has someone from the Lord Chamberlain's Men or the King's Men approaching a stationer (a member of the Stationers' Company, be he or she a printer, a bookseller, or what we now call a "publisher") with a manuscript to request that he or she oversee the production of a printed playtext. The seller is then, by and large, no longer part of the production process. The stationer enters the play in the *Stationers'*

Register. On July 26, 1602, for example, the *Register* reads: "*Ent. J. Robertes: lic. Pasfeild: a booke called the Revenge of Hamlett Prince Denmarke, as yt was latelie acted by the Lord Chamberleyn his servants.*" Once the text was entered (and a goodly number of extant early modern English books have no record of entry), it was approved for publication; any legal squabbles could be settled at the court of the Stationers' Company. The holder of the entrance held the "copyright"; he or she could transfer that right to another stationer. The myriad variations on the process oversimplified above are witnessed in the records of the court of the Stationers' Company, stationers being no less litigious than the rest of the population.

Which play of Shakespeare's was published first is, like so much about anything having to do with Shakespeare's plays, a matter of some dispute. Was it *The First and Second Part of the Troublesome Reign of John King of England*, first printed in 1591 with "W. Sh." appearing on the title-page of a 1611 edition, a play thought to be an early version of the Folio's *King John*? Or was it *Titus Andronicus*, published in three quarto editions starting in 1594 before its appearance in the First Folio of 1623, each early edition lacking Shakespeare's name on its title-page? The apocryphal *Locrine*, first printed in 1595 with "By VV. S." on its title-page, was excluded from the First Folio but appeared in the second issue of the Third Folio in 1664, and again in the Fourth Folio of 1685. A recent entry in the Shakespeare canon sweepstakes, *The Reign of King Edward the Third*, appeared in 1596 and again in 1599; neither edition mentions an author (or, for that matter, a company of players, or a theater). First prize for first Shakespeare seems, like other first prizes, to be "contested," with scholars ever willing to be judge and jury at the same time.

By 1598, however, with the appearance of the first quarto of *Love's Labour's Lost* and the second quartos of *Richard II* and *Richard III*, all of which have Shakespeare's name on their title-pages, William Shakespeare had arrived as an "author," something many published playwrights never achieved, something many published playwrights, perhaps Shakespeare, never sought.[2] Insofar as there is no record that Shakespeare ever received any direct remuneration for the publication of his plays (as opposed to *Venus and Adonis* in sixteen editions and *Rape of Lucrece* in eight editions, where the dedicatee might, or might not, have rewarded him indirectly), Shakespeare's income came from the stage, from paying audiences of varying sorts.

The title-pages of early modern English plays provide a wealth of information and, quite probably, a wealth of misinformation about

English drama in print. The title-pages of the eight early editions of *Richard III* (not counting the folios of 1623, 1632, 1663–4, and 1685) provide such a bounty, some of which may indeed be factual. The title-page of the 1597 first quarto reads as follows (vertical stokes indicate line breaks):

[ornament] | THE TRAGEDY OF | King Richard the third. | Containing, | His treacherous Plots against his brother Clarence: | the pittiefull murther of his innocent nephews: | his tyrannical vsurpation: with the whole course | of his detested life, and most deserued death. | As it hath beene lately Acted by the | Right honourable the Lord Chamber- | laine his seruants. | [ornament] | AT LONDON | ¶ Printed by Valentine Sims, for Andrew Wise, | dwelling in Paules Church-yard, at the | Signe of the Angell. | 1597.

The play's genre is identified at once. While we might think of the play as the last in the Shakespeare's second tetralogy of history plays, it was nothing of the sort to the play's first readers. The genre begins the title-page in large upper-case letters, followed in the next line by the play's titular hero, if hero he be. A list of Richard's main accomplishments is next, his "treacherous Plots against his brother Clarence: | the pittiefull murther of his innocent nephews: | his tyrannical vsurpation." Indeed, we will be treated to "the whole course | of his detested life, and most deserued death." As well, readers are informed of the playing company: "As it hath beene lately Acted by the | Right honourable the Lord Chamber- | laine his seruants." What is missing here is one fairly obvious element, the venue, the theater where the play was performed. If the prospective buyer did not know that the Lord Chamberlain's Men played at the Theatre, that's his or her tough luck. Nor are we given an author. That author, "William Shakespeare," appeared two years later in the second quarto of 1599. This is similar to the case of *Richard II,* where Shakespeare's name is omitted in the first quarto of 1597 but appears in the second quarto of 1598 (and succeeding quartos).

The date on *Richard III*'s third quarto is 1602, at least two years after the construction of that new theater south of the Thames. The Globe is not recognized by the stationer as having any power to attract book buyers. What receives stress is the "fact" that the play is "newly augmented," which in fact it was not. By 1605, two years after James I had issued a royal patent bringing Shakespeare's company directly under his patronage, making them the King's Men, one would have thought Matthew Lawe, who bought the rights to *Richard*

III on June 25, 1603, would have reflected its players' royal patron on the title-page of the 1605 quarto. But no, if it ain't broke, don't fix it. The text is presented is "*As it hath beene lately Acted by the | Right honourable the Lord Chamber- | laine his seruants.*" The title-page material on the 1612 edition of *Richard III* recognizes that the text of the play to be purchased is "*As it hath beene lately Acted by the Kings Maiesties | seruants.*" And so that title remains in the editions of 1622, 1629, and 1634, "*Newly augmented*" by a man who died in 1616. If it ain't broke, don't fix it.

The title-pages of early editions of *Romeo and Juliet* do not contain the name of an author or a venue. The earliest edition, printed in 1597, tells that not only is the play a "Tragedie," it is "*An* EXCELLENT conceited Tragedie." Not only are we told that it has "been often . . . plaid publiquely," but that the public presentation has been received, parenthetically, "(with great applause)." The company performing the piece was "the right Ho- | norable the L. of *Hunsdon* | his Seruants." The second edition of 1599 represents a fuller text, "*Newly corrected, augmented, and amended.*" Lord Hunsdon's Servants have been replaced by "the right Honourable the Lord Chamberlaine his Seruants." That this is true might strike a student of title-pages as somewhat bizarre, as more than a few printed plays of the period sometimes slap a new title-page on an early, uncorrected, non-augmented, and unamended text. Q2 *Romeo and Juliet* is very much "augmented, and amended." By the time of the 1609 quarto, the "Kings Majesties Servants" have replaced the Lord Chamberlain, and the play's venue is now "the Globe." There is a flurry of information on this title-page: A Title, the fact that it was played, the players who played it (by now "the Kings Maiesties Seruants"), a venue, a stationer (John Smethwick), the location of his shop, and a date. Missing are typographical ornaments and, oh yes, an author. The fourth quarto, undated but after the First Folio of 1623, has two versions of a title-page. The first contains all of the information from the 1609 quarto; the second issue adds, as last, "Written by *W. Shake-speare.*" The final quarto of the seventeenth century, printed in 1637, almost gets it right (as if there is a "right" and a "wrong" in pre- [or post-, for that matter] Enlightenment anything):

THE MOST EXCELLENT And Lamentable Tragedie, of ROMEO and | JuLIET. | As it hath been sundry times publikely Acted, | by the KINGS Maiesties Servants | at the GLOBE. | Written by *W. Shake-speare. | Newly corrected, augmented, and amended.* | [printer's device] | *LONDON,* | Printed by *R. Young* for *John Smethwicke,* and are to be sold at | his Shop in St. *Dunstans* Church-yard in Fleetstreet, under the Dyall. 1637.

At last, a title-page behaving itself with all the necessary information: a title, a playing company, a theater, an author, a state of the text, a printing location, a printer, a bookseller, the location of the bookseller's shop, and a date. It took English stationers 43 years to "get it right."

Shakespeare's arrival was not noted anywhere in the 1600 quarto of *Henry V*, nor in its 1602 second edition, nor in its edition of 1619 (dated 1608). *The Second Part of King Henry IV*, also published in 1600, was *"Written by William Shakespeare,"* as were *Much Ado About Nothing, A Midsummer-Night's Dream*, and *The Merchant of Venice*, all printed in that year. There follows a two-year gap in publication until 1602, when *The Merry Wives of Windsor* appears with Shakespeare's name. *Thomas Lord Cromwell*, "Written by W. S.," appeared in 1602 as well, and it was reprinted in 1613 with the same "W. S." attribution.

In 1603 appeared the first edition of *Hamlet*, and Shakespeare's name figures on its title-page. It was printed for Nicholas Ling by John Trundell. In the next year Ling had an edition "Newly imprinted and enlarged to almost as much againe as it was, according to the true and perfect Coppie." This too bore Shakespeare's name, with a text greatly enlarged. His name appears again on the first (and last) quarto of *The London Prodigal* (1605), a play that reappears in the second issue of the Third Folio (1664) and in the Fourth Folio (1685), while the initials "W. S." appear on *The Puritan* (1607), another play that reappears in 1664 and 1685.

In 1608 appeared *King Lear*, with "M. W. Shak-speare" in type twice the size of the play's title and with pride of place at the top of the title-page. Here is authorship with a vengeance. In that same year, as if to spite our author, *A Yorkshire Tragedy*, written by "VV. Shakspeare," made its way into print. The very next year brought *Troilus and Cressida*, "by William Shakespeare," and *Pericles*, also by "William Shakespeare" but with two ornamental leaves separating the "William" from the "Shakespeare." There follows a gap of some fourteen years, during which time Shakespeare died in 1616, before the appearance of the next previously unpublished play, a quarto edition of *Othello*, printed in 1622, a year before the First Folio. This quarto, presenting a play that had been acted at both the Globe and Blackfriars, is the only title-page that extols both the King's Men's open-air theater on the South Bank and its more private space with the Blackfriars. It also marks the virtual end of Shakespeare's plays in quarto, with no new plays appearing after the Folio "established" the canon in 1623. None of the folios marks the end of Shakespeare's plays in quarto. Separate editions kept pouring forth:

The Taming of the Shrew, 1631
Richard II, 1634
Richard III, 1629, 1634
Romeo and Juliet, 1637
1 Henry IV, 1632, 1639
Love's Labour's Lost, 1632
The Merchant of Venice, 1637
The Merry Wives of Windsor, 1630
Hamlet, 1625 (?), 1637
King Lear, 1655
Pericles, 1630
Othello, 1630

There are other plays that have wandered into and out of the Shakespeare canon, those plays in the so-called "Shakespeare Apocrypha," plays associated in one way or another with Shakespeare, often more in fancy than in fact. Many have argued their authorship using the latest "scientific" methods to prove their authenticity. These plays include *Arden of Feversham*, *Locrine*, *Edward III*, *Mucedorus*, *Sir John Oldcastle*, *Thomas Lord Cromwell*, *The London Prodigal*, *The Puritan*, *A Yorkshire Tragedy*, *The Merry Devil of Edmonton*, *Fair Em*, *The Two Noble Kinsmen*, *The Birth of Merlin*, and *Sir Thomas More*. A glance at the second edition of the *Riverside Shakespeare* (1997, first edition 1974) reveals that *The Two Noble Kinsmen* and *Edward III* have become part of the legitimate ("Fine word, 'legitimate,'" says the bastard Edmund in the second scene of *King Lear*) canon. The remainder, like many martyrs, await canonization.

What was it the printers of Shakespeare's early editions had before them as they set type? We have few ways of knowing precisely. Was it a manuscript in Shakespeare's hand, what is called a holograph, or was it a copy of that manuscript, perhaps one approved by the Master of the Revels, allowing the piece to be played? Was it a copy prepared for the bookholder (what we call today a "prompter"), with all the notations that person may have made during rehearsals concerning entrances, exits, properties, who's on-stage, who's off-stage, who had better be ready to go on-stage in five or six lines? Or was it, perish the thought, an amalgam of several "original" manuscripts?

It may be important here to stop and note the obvious. As much as Shakespeare and his fellow dramatists, speaking to us of eternal verities, are our contemporaries, and they are, they are also very much part and parcel of an early modern world, a world before the Enlightenment, a world where playmakers did not feel compelled to do things reasonably or efficiently. That said, suppose a play had reached the end of its run in the repertory. The odds of its being revived determined to be less than likely, the Lord Chamberlain's Men / King's Men decide to sell it to a stationer so that (1) they might reap some profit and (2) it might appear in print. Philip Henslowe, working for a rival company, kept a diary. In it he records acquisitions of play manuscripts, partial and full, along with the amounts he paid for them. Turning at random to the verso side of leaf 68, we find that Henslowe paid £3 3s. to Will: Haulton "in full payment of his play of ferrex and Porrex." He lent William Haughton 10s. in earnest for "A Boocke called the Ingleshe fegetives . . ." He paid another 20s. in earnest for the same play in the next entry. He "payd to Henry Chettle in full payment of six pounds for his booke of Damon & Pithias" (Foakes and Rickert 1961: 119–20). With that payment, a "full payment," the author had received his due, and the company no longer had any further financial obligation to him. The concept of royalties might at best have been an idle fantasy of a playmaker. When the play had run its course, Henslowe may well have sold it to a stationer, perhaps a bookseller, probably not a printer, though booksellers could print, and printers certainly could sell books. One would suppose, and supposition, alas, is all we have, that stationers paid roughly as much for the manuscript they would put into print as Henslowe and his counterpart at the Lord Chamberlain's Men / King's Men would pay for a playscript.

The manuscripts that the compositors (now called typesetters) had in front of them must have come from somewhere; presumably that somewhere is the playing house in which the plays were produced: the Theatre, the Globe, Blackfriars, other public venues, and the court, where the rewards were far greater. The process by which a dramatic manuscript moved from theater to printing house can be very simple or very complicated. Having graduated from Famous Playwriting School, an eager young author would approach a playing company with the manuscript of his play. If it was deemed playable and potentially profitable, the company would buy the manuscript. At this point the author is paid and exits. Having been paid, he has foregone any rights in the piece he has composed. The piece had yet to be fitted to the personnel of the company and the exigencies of its stage or stages. Shakespeare more or less outlines the process nicely in *A Midsummer Night's Dream*, commenting on but never satirizing his fellows in the Lord Chamberlain's Men. Peter Quince is at once the author and director. He has written the play and has, as well, cast it. The text with its characters represents Quince's authorial manuscript. Nick Bottom will be Pyramus, a lover, though he would prefer to play the role of a tyrant, explaining that he "could play Ercles rarely, or a part to tear a cat in." Francis Flute is called upon to play Thisbe, and he tries to excuse himself by saying he is growing a beard. Quince, ever resourceful, will provide him with a mask. Bottom volunteers to play Thisbe as well, unaware that in a play entitled *Pyramus and Thisbe*, the two title characters might just appear on that stage at the same time. Robin Starveling will play Thisbe's mother, and Tom Snout Pyramus's father. Quince himself will play Thisbe's father, with the script-challenged Snug playing the lion's part.

Shortly after they arrive in the woods to "rehearse most obscenely and courageously," Bottom has discovered flaws in the script, one of which is Pyramus's killing himself with his sword. But Bottom has solved the problem with a Prologue:

> Write me a prologue, and let the prologue seem to say we will do no harm with our swords, and that Pyramus is not killed indeed. And, for the more better assurance, tell them that I, Pyramus, am not Pyramus, but Bottom the weaver. This will put them out of fear.

More problems ensue. The lion will frighten the ladies, but not if Snug delivers a prologue as well. Then too, Pyramus and Thisbe meet by moonlight, so "one must come in with a bush of thorns and a lantern and say he comes to disfigure or to present the person of Moonshine." A wall is needed, insofar as Pyramus and Thisbe, "says the story, did talk through the chink of a wall." With these alterations in the parts from Bottom's foul papers, perhaps even his fair copy, the play is ready for the stage. The rehearsal lasts for twenty-odd lines. Bottom has exited and re-entered with his ass's head. All disperse but Bottom. The play as presented before the Duke and Hipployta on their wedding day at night is considerably different. Quince has turned from a playmaker with foul papers into a prompter with prompt copy. Before Theseus and Hippolyta the roles in this version are Pyramus, Thisbe, Wall, Moonshine, Lion, and Prologue. The show goes on and is received well by its actors if not by its audience. In addition to all the other issues to which Shakespeare is attending in his play, *A Midsummer Night's Dream* attends to the issue of text, how the exigencies of the theater and the company affect the way a play will be staged.

To return to London, what was it that Thomas Fisher brought to Richard Braddock's printing house west of St Paul's Cathedral on

Fetter Lane, one Braddock obtained when he married the widow of printer Robert Robertson in 1597 or 1598? There are several possibilities. It could have been a holograph. It could have been that manuscript copied and emended by a scribe in the playhouse before a copy was prepared for the bookholder. Either of these is closer to the playwright himself than to the theater for which that playwright wrote.

At some point in the process of page to page to stage, a manuscript would have had to be inspected by an official of the Master of the Revels. The officer would mark passages which contained offense and would order such passages to be deleted. Then the manuscript would be revised, resubmitted, and, with or without a bribe, approved for playing. Let us suppose that there are now two extant manuscripts, the author's and a scribe's. One has the seal of the Master of the Revels, one does not. From one of these copies a "prompt book" (a term whose use is first recorded in 1809) would be prepared. The bookholder or prompter (a word whose first use is attributed to Shakespeare, in *Othello*, 1.2.84: "Were it my cue to fight, I should have known it / Without a prompter") would sit to the side of the stage, following the action and the text, assuring himself that players who should be onstage were on-stage, and that players who were to be off-stage would be out of sight. This bookholder would prepare his prompt book in the course of rehearsal. Entrances and exits would appear in the prompt book at least several lines before they actually were to take place, giving the bookholder time to notify a tardy actor that he should be ready to enter, nod to an on-stage actor that it was time for him to exit. One "clue" to a prompt copy is thought to be the use of the abbreviation "*etc.*" in early texts. These often occur when a character is reading a letter. As the actor will have the document in front of him, the prompter need only make note of the few first words. When Polonius is reading Hamlet's letter to Ophelia to Gertrude and Claudius, the text reads: "*To the celestial, and my soul's idol, the most beautified Ophelia* – That's an ill phrase, a vile phrase; beautified is a vile phrase. But you shall hear. Thus: [*He reads.*] *In her excellent white bosom, these, etc.*" (2.2.117–20). Insofar as Polonius has the text in his hands, the bookholder needs only the beginning and end of Ophelia's letter to make sure his business is done. Problems might have arisen for the bookholder when the King's Men had two venues, the larger Globe theater on the South Bank of the Thames and the more intimate Blackfriars, well west of St Paul's, one whose smaller stage made different theatrical demands, many of which were the responsibility of the bookholder.

Let us return to the printing house, to the booksellers, to that area north of the Thames whose center was St Paul's Cathedral. In 1598 the lease for the Theatre ran out and Giles Alleyn, who owned the land on which the Theatre was built, refused to renew the lease. In December of 1598 Cuthbert and Richard Burbage arranged to have the building torn down. The lumber was transported to the south bank of the Thames in order to build a new theater, the Globe. Then as now, theaters suck money into what appear to be vast and bottomless pits, and the Burbages needed capital. They sold half the rights of the theater to Shakespeare, John Heminges, Augustine Phillips, Thomas Pope, and Will Kempe. Suppose, and what follows is supposition, that in and around 1598 the Burbages started unloading playtexts onto the stationers north of the river. Page and stage are often less far apart than we perceive them to be. What follows is fiction: sometime before 1600, the dates when Ben Jonson's *Euery Man Ovt of his Hvmovr*, and Shakespeare's *Henry V*, *2 Henry IV*, *Much Ado About Nothing*, *A Midsummer Night's Dream*, and *The Merchant of Venice* appeared, the Lord Chamberlain's Men needed to raise "capital" (a word just coming into use in the sense of accumulated wealth) for that new theater, and raise it they did by selling off a number of plays to stationers in order to turn stage to page and to turn playbooks into money.

What kind of manuscripts did the stationers receive from the Lord Chamberlain's Men? It seems ("seems madam, I know not seems") to be the case that in most instances the most expendable manuscripts were those authorial manuscripts, the papers closest to the author but furthest from the stage. Once a play had gone into production, once there was a copy with the Lord Chamberlain's seal, once there was a prompt book noting the entrances, exits, and stage actions, then "logically," the author's manuscript, those so-called "foul papers," would be the most likely (and the most expendable) of the extant manuscript copies of the play to be sent to the printer. The texts of some of the early editions of Shakespeare's plays were considerably shorter than their equivalents in later quarto editions and in the First Folio. This fact has engendered much debate. Were the early editions texts for touring? Were they transcribed at the theater by a cagey stenographer employing the latest form of early modern shorthand, then sold to an unscrupulous stationer? Were they early drafts of plays that were later revised and perfected by their author? The conclusion reached by Paul Werstine is that "these texts were open to penetration and alteration not only by Shakespeare himself and his fellow actors but also by multiple theatrical and extra-theatrical scriveners, by theatrical annotators, adapters and revisers (who might cut or add), by censors, and by compositors and proofreaders."[3] Werstine prefers, sensibly, "a narrative that includes post-structuralist differential reading of multiple-text works that keep in play not only multiple readings and versions but also the multiple and dispersed agencies that could have produced the variants" (Werstine 1990: 86).

Off it went, that manuscript, taken by the stationer to the printer. The printer may well have put the manuscript in a certain pile, on the basis of size and urgency. Playbooks and prayer books and sermons being relatively short, they may well have been printed concurrently with longer works, the monies received for the shorter books enabling the printer to meet his or her expenses, the larger works bringing in profit. Note, please, the capitalist vocabulary being forced upon a decidedly pre-capitalist economy. The printer would have contracted with the stationer to produce a certain number of books at a certain time in return for a certain sum of money. I would note here that each of the London companies – fishmongers', butchers', vintners' (including the Stationers') – had its own court and dealt with intra-company disputes in its own ways.

The type was set by a compositor. Those four leaves of each quarto sheet contained eight pages printed on two sides of a sheet of paper. Let's look at sheet B, the second sheet to appear. Often sheet A, the first sheet with the title-page and, possibly, a dedication, a list of characters (*dramatis personae*), and a prologue was printed last, in the (often vain) hope of finding a dedicatee, a patron, someone to offset some of the expenses of printing and to increase the possibility of some degree of profit. The typesetter would be obliged to set eight pages of type. Pages 1, 4, 5, and 8 would occupy one side of the sheet (the outer forme), and pages 2, 3, 6, and 7 the other side of the sheet (the inner forme). If the compositor set the pages in order, that is, if he set the play *seriatim*, he would have to set seven pages of type before one of the two formes could be fitted with "furniture" (pieces of wood to separate each page and provide ample margins) and sent off to the press for printing. Alternatively, and this alternative was just making its way into English printing, the compositor might determine how much of the manuscript would fit onto each of the eight pages he had to produce; he would "cast off" his copy. Then he could set one of the two formes all at once, send it off to the press, and turn to the other forme and set its four pages. When the press had printed the requisite number of sheets on one side, it would then be prepared to print the other forme. This method increased efficiency but was fraught with danger. If the compositor mis-estimated and did not cast off enough text for four pages, he would be forced to spread a sub-minimal amount of text over the four pages. In many dramatic texts of the period one can see pages with a good deal of "white space," space above and below stage directions, space in the last two lines of a prose speech, allowing it to occupy another line. The worst-case scenario is that the compositor might feel compelled to add the odd word, phrase, or clause to fill out a speech and get it to a new line. The prospect of Shakespeare's quartos containing material "written" by a compositor trying to fill out a page, a forme, fills bibliographers with horror. Equally horrific is the alternative scenario, a compositor biting off more manuscript than he can set into type. One can find formes in early modern printed plays where the type is so tightly set that often two words look like one. What happens after the compos-itor has set his type as tightly as he can and there is still manuscript text that needs to be set? Are all of those "additions" that we find in a Folio play with an earlier quarto edition really authorial, "possibly by another author," or do they derive from the original manuscript, unable, due to the exigencies of casting off copy, to appear in its earlier printed text?

Shakespeare's pre-Folio texts begin to come to a close in 1619 with the publication of the so-called "Pavier quartos," named after the printer Thomas Pavier. These 10 plays were published in new editions by the stationer Thomas Pavier, who held the rights to several of the plays. *2* and *3 Henry VI* were printed as *The Whole Contention Between the Two Famous Houses, Lancaster and York*. Reprinted were *Pericles, A Yorkshire Tragedy, The Merchant of Venice, Sir John Falstaff* (*The Merry Wives of Windsor*), *King Lear, Henry V, 1 Sir John Oldcastle*, and *A Midsummer Night's Dream*. The King's Men, in negotiations for the printing of the First Folio, persuaded the Lord Chamberlain to write a letter to the Stationers' Company saying that in the future "no play that his majesty's players do play" should be printed without consent of the King's Men. Pavier did a double reverse and put earlier dates, some those of the original publication, on the remaining eight plays. Thus 1608 is the date on the texts of *King Lear* and *Henry V*, with a date of 1600 for *The Merchant of Venice, Sir John Oldcastle*, and *A Midsummer Night's Dream*. Whether these publications were "illegal" is dubious. Perhaps they reflected a degree of business acumen on the part of Pavier, first, to take advantage of Shakespeare's death to sell some copies of his plays and, second, to co-opt (not a term in use in early seventeenth-century English) the cartel that was in the process of preparing the First Folio: William Aspley, Edward Blount, Isaac Jaggard, William Jaggard, and John Smethwicke. Sonia Massai (2007) offers an alternative account of the circumstances that led Pavier to change his original plan to publish 10 Shakespearean and pseudo-Shakespearean plays as a collection and opt instead for individual title-pages and for a bizarre mixture of genuine and fake imprints for each play. Massai sees the publication of the quartos not as a deterrent to the First Folio but rather as a marketing device to whet the play-reading public's hunger for the larger collection that would appear in 1623. Such a theory makes sense of Pavier's poor effort to cover his tracks. Why, asks Massai, would the Shakespeare's company use the Jaggards to print the Folio if these same Jaggards had "betrayed" the King's Men by publishing the 1619 "collection"? Why, Massai continues, would the King's Men present the Jaggards with annotated copies of the Pavier quarto edition of *A Midsummer Night's Dream* and, possibly, *King Lear* for use as copy for the First Folio? The Pavier quartos provide more questions than they do answers. Moreover, they suggest that a re-interrogation of earlier Shakespearean quartos might well be worthwhile.

One year before the publication of the First Folio appears the final quarto, a 1622 edition of *Othello*, entered into the *Stationers' Register* on October 6, 1621, by Thomas Walkley and printed by Nicholas Okes with a 1622 date on the title-page. Its text differs from the Folio in its brevity and in many readings, indicating that the Folio text came from a different source. These two texts would be conflated in 1630 when Augustine Mathewes printed a second quarto edition for Richard Hawkins.

This chapter has considered Shakespeare. Further answers might be provided by any number of the more than eight hundred plays printed in a variety of editions from 1516 onward, not to mention the twenty-odd Latin plays that appeared in print, or the 121 plays entered in the *Stationers' Register* that are not extant, or the 187 plays that at one time or another were headed for print but have not survived. Very much as in the world of the twenty-first century, if something can go wrong, it will. If someone is tempted by the siren of self-interest, she or he will, in time, succumb. Such are the people who put these texts together, took them from manuscript to print. Their families wanted a roof and food; their government wanted them to believe that their queen, then their king, were direct descendants of Adam and Eve. That the men and women of the Stationers' Company were able to present us with as many texts as they have in as good a condition as we have them is – war, famine, pestilence, and death notwithstanding – something of a miracle.

Notes

1 There were 36 plays in the 1663 volume, which, apparently, was not a financial success. It was reissued in 1664 with an additional seven plays appended: *Pericles, The London Prodigal, Thomas Lord Cromwell, Sir John Oldcastle, The Puritan, A Yorkshire Tragedy,* and *Locrine.* These seven plays were reprinted in the 1685 folio.
2 In *Shakespeare as a Literary Dramatist,* Lukas Erne (2003) posits a Shakespeare who, when he hit his stride from about 1596–7 on, was a writer very much interested is the printing and marketing of his plays. This may well be true, but solid documentation is difficult to come by. Shakespeare may well have been interested in having his plays printed, but he most certainly did not seek with success to have his name on title-pages. The first extant printed play with Shakespeare's initials on the title-page is *Locrine* (now well outside the canon) in 1596. His name appears in 1598 on the title-pages of *Richard II* and *Richard III,* each in its second edition. There seems to be no correlation between the publications of Shakespeare's play and outbreaks of the plague, which shut the theaters and turned out-of-work playmakers into "authors." Shakespeare's name appears four times in the *Stationers' Register*: on August 23, 1600, in the entries for *2 Henry IV* and *Much Ado About Nothing,* on November 26, 1607, for *King Lear,* on May 2, 1608, for *A Yorkshire Tragedy,* and on November 8, 1623, for eight comedies, two histories, and six tragedies. I have not considered authorial appearances in any of the eight editions of *The Rape of Lucrece* or the sixteen editions of *Venus and Adonis.*
3 Paul Werstine (1990) has skillfully delineated the problems attendant upon the categorization of play manuscripts (actual and lost). In a companion article, Marion Trousdale (1990) deals with various misconstruings of evidence on the part of early- to mid-twentieth-century bibliographers and editors.

Chapter 4

The Life of the First Folio in the Seventeenth and Eighteenth Centuries

Anthony James West

The First Folio, the first collected edition of Shakespeare's plays, has had a very rich and varied life since its publication in 1623. This life is fascinating not only in its own right, but also for the light it shines on Shakespeare's reception and changing reputation. This chapter focuses on its life during its first two centuries, when it shifted from not being widely regarded as distinctive or special to being generally recognized as of unique and immense importance. By 1800, the Folio stood apart in a class of its own from all other English books.[1]

The Folio contains 36 plays, that is, all of the traditionally accepted dramatic works of Shakespeare, except *Pericles*. The plays were gathered for publication by John Heminges and Henry Condell, fellow players of Shakespeare in the company of the King's Men. It was printed in London over a two-year period by William Jaggard and his son, Isaac. It is folio in format, printed in two columns, on 908 pages – a big book. Its preliminaries, the first nine leaves, contain the laudatory verse ("The Figure, that thou here seest . . .") by Ben Jonson and, on the title-page opposite, the "Figure" itself: the now iconic portrait of Shakespeare engraved by Martin Droeshout. The book is printed on medium-quality paper and, while the text is clear and (in an undamaged copy) perfectly legible, the quality of the printing cannot compete with the Gutenberg Bible or fine Italian printing. Probably about 750 copies were printed; 230 survive. The Folio was issued unbound at 15s.; a copy bound in plain calf, typically on heavy boards, cost £1 (the equivalent, at the time, of 44 large loaves of bread; a quarto cost the equivalent of one loaf).

To place it briefly in a historical context: Queen Elizabeth died in 1603; Shakespeare died in 1616; the *Mayflower* landed at what became Plymouth, Massachusetts, in 1620; and King James I and VI was succeeded by Charles I in 1625. The following years were marked by the struggle between the crown and Parliament, and between the Royalists and the Puritans, leading to the Civil War and the closure of the theaters in 1642. In a book context: the King James Bible was published in 1611; Ben Jonson published his *Works*, a trail-blazing literary folio including his plays, in 1616. The publication of the First Folio in 1623 was followed only nine years later by the Second Folio, in 1632, then by the Third, in 1663; the second issue of the Third Folio (1664) contained *Pericles* and the apocryphal plays; the Fourth Folio (1685) retained them.

The First Folio is an immensely important book. It is intriguing to ask: "What if it had not been published?" The short answer is, because no Shakespeare play manuscripts survive and because the Folio published 18 plays for the first time, for which it is the sole source, that without it we would lack half the dramatic works, including *The Tempest, Measure for Measure, As You Like It, All's Well, Twelfth Night, Coriolanus, Julius Caesar, Macbeth, Antony and Cleopatra*, and *Cymbeline*. Further, it offers better texts for over half the other plays, already published as quartos. From a collector's point of view, it is the first edition of the 18 plays and, increasingly from 1800, a "must have" volume. From the point of view of publishing history, it is the first English folio containing only plays. Culturally, it illustrates the rise of the printed book and reading as a popular activity to join the theater and playgoing. Sir Sidney Lee, the leading Shakespearean at the start of the twentieth century, called it "the greatest contribution made in a single volume to the secular literature of any age or country" (Lee 1902a: xi). William Jackson (of *STC* [Pollard et al. 1926] and other fame) wrote that it is "incomparably the most important work in the English language" (Unger and Jackson 1940: III, 935). As we shall see, during the eighteenth century, it became central to the editing of Shakespeare plays and to Shakespeare studies. By the end of that century it became increasingly sought-after and expensive as a collectable book.

Early Records, Owners, and Readers

The documentary records of the Folio in the seventeenth century offer us enough to form a picture of its early life and the kinds of people who owned and read it. There are quite a few records in the first decade or so; there is relative silence from the 1630s, through the Civil War and the Restoration, till 1687; then, more records again at the end of the century.

Three records – one announcing the future Folio, the second recording the right to publish some of the plays, and the third showing marked-up proof-sheets – predate the Folio's publication. The October 1622 listing of English books, attached to the English version of the catalogue of the annual Frankfurt book fair, mentions a one-volume book of plays by William Shakespeare printed by Isaac Jaggard in folio. The fact that this entry occurs over a year before the Folio appeared may suggest the Jaggards had planned to publish it earlier than November 1623. For publication rights, the principal publishers, Isaac Jaggard and Edward Blount, whose names appear on the Folio's title-page, negotiated with the playhouse (for manuscripts) and with the owners (for the plays already printed). The second record, dated November 8, 1623, is their entry at the Stationers' Company for "Master William Shakspears *Comedyes, Histories, and Tragedies* soe manie of the said Copies as are not formerly entered to other men." The "said Copies" embraced eight comedies, two histories, and six tragedies. Difficulties over the rights to one play, *Troilus*, delayed its printing; this caused its position in the Folio to be changed and explains its absence from the "Catalogue" of plays on a preliminary leaf. The third record is a number of sheets that have been marked up by the proof-reader for correction; the leaves then survived in bound copies of the Folio. The occurrence of marked-up pages is not unusual in early printed books, probably explained by the high cost of paper. There are examples in folios in Paris, and at the Folger and Huntington Libraries (for illustrations, see Hinman's edition [1996: 920, 922]; Blayney 1991: 16; also, for the crossing out of a cancelled leaf, Hinman 1996: 916).

After the book was printed, Isaac Jaggard sent the sheets for the deposit copy to the Bodleian Library. The dispatch of the sheets to the Oxford binder, William Wildegoose, was recorded in the Bodleian Binding Record, on February 17, 1624. The copy, West 31,[2] has the original Wildegoose binding today. It has a gash on the fore-edge, where the chain was attached. As was normal at the time, the Folio was chained to a fixture in the library.

The copy now in Glasgow University Library (West 11) has some very interesting early (as yet undated) annotations. Comments against 11 of the names of the principal actors in the preliminaries suggest the annotator knew or had seen some of them. Comments in the comedies give an early response to plays, such as "starke naught" (*Two Gentlemen*), "pretty well" (*Tempest*), and "very good; light" (*Merry Wives*).

There are records of at least two early gifts of the Folio. The older Jaggard, who had become blind, died just before the Folio was published. He arranged for the gift of a copy of the Folio to Augustus Vincent, whose *Discoverie of Errours* went through the Jaggard press at the same time as the Folio. Vincent records the gift, "1623," in Latin, on the title-page. Henry Folger, who formed the Folger Shakespeare Library in Washington, DC, paid a very large sum for this copy early in his collecting career. When he numbered his copies, he gave this one pride of place as No. 1. The other gift is recorded, perhaps in 1626, in the Donors' Book of the Vicars' Choral Library at Hereford Cathedral. The donor was Philip Traherne, mayor of Hereford in 1622. There is a literary association: Traherne was the uncle of, and responsible for the education of, the poet Thomas Traherne.

There are several records of very early ownership. The first recorded purchase is in the accounts of Sir Edward Dering, of Surrenden Hall, Kent. On December 5, 1623, Dering entered that he purchased in London for £1 each two copies of the First Folio. Dering was an antiquarian, an MP, and deeply involved in the political and religious controversy of the times. From the evidence of his other book purchases and his playgoing, he clearly loved Shakespeare and the drama. What is important here is that he put on plays at home in Surrenden, and that in West 198, in the library at Padua University, there are three plays marked up for performance. The plays, quite possibly marked up at Surrenden, are *Measure for Measure*, *Winter's Tale*, and *Macbeth*. Another early purchase was by Thomas Longe: his autograph ("Oxford," but no date), and the fact that the price he paid was 15s., is on the title-page of West 129 in the Folger Library. Bibliographical evidence suggests he may have bought his copy even before Dering. This Longe may well have been a fellow of All Souls' College in 1607 and vicar in a village near Oxford in 1617. There are suggestions of other very early purchases – Lee mentions the earl of Bridgewater and Lord Arundell, for example (Lee 1902b: 28, 27) – but I have not found solid evidence.

While Longe was a parish priest, John Cosin was a bishop and moved in royal circles. He became bishop of Durham and master of Peterhouse, Cambridge. Lee thought he bought his copy, West 7, "*c*.1630" (Lee 1902b: 27). It was deposited for a while in the Peterhouse

Library (it has a Peterhouse press-mark) when Cosin escaped to France with other supporters of Charles I. The volume is distinguished by having probably the longest single provenance of any copy. It is also distinguished for being effectively in the same library for longer than any other Folio. It is unfortunately marked in another way. It was stolen from the University of Durham in 1998.

One purchaser, John Buxton, who had trained as a lawyer at Gray's Inn, gives us evidence of what a First Folio was worth to a middle-class, well-to-do, but not overly wealthy professional. Like Dering, he loved Shakespeare and drama. His account book shows, in about 1627, he traded one copy of the First Folio for a better one; it also shows he frequented the theater and collected plays. The purchases he made with his wife at the Stourbridge Fair in 1629, buying items for his new home, give us an idea what the Folio's equivalents were. For prices each close to what he must have paid for his Folio, he purchased a brass chafing dish and chafer, a baking pan, four skillets (these cost £1, i.e., the same as a bound Folio), and a dozen stools and a round table (McKitterick 1997: 200–3).

The sexes vie for the first record of a First Folio reader. We owe to Richard James, often cited by scholars on the Falstaff/Oldcastle issue, the story of "A young Gentle Lady . . . having read ye works of Shakespeare" asking him an intelligent question on Falstaff's survivability. Other than this gentle lady there is only little documentary evidence of female readers or owners in the seventeenth century. Her reading of Shakespeare's works probably dates from the mid-1620s. About the same time, an unidentified Scot gave an extraordinarily careful reading of all the plays in West 201 (now held by Meisei University Library in Tokyo). In addition to reading them closely, he annotated them copiously: there is hardly a blank space throughout the text that is not covered by his handwriting. The Japanese bibliographer, Akihiro Yamada, who painstakingly transcribed the annotations, dates them from the "1620s or around 1630" (Yamada 1998: xix). One might hope they would give early insightful interpretations, but unfortunately the Scot's commentaries are mostly mundane. (Some merely copy the text; many simply say what is happening.)

Two other early references to the Folio can be mentioned. Humphrey Dyson (d. 1633), a book-collector and owner of Jonson's *Works*, certainly consulted, if he did not own, a First Folio: he noted in his copy of the *Troilus* quarto that it was "Written by William Shakespeare and printed amongst his workes." William Prynne, strict Puritan, writing before 1633, objected that playbooks had "grown from Quarto to Folio" and was incensed that Shakespeare's plays were printed on paper "far better than most Bibles." Prynne's attitude was one common at the time and is indicative of the climate of opinion into which the First Folio was ushered. For example, Thomas Bodley, writing a bit earlier, wanted to exclude playbooks from his new library in Oxford; hardly one in forty was worth keeping; and the more he thought about it the more he was against admitting such "baggage bookes" to "so Noble a Librarie." Despite puritanical attitudes, there was good demand for Shakespeare in the 1620s. The first Folio sold out in nine years. The Second Folio was published in 1632.

Sir John Suckling (1609–42), poet and dramatist, demonstrates the shift toward Shakespeare the playwright in print. In about 1638 Suckling posed for a full-length portrait by Van Dyck. This very fine painting is in the Frick Museum in New York City. Suckling is conspicuously holding open a Folio, labeled "Shakespere" (see West 2005). (It is not proven whether it is a First or Second Folio, but the message is the same. Also, I have found no evidence Suckling owned a Folio.) Suckling had been one of the first to recognize Shakespeare's genius and his pre-eminence – even over the much-admired Jonson. The presence of the Folio is a tribute to Shakespeare and an acknowledgment of Suckling's frequent borrowings from Shakespeare in his own dramas. Its presence also "reveals," as David Scott Kastan puts it, "that the prestige he offers is already less a function of memorable plays enjoyed in the theater by millions (even by 1638) than of their existence in print" (Kastan 2001: 11).

Mid-Seventeenth-Century Owners and Readers

As mentioned above, there are few records of the First Folio in the mid-years of the century. No doubt this is partly explained by the Civil War and the closing of the theaters. Also, there were as yet no book auctions, so no sale catalogues. Clearly the demand for Shakespeare declined after the 1620s: whereas the Second Folio followed the First after nine years, there was a gap of 31 years before the appearance of the Third in 1663. Gary Taylor called 1659 "the nadir of Shakespeare's posthumous history" (Taylor 1990: 12). But the picture is mixed, as the three following instances show. In 1657, a book listing the *Most Vendible Books* included "Mr *Shakspear's* Playes. folio," *King Lear*, and *Richard II* (London 1657). Pepys, who bought a (presumably) Third Folio in July 1664, saw 37 performances of Shakespearean or semi-Shakespearean plays during the 1660s. The copy of the Folio in the Philadelphia Free Library contains valuable annotations – some apparently before, some after, 1650. They attempt to remove obscenities or confusions, improve the meter, and identify Shakespeare's sources.

The lives during this time of two particular First Folios have important things to tell us. The first concerns the perception of the First Folio and seventeenth-century student reading. In 1664, the Bodleian sold a parcel of "superfluous Library books" to Richard Davis, an Oxford bookseller. It is believed that among the books was West 31, the deposit copy referred to earlier, and the reason for selling it was the belief that the Third Folio had made it obsolete. Certainly, the second issue of the Third, with the addition of seven plays all purportedly by Shakespeare, gave this impression (*Pericles* is the only one now accepted). When the deposit copy was purchased back by the Bodleian in 1906, with the help of public donations, Oxford scholars analyzed the relative wear and tear of the plays. They concluded the tragedies were the most read, and the comedies the least read, by seventeenth-century Oxford students; and the four most-read plays were *Romeo and Juliet*, *Julius Caesar*, *I Henry IV*, and *Macbeth*.

The copy now in the Dr Williams Library in London was purchased probably between about 1650 and 1665 by Dr William Bates. What is significant is, first, that he was a nonconformist minister and, second, that he was an avid reader – he was called "a devourer of books" in his funeral oration. The text has been marked throughout the volume, most likely before Bates owned it – demonstrating a very close reading of the plays. Bates's library was purchased in 1699 by another nonconformist minister, Dr Daniel Williams. Williams left his library to the public. Thus the Bates/Williams Folio is distinguished both for its nonconformist association and for having been the longest in a public library.

Owners, Attitudes, and the Folio's Standing at the End of the Seventeenth Century

The English book market was revolutionized in 1676 by the start of book auctions. The growth in the trading of books was astounding. A listing of *British Book Sale Catalogues* (Munby and Coral 1977) records 13 sales in the 1670s, 157 in the 1680s, and 237 in the 1690s. A sale catalogue of 1687 lists 74 sales of libraries in the first decade of book auctions. Despite all this activity, I have failed – having gone through most of the extant catalogues – to find the sale of a First Folio until 11 years after auctions began. I have no explanation for this.

In the 1680s and 1690s at least five First Folios were auctioned. The sellers and buyers tell us something about the kinds of people who owned the Folio. The following is from the catalogues in the Bodleian and British Libraries. It includes two prices.

- In May 1687 "the several Libraries of the Honorable Sir William Coventry, and the Honorable Mr. Henry Coventry, Sometime Secretary of State to King Charles II" were auctioned. A "Mr Harinton" bought "William Shakespears Works [Lond.] 1623" for 8s. 6d.
- In March 1688, the "Books . . . contained in the library of a Learned, and Eminent Citizen of London" were sold. It included "Shakespears Comedies, Histories and Tragedies, 1623."
- In May 1690, the "English part of the library of the late Duke of Lauderdale" was sold, including "Will. Shakespears Commedies, Histories and Tragedies – Lond. 1623."
- In May 1695, the library of "Rev. Doct. V. D. Jo. Scott" was sold, including "Shakespears Comedies, Histories and Tragedies – 1623."
- In February 1699, two libraries were sold together. "Shakespear's Plays and Poems – 1620," from the "Hamden" library, was bought by "Mr Frasier" for 18s. Wrong dates sometimes occur in sale catalogues. Since no separate date is given, the "Poems" could refer to the verses on the preliminary leaves. Despite the questions, I cautiously assume this is a First Folio.

Former and new owners included a duke, a former secretary of state, two honorables, a reverend doctor, a learned and eminent citizen of London, and (presumably) three "Mr"s. It is not clear which of the Coventry brothers owned the Folio, or whether he had bought it or inherited it from his father, the lord keeper; they were both members of Parliament, where their performance together was celebrated in a poem by Andrew Marvell. Sir William was the Coventry famously chronicled by Pepys in his diary. John Maitland (1616–82), duke of Lauderdale, was close to Charles II and was particularly involved with Anglo-Scottish affairs; he possessed an enormous library and was known for his learning and scholarship. John Scott (1639–95) was a rector in London; he published sermons and several books on religion. I have not traced the other vendors or buyers. To summarize ownership in the seventeenth century as a whole, practically all owners were among the aristocracy, the wealthy or at least well-off, middle-class professionals, and the clergy. I have found no evidence of owner-ship among important writers, except Congreve (see below).

Where the Folio is listed in sale catalogues tells us something of the values of the time, and, by extension, something of the attitudes toward Shakespeare and his plays. Books in Latin, in folio format, and on theology are listed first; books in French, Italian, then English, in smaller formats, and on other subjects are listed later. The cata-logues have no heading for drama or even literature. In the sales above, the Folio is listed under "Miscellanies, viz. History, Philology, etc.," under "English Divinity, History and Miscellany," under "Mis-cellanies in Folio," and under "English books Divinity, History, Etc." It certainly strikes us as odd to find what is now the revered First Folio appearing as a "Miscellany" or under "Etc."

The interconnection between the recognition of Shakespeare and the recognition of the First Folio, where the reputation of one moved with and fed the reputation of the other, was hardly visible in the seventeenth century. Perceptive critics wrote approvingly of Shake-speare's distinction or merits: Humphrey Moseley, in the preliminaries of Beaumont and Fletcher's *Comedies and Tragedies*, 1647, showed high regard for the "sweet Swan of Avon"; Dryden's admiration of Shakespeare in *An Essay of Dramatic Poesy*, 1668, probably did more for Shakespeare's seventeenth-century reputation than anything else; Aphra Behn in *The Dutch Lover*, 1673, said *"We all well know that the immortal* Shakespears *Playes ... have better pleased the World than [Jonson's] Works"* (quoted by Taylor 1990: 28); William Davenant in his edition of *Hamlet*, 1676, refers to "the incomparable Author"; Nahum Tate in the prologue to his 1689 edition of *Lear* expresses his "Zeal for all the Remains" of Shakespeare; and Gerard Langbaine in his account of some 200 English dramatists, 1691, wrote: "I esteem his Plays beyond any that have ever been published in our Language" (Langbaine 1691: 454). But none of these or other favorable remarks refers to or is connected with the First Folio. Rather, interest in and demand for Shakespeare is shown by the publication of the Third Folio (two issues: 1663/4) and of the Fourth Folio (1685).

Records in copies of the First Folio, or about it, in the latter part of the century, at least those I have so far seen, tell little about the response of readers to Shakespeare. However, six First Folios, associ-ated with the theater and/or the text, tell us something about interest in Shakespeare's plays.

William Cartwright, former actor, left his library in 1687 to Dulwich College in London. His library included the Dulwich First Folio, a fact that has only recently been proven. According to William Jaggard, bibliographer, Cartwright wrote in a letter, November 30, 1623, to his close friend Edward Alleyn that he had bought a Folio for a sovereign (Jaggard 1911: 495). (There is doubt about the authenticity of this letter. Jaggard said it was at Dulwich, but I have been unable to trace it.) Alleyn, founder of Dulwich College and builder of the Fortune theater with Philip Henslowe, was a leading actor. We can probably assume that both Cartwright and Alleyn used the Folio, which remains in the College Library today.

The copy in the Bibliothèque Nationale in Paris has what appear to be post-Restoration comments on the comedies and some apparently early corrections to the text. (The purchase of this copy, which went to the Bibliothèque Royale, by a French book-dealer in 1841, shows, incidentally, the spread of Shakespeare's reputation abroad in the nineteenth century.) The comments, written against the comedies on the catalogue leaf in the preliminaries, are: on *The Tempest*, "better than Dryden"; on *Midsummer* and *Taming*, "pretty good"; on *Merry Wives*, *Merchant*, *As You Like It*, and *Twelfth Night*, "good"; and on the rest, "*Ind*[different]." This copy also contains a proof-sheet in *Hamlet*.

Another copy is distinguished by having remarkable theatrical and literary associations. It was owned by Charles Killigrew (1655–1725). He was Master of the Revels and, from 1682, patentee of Drury Lane, London's most successful theater. The copy passed, on a date unknown, to William Congreve (1670–1729), one of England's most successful dramatists. Both men signed the copy. Congreve's use of the volume is evidenced by his annotations. In Act II, scene i, of *As You Like it* (Q5v, paginated 190), on the outer margin, are the two main annotations, in Congreve's hand, both in speeches by the First Lord, both referring to Dryden plays. The first, "*Spanish Friar*," is against the two lines, "Almost to bursting, and the big round tears / Cours'd one another downe his innocent nose." The second (slightly cropped), "Anthony [sic] in all for love by Dryden," is against the five lines, "Left and abandoned . . . Sweepe on you fat and greazie Citizens." Congreve left the Folio, with his library and estate, to Henrietta, his mistress. Henrietta in turn left it to her (and Congreve's) daughter, Mary. Mary married the duke of Leeds and the volume stayed in the family till it was sold at Christie's in November 1990. It was bought by Meisei University, Tokyo, where it is today. According to a questionnaire in the Sidney Lee archives, the first half of the volume was apparently dented by a bullet – a unique distinction, as far as I know, among First Folios.

Three copies show interest in the text. The first, Folger copy 73, belonged to someone with theatrical interests "in or before the 1670s": the reader wrote lists of *dramatis personae* by two comedies, drew attention to comic scenes he enjoyed, and commented that *Taming of the Shrew* might be made into "something prety . . . in Pastorale" (Blayney 1991: 34). The other two, both marked up for performance, unfortunately survive only as fragments. One consists of a single leaf in *Hamlet* (oo5 or pp. 265–6), including the "To be, or not to be" speech, sold by Sotheby's in July 1983 (West 2003: 323). The markings cut some seventy lines, including all of Hamlet's speech to the players, and contract Polonius's speech beginning, "Ophelia, walke you heere." The Sotheby's catalogue says the text incorporates some of the substantial revisions found in the 1676 quarto, but gives the opinion that the markings "almost certainly" predate 1676.

The fragments of the third (so-called Nursery) copy are geographically apart. Two plays, separately bound, *Midsummer Night's Dream* (heavily cut) and *Comedy of Errors*, are at Edinburgh University. Six leaves from *Hamlet* are in two copies, West 130 and 140, at the Folger (West 2003: 197–8, 320). Blayney (1991: 35) illustrates two marked-up pages from *Hamlet*. (One is tempted to speculate that the single leaf from *Hamlet* mentioned above might also have come from the Nursery Folio.) According to Blayney, "the actors named in the 'calls' for entrance [in *Comedy of Errors*] suggest that the play was performed around 1672 at the Hatton Garden theatre known as the Nursery" (Blayney 1991: 34). It seems that little or none of the textual interest in the seventeenth century, in contrast to that of the eighteenth century, represents any serious attempt to edit the plays.

Information on market prices of First Folios is scarce and may not be very reliable, but what exists is indicative. With two prices from the sales mentioned above and one from a nineteenth-century bookman, I have three First Folio prices between 1687 and 1699: 8s. 6d., 14s., and 18s. It is noteworthy that all are below the issue price for a bound Folio. One obvious comparison is with prices of the other three Folios (F2–4). From 1678 to 1699, among 50 F2–4 sales, there was nothing to differentiate their prices from those of F1; all 13 F2–4 prices I found were within the 8s. 6d.–18s. range of F1, except for one F3 at £1 8s. 6d. A copy of the catalogue of the Hamden sale in the British Library, in which the presumed First Folio achieved the 18s., is copiously annotated on interleaves. The prices given for two other folio collected dramas and for other literary folios permits a direct comparison, in the same sale, with the Folio's 18s.: Beaumont and Fletcher's *Works* fetched 17s. 6d. and Ben Jonson's *Works* in two volumes fetched 11s. 6d.; the folios of *Paradise Lost*, Chaucer's *Works* and *Life*, and two editions of Cowley's *Works* ranged between 7s. and 14s. In short, to the extent that these comparisons, which ignore differing condition, are valid, the standing of the First Folio in the market place at the end of the seventeenth century was not distinctive – either from the other Shakespeare Folios; or from Beaumont and Fletcher's, and Jonson's, *Works*; or from other literary folios. Roughly the same can be said of Shakespeare's reputation. While it may have been on the rise, one could scarcely say it greatly outshone those of his rivals.

Eighteenth Century: Shakespeare's Reputation, the Book Market, Editors, and Owners

Shakespeare reached the heights of fame somewhat before the First Folio. (For a concentrated coverage of his eighteenth-century apotheosis to the position of iconic bard, see West 2001: 20–2.) Suffice it to say here, with Gary Taylor, that "after a slow but steady upward climb, Shakespeare's coronation as the King of English Poets finally occurred . . . at some time between the death of Alexander Pope (1744) and the birth of William Wordsworth (1770)" (Taylor 1990: 114). As we shall see, the Folio's fortunes were stirring in these middle years, but the takeoff came a little later.

A necessary context in which to view the history of the First Folio is the book market. It grew prodigiously during the century, in part due to changes in taste and values, and the growth of serious book collecting. Booksellers and auctioneers flourished. There were some 150 booksellers in London during the middle 50 years of the century. Retail (as opposed to auction) catalogues became important from the 1730s; retailers and auctioneers together produced some 2,400 book catalogues in the century. One third of these was concentrated in the 1780s and 1790s. English books came to be placed first in catalogues. Secular subjects overtook theological. All of these factors favored the First Folio.

The great editing tradition of Shakespeare's plays began early, with Rowe (1709, then 1714), who owned a Second Folio, though primarily used a Fourth. It stretched all through the eighteenth and nineteenth centuries, from Pope (1723–5, 1728), Theobald (1733), Hanmer (1743–4), Warburton (1747), Johnson (1765), Capell (1767–8), Johnson–Steevens (1773, 1778), Johnson–Steevens–Reed (1785), Malone (1790), and Johnson–Steevens–Reed (1793), to Reed (1803, 1813), and Boswell the younger/Malone (1821), and on through Knight, Halliwell-Phillipps, Dyce, Cowden-Clark to Furness (father and son). An outstanding feature in the Folio's life is its connection with this tradition: *all* these editors after Rowe (except Warburton) owned a First Folio, some of them more than one (West 2003: 392).

Some of the copies are very noteworthy. Sir Thomas Hanmer was the first to buy one, West 74, now at the Folger: his bookplate is dated 1707; the volume contains stage directions in his hand. West 17 in the British Library was owned successively by Lewis Theobald, Dr Johnson (who "did not much improve its condition," according to Charles Burney [ms note (n.d.), signed by Charles Burney, on verso of first original leaf of West 17, one of the Folios in the British Library]), and George Steevens. It was given to Steevens by Jacob Tonson, who with his successors owned the copyrights and held a monopoly of eighteenth-century Shakespeare publishing. Edward Capell bought his copy about 1720; he gave it, with the best part of his library, to Trinity College, Cambridge. For his great variorum edition, Malone purchased a copy around 1780. When he died in 1812, James Boswell the younger continued to use it to complete the revision of Malone's *Variorum* edition in 1821. It then went to the Bodleian. It is a distinguished copy. It has a state 1 Droeshout portrait, which is very rare. When Malone had it rebound, he had "EM" stamped in gold on the covers and gave the copy pride of place in his library ("M[alone] 1" on the spine). He also grangerized it: bound in among the preliminaries are about twenty leaves of manuscript and engravings, including some of Shakespeare.

Connected to, and an integral part of, this editing tradition is the most significant textual event in the First Folio's life: the recognition of its textual primacy over the Second, Third, and Fourth Folios. By "primacy" I mean that it alone, among the four, has textual authority. The later three are derived from it. Capell said he made this discovery in 1745, but he was slow to publish it. Dr Johnson, in 1765, was the first to publish: "The truth is, that the first is equivalent to all others, and the rest only deviate from it by the printer's negligence. . . . I collated them all at the beginning, but afterwards used only the first" (vol. I, [D1]v). This was the turning point in the First Folio's life. As the century progressed and its textual primacy came to be more widely recognized, the Folio became increasingly set apart in reputation.

As with the editors, actors liked to own a First Folio. David Garrick purchased a copy around 1760 and it seems he used it for performances at Drury Lane. It is now held by Queen's College, Oxford. It contains his bookplate. Another copy was probably owned by the actor John Henderson (d. 1785). This copy, West 21, in the Sir John Soane Museum, has further distinction through its succession of ownership. It was bought and used by Isaac Reed for his 1803 edition. When he died in 1807, John Philip Kemble, one of the all-time great Shakespearean actors, purchased it. Then, when James Boswell the younger relinquished the Malone copy in 1821, he replaced it by buying this copy in the Kemble sale for a very high price. He defended the price by saying he paid it to obtain what was at the same time "a memorial of Shakespeare and of Kemble" (MS at the Museum). He commissioned for it perhaps the best binding of any Folio in the world. The tradition of actor-ownership continued. Edmund Kean was presented with a copy when he was acting in New York in 1820; it was one of the first to be on American soil; later it was sold in London and has disappeared. William E. Burton, comic actor and theater manager, also took a copy to America. On his death, Edwin Forrest (d. 1872), considered the first great American actor, purchased it and so revered it he had a glass case and stand specially made for it and kept it within arm's reach of his desk. Unfortunately, after Forrest's death it was in a fire; its charred remains are at the University of Pennsylvania.

Since not many First Folios changed hands before the last two decades of the eighteenth century, the profile of owners stayed pretty much the same as in the seventeenth century. Steevens wrote in 1793, "Most of the first folios now extant, are known to have belonged to ancient families resident in the country" (I, 445, n. 6). One can say, as a generality, most copies were privately owned by the peerage and landed gentry, and increasingly by middle-class, professional, and educated men, including MPs, churchmen, and scholars. Among the notable purchasers was George III, around 1770. His copy was presented to the nation by George IV; it is now in the British Library as part of the King's Library, visible in glassed-in stacks as one enters the building. Two copies were owned by prime ministers: around 1740, the first duke of Newcastle purchased a copy – today one of the few in private hands (West 43); apparently around 1760, the second earl of Sherburne, afterwards first marquess of Lansdowne, purchased the copy now in the Guildhall. Some were purchased in the formation of libraries. Around 1760, Clayton Mordaunt Cracherode purchased a copy for his important library, which he bequeathed to the British Museum (Library). The copy in the great library at Longleat was possibly bought by the second marquess of Bath at the end of the eighteenth century. Also at the end of the eighteenth century or at the beginning of the nineteenth, the eleventh duke of Norfolk purchased the copy still in another great library, that in Arundel Castle. The shift from private to institutional ownership became pronounced as the century progressed: in addition to copies mentioned above, in 1779, Capell gave his copy to Trinity College; in 1784, the Society of Antiquaries received a copy that is now in the National Library of Scotland; and in 1799, Eton College received its copy. Few women owned a Folio. Three who did marked and dated their ownership. Elizabeth Brocket dates two of her signatures, 1702 and 1712, in a copy that stayed in her family till 1907 (West 81). Elizabeth Okell inscribed "her Book 1729" in her copy (West 136). Around 1790, Mrs Anne Damer, sculptress, purchased a copy in which she placed her artist-designed bookplate, dated 1793 (West 76). As in the seventeenth century, no major writers owned a copy (other than those among the editors).

Early and Middle Years of the Eighteenth Century

The First Folio makes little mark in the early years of the century. I have so far found little internal information of interest recorded in copies. For the first eight decades, few copies sold. In the first six decades, I have found hardly any reliable price information. What little there is suggests no significant change in First Folio prices. Three offer prices (two at £1 5s. and one at £1 17s. 6d.) of the Fourth Folio in the 1730s give evidence that it was still the preferred edition; in fact one of these, and one in 1770, were promoted in the catalogues as the "best Edit[ion]." The first solid evidence I have seen of a premium for the First Folio was £3 3s., paid in 1756 for the copy belonging to the late Martin Folkes, president of the Royal Society (on the eighteenth day of the sale; this large library, "rich in works on natural history, coins, medals, inscriptions, and fine arts" [West 2003: 110], is typical of an inquiring, erudite, eighteenth-century, English gentleman). Sidney Lee in his *Census* (1902a) says this copy had been owned c.1730 by Lewis Theobald and was bought at the Folkes sale by George Steevens; if Lee is correct, it was a second copy for both editors. It is now in the John Rylands University Library of Manchester.

Some events in the 1730s to 1770s can quickly suggest the mid-century progress of Shakespeare's reception and public recognition. In these five decades, seven new, major editions of the plays, prepared by as many distinguished editors, appeared. In 1736 a Ladies Club was formed to persuade theater managers to put on more Shakespeare. In 1733–55, the frequency of Shakespeare performances reached an all-time peak. In 1741 his monument was erected in Westminster Abbey. In 1751–6 the first academic lectures on Shakespeare in an English university were given (in Oxford). In 1755 a two-volume Shake-spearean novel was published. In 1774 the first public lecture on Shakespeare was given. In 1776 the first complete French translation of Shakespeare came out. From 1747 to 1776 David Garrick – one of the all-time great Shakespearean actors, a great theater manager, a great promoter, and a man who concerned himself with the text – ran the Drury Lane theater (in rivalry with Covent Garden). (For sources of these events and dates see West 2001: 22–3.) Garrick did more than anyone in the eighteenth century for Shakespeare and by extension also perhaps for the First Folio. (In the nineteenth century, Halliwell-Phillipps's role is comparable.) Undoubtedly, the most significant event affecting the public perception of Shakespeare was Garrick's 1769 Jubilee bonanza in Stratford-upon-Avon. Taylor called it his "marketing masterpiece," adding "it was reported in newspapers throughout Europe [and] spawned Stratford's literary tourism industry" (1990: 119).

As for the market place, only a few First Folios appeared at auction in the middle years, though we know that the editors procured copies – Theobald perhaps two copies in the 1730s, Dr Johnson one in the 1740s, Steevens one in 1756; and he was given one in 1765. Garrick bought his around 1760. First Folio prices began to stir in the 1760s. The average of four reasonably reliable prices was £5 8s., the low (Garrick's) £1 16s., the high (Cracherode's) £8 18s. 6d. A comparable and reliable price in the 1770s was £5 5s.

In 1765, I found an example of all four Folios in the same catalogue; at least three of these were purchased by a different person. But around this time collectors began the custom of procuring all four Folios for their library. In 1765, Steevens was given West 17. When it was sold in 1800, the three other Folios were in his sale. By at least the end of the first quarter of the next century, there is evidence that the four Folios together were regarded as a package: a bookseller advertised the four as a set in 1824. At least thirty collectors in the nineteenth century sold their First Folio accompanied by the other three. Package prices for the four were the norm in the twentieth century.

Two copies have mid-century annotations of note, one concerned with the text, the other with performance. West 128 in the Folger, in addition to some early eighteenth-century manuscript, in a similar hand to autographs of the name Lister, has mid-century manuscript throughout the volume. It shows a close reading of the plays: some seems to refer to commentary by mid-century editors; readings are changed by both erasures and additions. One could speculate the person was considering another new edition. As the copy's description in West (2003) says, these extensive markings are typical of the eighteenth-century preoccupation with Shakespeare's text. As Brian Vickers put it, "Suggesting emendations" became "almost a national pastime" (Vickers 1995: 21). The other copy, West 173, owned by a private collector in New York City, was annotated by someone who paid attention to who played the parts in performances he presumably attended. He provides lists of actors paired with the printed or manuscript names of the parts. In *Coriolanus* Charles Kemble is mentioned, and under "1756" is a pair of lists with Garrick as Bastard and Mrs Cibber as Constance. In other places Garrick is shown as King Henry IV, and Kean as Hamlet and Timon. One paired list in *Twelfth Night* bears the date "Dec. 10. 1771." This copy has four other Shakespeare associations. It was owned by William Macready's manager; from 1883, it was owned by Mrs Mary Cowden Clarke, during the years she was editing Shakespeare; Mrs Clarke gave it to Frederick Haines, a trustee of the Shakespeare Birthplace Trust; and it is presently owned by the curator of rare books at the Globe.

The Last Two Decades of the Eighteenth Century

The last two decades of the century are treated separately because in these years the First Folio consolidated the pre-eminent position it has held ever since. Interest in and demand for Shakespeare were necessary conditions. Both conditions were amply met. As we have seen, the 13 years from 1790 witnessed the culmination of the century's great Shakespeare scholarship – with the magisterial editions of Malone,

Steevens, and Reed. In seven years within the 1790s, 15 editions of the plays appeared. By the 1790s, high demand crossed the Atlantic: the first edition of Shakespeare was printed in America. From the 1780s to the present, the price of the Folio and the reputation of Shakespeare appear to be tied.

Five central features of the First Folio's life become apparent in these two decades. The first is high price and frequency of sale. If one had to choose the moment when the Folio took off, it would be in April 1787 on the ninth day of the sale of Richard Wright, MD, fellow of the Royal Society. The sale of his library lasted 12 days. As with Folkes' forty years earlier, here is a typical sale of the large library of an eminent and learned man. The First Folio achieved a new record price of £10, the highest since Cracherode's purchase c.1760. It is a fine copy with all original leaves present. Just over a hundred years later it went to the Library of Congress. From that sale, prices never looked back. In 1790, Steevens wrote with heavy irony to Isaac Reed that he anticipated paying "the small charge of twenty guineas" (West 2001: 27; and 23, n. 95). In 1793, Steevens records his perception of the Folio as "the most expensive book in the language" (447). In the 1790s the average price for eight copies, all apparently in good condition, was over £30. New records were set in 1790 (£35 14s.) and 1792 (£73 10s.). The sales rate accelerated in the 1780s. Before then, I have recorded three or fewer per decade. In the 1780s there were at least six sales and in the 1790s at least ten. The perception of the Folio among dealers had changed: in 1781 a First Folio was advertised on the front cover of a sale catalogue (illustrated in West 2001: 28): in short, by this time the Folio was well enough known that it could be used to draw people to the auction.

During the eighteenth century, book collecting became a favorite pastime of the English wealthy. By the end of the century, Sidney Lee said it was growing to be "a passion" among noblemen (Lee 1924: 97). At the same time the Folio became a collectable. It is difficult to pinpoint when this happened, but by the last two decades most of the sales in which it appeared were of collections. Its position as a collectable was consolidated at the sale in March 1790 when the duke of Roxburghe famously paid the extraordinary sum of £35 14s., the record just mentioned. The copy is now in the Huntington Library. The duke was one of the greatest of all book collectors. He had purchased a First Folio around 1780, but gave it away when he acquired this better copy. The latter fetched £100 at the celebrated sale of the duke's library in 1812. The remarkably high £73 10s., the other record just mentioned, was also paid by a well-known collector, Henry Constantine Jennings. During the nineteenth century the Jennings copy, now in the Elizabethan Club, Yale University, was in the great collections of George Hibbert and Henry Huth.

The combination of high market value and the demand of collectors for copies in good condition made it profitable to conserve damaged copies. West 69 (at the Folger) illustrates the beginning of what became a veritable mini-industry. In about the 1780s Roger Payne, a leading binder, well known for both his good bindings and his detailed bills, rebound West 69, one of at least six he so treated. What his bill reveals is typical of the treatment accorded many Folios. He inlaid six leaves, strengthened the title-page (with over forty pieces!), repaired leaves (including margins) throughout the volume, and spent *seven and a half days* cleaning the leaves. His total bill approached £5. (In short, collectors were prepared to pay a premium, for these services, of about 20–30 percent of the going market price.) Today few First Folios remain untouched by the conservator. Most have undergone considerable treatment, very often more than once. Until well into the twentieth century, much harm was done. Original or old bindings were replaced in the contemporary fashion. Rebinding was usually accompanied by trimming, and this meant the diminution or disappearance of margins and marginalia. Leaves were bleached, and this meant the loss of such historical information as owners' and readers' annotations. (See "Enemies of First Folios," West 2003: 293–6.)

The fourth feature in the Folio's life concerns emigration. Combinations of Shakespeare's and the Folio's fame, and the accumulation of necessary wealth, led to the Folio becoming global. In 1791, Judge William Parker of Exeter, New Hampshire, inscribed his name and the year in a copy now in the Scheide Library at Princeton. Thus began the exodus of copies from England to America. By 1850, at least six copies were owned by Americans; by 1876, at least 18; by 1888, there were 13 in New York City alone. Today, of the 230 extant copies, nearly two-thirds are in America, with 82 of them in the Folger Shakespeare Library. In the nineteenth century, copies went to three Commonwealth countries (Australia, New Zealand, South Africa) and three continental (France, Germany, Italy). In the twentieth, single copies went to Canada and Switzerland, and 14 to Japan.

Finally, in the last two decades of the eighteenth century the Folio became distinct from all other English books. After the Roxburghe purchase in 1790, it became an icon. In the market place, no English book rivaled its price. The other three Folios tended to sell for around one to two guineas (seldom more), compared to the First Folio's £10 (1787) and an average of over £30 in the 1790s. The folio prices of other dramatists (Ben Jonson, Beaumont and Fletcher, and Davenant) and other literary figures (Chaucer, Spenser, Cowley) tell the same story. (By contrast, £100 in 1793 for a Gutenberg Bible may temper any awe concerning First Folio prices.) Since the end of the eighteenth century, the divergence of First Folio prices from those of comparable books has continuously increased.

By the end of the century, most of the main features that character-ize the life of the First Folio were established or had at least been heralded. As we have seen, these include centrality to editing the plays, high sales rates and prices, being sought and fought over by collectors, selling in sets of the four Folios, types of owners, emigra-tion, and an immense amount of conservation. Its life since has been largely an amplification of these features. In addition, they generated some logical or related outcomes, such as printing of First Folio facsimile editions, listings and censuses of copies, a massive shift from private to institutional ownership, the concentrated collecting of one-third of the copies by Henry Folger, and a central role in the New Bibliography. But by the end of the eighteenth century, the First Folio had "arrived." From then on its reputation and that of Shakespeare continued to rise – together – in closely related trends.

Notes

1 The principal sources for this chapter are West (2001, 2003), the first two volumes in *The History of the First Folio* series. The third volume will describe all copies of the First Folio in detail and provide more information about subjects covered in this chapter.
2 Copies are referred to by the numbers in the new *Census* of First Folios, West (2003).

Part II

Theories of Editing

Chapter 5

The Birth of the Editor

Andrew Murphy

No text of Shakespeare's has ever appeared without, in some sense, being "edited." Indeed, the playwright may have been his own first editor, if (as seems likely) he himself brought the narrative poem *Venus and Adonis* to the Stratford-born printer Richard Field for publication in 1593. Every text that came to print in quarto needed some element of preparation before it reached publication, and so too did the First Folio and the three further collected editions which followed it in 1632, 1663/4, and 1685. We know what the folio editors did, thanks to an extensive study carried out by N. W. Black and Matthias Shaaber (1937). In their *Shakespeare's Seventeenth-Century Editors, 1632–1685*, they track the changes made by the anonymous printshop workers who helped to shape the text of the plays by, for example, retrieving Greek and Roman names that had been scrambled in F1, correcting obvious typographical errors, and even adding entrances and exits.

While we know what work these early editors carried out, we do not know their identities, nor do we really know what explicit "program" they were following as editors. Black and Shaaber have proposed (specifically of those involved in editing F4) that "their object was to produce a creditable specimen of the printer's art and a book that buyers could read with ease" (1937: 59) and, intuitively, it seems right to think that the earliest of Shakespeare's editors had little more in mind than this laudable aim. From the beginning of the eighteenth century, however, the nature of Shakespeare editing would change radically, and the purpose of the present chapter is to track the emergence of the editor as a public figure in his own right and to trace, in this period, the evolution of editing as a discipline with its own clear theoretical underpinnings.

By the opening decade of the eighteenth century the publisher Jacob Tonson had acquired a majority stake in the rights to Shakespeare's plays. Shakespeare had been dead for almost a hundred years, and so, to generate some renewed interest in the plays, Tonson invited one of the foremost dramatists of the day, Nicholas Rowe, to prepare the text for publication. The title-page of the first of the six volumes of the edition advertised it as being "Revis'd and corrected. . . . By N. Rowe, Esq." Rowe thus became the first of Shakespeare's editors to be publicly identified. In dedicating his edition to the duke of Somerset, Rowe also became the first person to comment on the nature of the task he had undertaken as an editor of Shakespeare:

> I have taken some Care to redeem him from the Injuries of former Impressions. I must not pretend to have restor'd this Work to the Exactness of the Author's Original Manuscripts: Those are lost, or, at least, are gone beyond any Inquiry I could make; so that there was nothing left, but to compare the several Editions, and give the true Reading as well as I could from thence. This I have endeavour'd to do pretty carefully, and render'd very many Places Intelligible, that were not so before. (I, A2r–A2v)

Rowe points here to two important facts concerning the Shakespeare text: first, Shakespeare's own manuscripts have not survived, so there is no "original" text for editors to work with; second, even in Shakespeare's own time many of the plays appeared in multiple editions, which frequently differ from each other in a variety of ways, some minor, some major. Rowe set himself the task of divining the "true" reading of the text through an examination of the various printed editions he had to hand.

In fact, Rowe's study of the early editions was neither comprehensive nor systematic. He used F4 as his base text, and where he found significant variation between F4 and one of the early editions he happened to consult, he emended as he saw fit. Thus, for example, the Second Quarto of *Hamlet* includes a scene in which Hamlet questions the purposes of Fortinbras's army and lapses into a soliloquy ("How all occasions do inform against me . . .") which the folio texts lack. Rowe incorporated this scene into his own text, but he derived it, not from Q2, but from a 1676 quarto performance edition. He also happened upon the quarto prologue to *Romeo and Juliet*, again lacking in the folio texts, and he included this in his own edition, though, somewhat oddly, he placed it at the end of the play, rather than the beginning.

Detailed analysis of the early texts was not Rowe's central concern. But we should not be surprised by this. He was, after all, a dramatist by profession and it is the concerns of a dramatist that he brings to the editorial project. He systematized the text in a variety of different ways, providing *dramatis personae* lists for all of the plays, adding indications of location to some scenes, and standardizing many of the variant character names. His enduring influence on the text is seen in, for example, the traditional ordering of *dramatis personae* lists by social rank and gender – a convention which persisted far into the modern era.

From the point of view of the Tonson publishing firm, Rowe's text was a success: it appeared in a second edition in its year of first publication (1709) and a third edition was published in 1714. With the centenary of F1 coming on the horizon in 1723, the firm began planning a completely new edition and the same marketing strategy was deployed again, with the dramatist Rowe being replaced by the foremost poet of the day, Alexander Pope. Like Rowe, Pope prefaced his edition with an account of his editorial practice. Pope's assessment of the textual situation was decidedly gloomy. Shakespeare had suffered grievously, in his view, from "the excessive carelessness of the press" (I, xv). In addition to this, the theatrical provenance of the plays was, in itself, a decided liability. The source texts for the earlier editions were likely, in Pope's view, to have been cobbled together from "the *Prompter's Book*, or *Piece-meal Parts* written out for the use of the actors," texts which "had lain . . . in the playhouse, and had from time to time been cut, or added to, arbitrarily" (I, xvii). Where speeches were, in Pope's view, assigned to the wrong character, this was probably because "a governing Player, to have the mouthing of some favourite speech himself, would snatch it from the unworthy lips of an Underling" (I, xix).

Like Rowe, Pope did not analyze or make use of the early texts in any kind of systematic fashion. Rather, he cherry-picked from these texts the readings he found to be most appealing. He also used his own reading of the textual history of the plays to justify excising passages he considered to be unworthy of Shakespeare. Most of this material was "degraded" to the bottom of the page, though some text was simply deleted from the edition without comment. In the case of *Love's Labour's Lost*, for example, in excess of 200 lines were removed from the main body of the text and a further four complete scenes were marked as being of doubtful provenance. Pope carried forward some of Rowe's innovations, offering further details of the locality of particular scenes and regularizing the division of the plays into discrete acts and scenes. Just as Rowe had brought a theatrical mindset to the business of editing, so Pope brought a poetic sensibility to his task, and he intervened repeatedly to enforce a greater sense of metrical regularity in the text.

In essence, Pope's central aim as editor was to refashion Shakespeare according to the norms and aesthetic expectations of the early eighteenth century. In this manner, he acted as Shakespeare's artistic partner, rather than his textual servant, and this sense of the relationship between the two writers is nicely caught by Pope's contemporary, George Sewell, who observed that "When a Genius of similar Fire and Fancy, temper'd with a learned Patience, sits down to consider what SHAKESPEAR would *Think*, as well as what he could *Write*, we may then expect to see his Works answer to our Idea of the Man" (viii). What Pope provided was very much a text in keeping with an eighteenth-century idea of what Shakespeare should be.

Pope's edition prompted the publication of the first book-length study dedicated wholly to textual issues in Shakespeare. This was Lewis Theobald's *Shakespeare Restor'd: or, A Specimen of the Many Errors as well Committed, or Unamended, by Mr. Pope in his Late Edition of this Poet* (1726). As the combative title indicates, Theobald was highly critical of Pope's work as an editor. In particular, he took Pope to task for repeatedly "*substitut*[*ing*] *a fresh Reading*" where "there was no Occasion to depart from the Poet's Text" (1726: 134). Pope responded by making Theobald the crowningly dull hero of his mercilessly satirical *Dunciad*. The publicity generated by the dispute was enough to prompt the Tonson firm (much to Pope's disgust) to invite Theobald to produce his own edition of Shakespeare.

Though Theobald had had some modest success as a writer for the London stage, his professional training was in the law. His approach to the text was much less aesthetically oriented than Rowe's and Pope's had been. For Theobald, as might be expected given his background, *precedent* was of greater value than immediate contemporary aesthetic judgment. Thus, for example, where Pope complained of the early quartos that "every page is . . . scandalously false spelled" (I, xv), Theobald was able to recognize that language, spelling conventions, and grammar evolve over time and that what constitutes an error in need of correction in one era may be perfectly acceptable usage in another. For Theobald, one of the first duties of an editor was to familiarize himself with the cultural and historical context of his author, and he recognized that this requires a careful course of reading and scholarship. For his own part, he tells us, he

> purposely read over *Hall* and *Holingshead*'s Chronicles . . . ; all the novels in *Italian*, from which our Author had borrow'd any of his plots; such Parts of *Plutarch*, from which he had deriv'd any Parts of his *Greek* or *Roman* Story: *Chaucer* and *Spenser's* Works; all the Plays of *B. Jonson, Beaumont* and *Fletcher*, and above 800 old *English* Plays, to ascertain the obsolete and uncommon Phrases in him: Not to mention some Labour and Pains unpleasantly spent in the dry Task of consulting Etymological *Glossaries*. (I, lxvii–lxviii)

Theobald's reading enabled him to view the Shakespeare text within the context of its own time, rather than looking at it through the lens of eighteenth-century aesthetic criteria. He also pioneered the "parallel passages" approach to editing Shakespeare: supporting corrections and conjectures in some instances by drawing evidence from elsewhere within the Shakespeare canon.

In formulating his editorial strategies, Theobald was influenced by models drawn from classical textual scholarship and, in particular, by the work of Richard Bentley, editor of Horace, Terence, and Manilius. In some respects, Theobald's understanding of the relationship among the earliest texts was more complex than that of his predecessors. He certainly registers the fact that, in the absence of authorial manuscripts, errors are "transmitted down thro' a Series of incorrect Editions" (I, xli) and he claims also to have carefully collated the early texts. However, like Rowe and Pope, he tended to be rather indiscriminate in his use of materials drawn from these texts. He also followed the practice of basing his own text on the edition of his immediate predecessor; thus Pope's edition served as his base text and he accepted many of the poet's emendations – particularly his regularizations of Shakespeare's meter.

Theobald's immediate successor as a Tonson editor was the cleric William Warburton, whose edition appeared in 1747. Warburton was an associate of Pope's and the title-page of his edition declared that it was "By Mr. Pope and Mr. Warburton." In his preface, Warburton observes of Pope (who had died in 1744) that "he was willing that *his* Edition should be melted down into *mine*, as it would, he said, afford him (so great is the modesty of an ingenuous temper) a fit opportunity of confessing his Mistakes" (I, xix). In fact, Warburton did not base his edition directly on Pope's, but rather again followed the practice of using his predecessor's edition as his base text. He was witheringly dismissive of the work of other editors (of Theobald, whose text he was, of course, using, he observed that he had neither "common Judgment to see, [nor] critical Sagacity to amend, what was manifestly faulty" [I, xi]), and he made a very large number of changes to the text, often with little real justification. We have seen that Theobald brought his legal training to bear in the manner in which he attended to the text, but it was a certain kind of legal mindset that he drew upon, rather than direct knowledge of the law as such. Warburton was formidably learned in the fields of theology and church history, but he generally deployed his learning simply to generate unnecessary changes and annotations within his edition. The later eighteenth-century editor Edmond Malone, commenting on Warburton's edition, expressed amazement at the fact "that the learned editor should have had so little respect for the greatest poet that has appeared since the days of Homer, as to use a commentary on his works merely as *'a stalking-horse, under the presentation of which he might shoot his wit'"* (I, lxviii). Ultimately, Warburton's edition was neither a critical nor a commercial success. A second edition of Warburton was never issued; by contrast, Theobald's text had reached its eighth edition by 1773.

Following what must be considered the failure of Warburton's text, the Tonson group would appear to have turned back to the trusted formula of employing a high-profile contemporary writer to serve as editor of Shakespeare. The editor in question was Samuel Johnson, who took up the task soon after his *Dictionary* appeared in print. It would take him the best part of a decade to complete his work. Johnson's assessment of the textual situation was bleak and, like Pope, he laid the blame in large measure at the door of Shakespeare's fellow actors: "his works were transcribed for the players by those who may be supposed to have seldom understood them; . . . they were perhaps sometimes mutilated by the actors, for the sake of shortening the speeches" (I, C7v). However, Johnson's general textual orientation was much closer to Theobald's than it was to Pope's. His primary instinct was to try to make sense of the text as he found it on the page, and to resist emendation as far as he possibly could:

> my first labour is, always to turn the old text on every side, and try if there be any interstice, through which light can find its way. . . . In this modest industry I have not been unsuccessful. I have rescued many

lines from the violations of temerity, and secured many scenes from the inroads of correction. I have adopted the *Roman* sentiment, that it is more honourable to save a citizen, than to kill an enemy, and have been more careful to protect than to attack. (I, D8v–E1r)

While Johnson was indeed cautious in his approach to emending the text – and certainly, by contrast with Warburton, he was a paragon of restraint – there were some areas in which he gave himself free license. Thus, for example, he observes that he "considered the punctuation as wholly in [his] power" (I, E1r) and he made extensive changes to the pointing of the text. In an interesting study of Johnson's edition, Arthur M. Eastman indicates the extent to which he greatly simplified the punctuation of the plays, getting rid, in particular, of "the hundreds of pairs of parentheses that his precursors had used either in lieu of dashes or commas or, as if to emphasize thought divisions, along with them" (1950: 1115). Eastman also notes that Johnson restructured the text to break up extended sentences into smaller units. The final effect of these changes, Eastman suggests, is to make the text far more easily readable by a non-specialist audience. In this sense, Johnson sits squarely in the eighteenth-century tradition of refashioning the text in a way that makes it more intelligible to readers.

We have seen that Theobald observed generally of the early texts that errors are "transmitted down thro' a Series of incorrect Editions." There is a suggestion in this comment that, the farther one gets away from whatever text might be considered the most authoritative of the early editions, the more it is the case that unnecessary or incorrect variations accumulate within the printed text. Johnson was the first of Shakespeare's editors to formulate this principle as an explicit statement of textual authority and priority. Discussing Theobald's handling of the folios, he observes:

> he mentions the two first folios as of high, and the third folio as of middle authority; but the truth is, that the first is equivalent to all others, and that the rest only deviate from it by the printer's negligence. Whoever has any of the folios has all, excepting those diversities which mere reiteration of editions will produce. (I, D1v)

There are some obscurities in what Johnson is saying here, but his fundamental point is that, taking the four folios as a group, F1 has a status and authority which is wholly different from that of the other three. Of course, the textual status of F1 is itself complex. For example, in most cases it is difficult to do more than speculate as to what might be the source of the texts that F1 reproduces. We can ask whether it might be that some of the plays were printed from Shakespeare's own manuscripts, or from a copy made for use in the theater, or from a quarto edition published in advance of F1, or from a quarto marked up with reference to a manuscript source, or, indeed, from a manuscript marked up with reference to a quarto, but answering these questions, as both Thomas L. Berger and Paul Werstine indicate in their respective chapters in this volume, is a very difficult business. For this reason, F1 cannot in itself be thought of as a final point of origin for the plays that it reproduces. However, Johnson's argument is concerned with the relationship specifically between F1 and the other three folios, and what he proposes is that F1 has absolute priority over these editions because, being the first text in the sequence, it is necessarily closer to the original source texts, whatever these may have been. In Johnson's view, the changes made in F2–F4 can be of no real authority because they amount to little more than the speculations of the press correctors who prepared these editions for publication, with each edition being founded on its immediate predecessor. The farther one moves along the folio line of descent, then, the greater the cumulative level of intervention – whether speculative correction or typographical or other errors.

In mapping out this line of descent from folio to folio and in privileging F1 as being a text of absolute authority relative to its successors, Johnson was elucidating a principle that would become fundamental within later editorial thinking. But, though he recognized the principle in theory, he cannot really be said to have followed it himself in practice. The logic of his own position would suggest that he should have broken with the tradition of using the work of his immediate predecessor as his base text. After all, the sequence Rowe–Pope–Theobald–Warburton was simply an extension of the sequence F1–F2–F3–F4. If Johnson saw an accumulation of error and unauthorized intervention from F2 to F4, logically that process continued to develop through Rowe (who, as we have seen, based his text on F4) and on to Warburton. In fact, however, Johnson simply followed the traditional practice of marking his own changes in the text of his predecessor. Or, at least, that is partly what he did, in that he began by using a copy of Warburton's edition, but then, reaching the eleventh play in his edition (*The Taming of the Shrew*), he switched to the fourth edition of Theobald's text, thus, confusingly, founding his own edition on two very different base texts.

By contrast with Warburton's edition, Johnson's was very long-lived. His text appeared in several further editions, re-edited first by George Steevens and then by Isaac Reed. Steevens, in his later editorial work, offered a significant interrogation of the principle of establishing a clear hierarchy of authority within a line of textual descent, and we shall return to this issue in due course. First, however, it is instructive to examine a new Tonson text, edited by Edward Capell, which appeared just three years after Johnson's first edition. Capell recognized the same principle of textual descent as Johnson had done, but he explicitly extended it to the quartos as well as the folios, observing that

> The quartos went through many impressions . . . and, in each play, the last is generally taken from the impression next before it, and so onward to the first; . . . And this further is to be observ'd of them: that, generally speaking, the more distant they are from the original, the more they abound in faults; 'till, in the end, the corruptions of the last copies become so excessive, as to make them of hardly any worth. (I, 13)

Unlike Johnson, Capell made the link between this process of descent among the early texts and the textual tradition of his own century. Writing of Rowe's edition, he noted that he "went no further than to the edition nearest to him in time, which was the folio of 1685, the last and worst of those impressions" (I, 16). Capell argues that "the superstructure cannot be a sound one, which is built upon so bad a foundation as that work of Mr. ROWE's, which all [other editors], in succession, have yet made their corner-stone: The truth is, it was impossible that such a beginning should end better than it has done: the fault was in the setting-out" (I, 19).

In his own "setting-out" Capell decided to break decisively with this tradition. Before he began the task of editing he gathered together the largest collection of the earliest texts of the plays that had yet been assembled. He then began an extensive program of collation: "first of moderns with moderns, then of moderns with ancients, and afterwards of ancients with others more ancient." The outcome of this process was that he formed a resolution:

> to stick invariably to the old editions, (that is, the best of them) which hold now the place of manuscripts, no scrap of the Author's writing having the luck to come down to us; and never to depart from them, but in cases where reason, and the uniform practice of men of the greatest note in this art, tell him – they may be quitted. (I, 20)

Capell became the first editor to build his edition from the ground up, drawing directly on a wide range of the earliest published texts (the manuscript copy of his edition is preserved in the collection of the Wren Library at Trinity College Cambridge). His general plan was to use the earliest quartos, where these seemed the best texts, coupled with the F1 texts for plays which appeared for the first time in that edition. The exceptions to this general rule were *2 Henry IV*, *Othello*, and *Richard III* – in each of these cases Capell felt that F1 offered a better text than the available quartos.

By using the earliest texts as the sources for his edition, Capell succeeded in clearing out a very large number of errors which had been accumulating in the plays ever since the Renaissance. However, from the point of view of later editorial practice, there are two problematic aspects of Capell's work. First, as we have seen, Capell places a high premium on the early quartos, relying on them to provide the base text for almost half of the plays in his edition. But, as already noted, the question of what kind of source text lies behind any given early printed text can be enormously difficult to determine, and the fact that F1 appeared later than a particular early quarto does not necessarily mean that any specific F1 play is of lesser authority than its early quarto equivalent. As we have seen, it is possible to imagine a scenario whereby the source text of an F1 play could be, for instance, a copy of an early quarto corrected against a manuscript held by the King's Men company. In such a case, which would be the better edition to adopt as the base text for a new edition? Many editors would say that, in a case such as this, F1 should have priority.

Capell, as a pioneer in this field of study, was not best placed to map the lost history of what texts lay behind the early printed editions. But, then again, as Paul Werstine demonstrates in his chapter in this volume (and elsewhere), the signature note of twentieth-century editorial theory is a misplaced confidence in the idea that simple mechanisms can be devised for compelling a printed text to yield up the secrets of its original sources. Capell certainly went as far as anyone could in his era in bringing the Shakespeare text back to something like its historical fundamentals. Subsequent editors have come up with different narratives in determining whether a given quarto or F1 text has higher authority. But, in some respects, one could argue that, while these narratives may often be better informed than Capell's, they do not always offer any greater guarantee of certainty.

A second problem that has been identified with Capell's work is that he does not entirely stick to the principle of building his text exclusively from the earliest sources. In fact, he is quite explicit about this in the introduction to his edition, where he observes that errors in the earliest texts meant that he regarded it as "proper and necessary to look into the other old editions, and to select from thence whatever improves the Author, or contributes to his advancement in perfectness." Capell's rationale here is that the very fact that the later editions "do improve [the text] was with the editor an argument in their favour; and a presumption of genuineness for what is thus selected, whether additions, or differences of any other nature" (I, 21). The general principle here seems to be, as R. B. McKerrow has succinctly put it, that "if an editor likes a reading, that reading is (a) good, and (b) attributable to Shakespeare" (1933: 116).

There is a clear tension here between, on the one hand, Capell's enunciation of the principle that only the earliest texts have authority and that subsequent editions simply introduce error and corruption, and, on the other, his assertion that anything found in any edition that serves, in his view, to improve the text is necessarily recoverable as part of the genuine text. But this contradiction actually draws attention to a conundrum that is faced by all editors of Shakespeare who effectively follow in Capell's footsteps (which is to say, pretty much all editors of Shakespeare). All such editors seek to establish one of the earliest editions as their authoritative base text. But all editors inevitably encounter elements within their base text which clearly seem to constitute errors. Problematic aspects of the texts exist on a spectrum from the relatively straightforward to the convolutedly complex. Thus, for example, an editor encountering the word "aud" in the text may feel reasonably confident that it should be corrected to "and," arguing that no word "aud" appears to exist in the English language, that the context requires a conjunction, and that the likely explanation for the error is that the "u" is simply a turned "n." It may well even be possible to produce physical evidence in support of this change – if, for instance, "u" and "n" in the particular typeface being examined have features which enable them to be distinguished from each other. But things become more complicated when we look at a less straightforward (but still far from complex) instance. Take the well-known case of the Hostess's (Mistress Quickly's) description of Falstaff's dying moments in *Henry V*: "his Nose was as sharpe as a Pen, and a Table of greene fields" (TLN 838–9). It is extremely difficult to make sense of this wholly in its own terms. and most editors emend the text here to a reading suggested originally by Theobald: "his nose was as sharp as a pen, and a [i.e., he] babled of green fields" (IV, 30).

Editors in the modern era who choose to incorporate Theobald's emendation into their own text (as most editors do) are essentially following the same principle as Capell; the only real difference is that modern editors are less likely to assert as confidently as Capell would have done that, since Theobald's emendation makes sense, it must necessarily be what was written in the lost original manuscript.

The problem of correction and the necessity of accepting emendations from texts which, strictly speaking, have no authority was recognized by George Steevens, who, as we have seen, was responsible for a number of the revised editions of Samuel Johnson's text. Steevens was a wayward and eccentric figure, but he frequently brought a lively, pragmatically driven mindset to the business of editing. In the "Advertisement" to his 1793 edition, he observed that "Every re-impression of our great dramatick master's works must be considered in some degree experimental" (I, x) – a nice contrast with the attitude of blank certainty with which so many of his predecessors (and, indeed, successors) operated. Steevens generally adopted a much more re-laxed attitude to the business of emendation, and he declared that he did not "hesitate to affirm, that a blind fidelity to the eldest printed copies, is on some occasions a confirmed treason against the sense, spirit, and versification of Shakspeare" (I, xvi). On this basis, Steevens argued strongly against the elevation of F1 to a status wholly distinct from its successors. His particular point was to argue for the value of consulting F2 in cases where F1 was thought to be defective, and he noted that "it is on all hands allowed that what we style a younger and inferior MS. will occasionally correct the mistakes and supply the deficiencies of one of better note, and higher antiquity. Why, therefore, should not a book printed in 1632 be allowed the merit of equal services to a predecessor in 1623" (I, xxvi).

Part of what motivated Steevens in championing F2 was, charac-teristically, a desire to annoy his one-time collaborator and sometime adversary, Edmond Malone, who published an edition of Shakespeare in 1790. Following the same logic as Johnson and Capell before him, Malone dismissed F2 as worthless, but Steevens took great delight in pointing out that, despite this dismissal, Malone incorporated many F2 changes into his edition. Thus, Steevens predicted that the "numer-ous corrections from it admitted by that gentleman into his text, and pointed out in his notes, will, in our judgement, contribute to its eulogium" (I, xviii–xix). As Steevens' jibe makes clear, Malone was caught in the same bind as other editors: he privileged the earliest texts as authoritative, but nevertheless found himself having to draw on later texts in making sense of some of the problems he encountered with his base texts. Malone's own editorial procedure was curiously hybrid. Unlike Capell, he did not create his text absolutely from scratch, but rather used a copy of the 1785 Johnson–Steevens edition. In common with Capell, however, he did gather together an extensive collection of early texts, and he collated these texts in a way that was far more systematic than his predecessors. He explains his method of finalizing the text in the preface to his edition:

> Having often experienced the fallaciousness of collation by the eye, I determined, after I had adjusted the text in the best manner in my power, to have every proofsheet of my work read aloud to me, while I perused the first folio, for those plays which first appeared in that edition; and for all those which had been previously printed, the first quarto copy, excepting only in the instances of *The Merry Wives of Windsor* and *King Henry V*, which, being either sketches or imperfect copies, could not be wholly relied on; and *King Richard III.* of the earliest edition of which tragedy I was not possessed. I had at the same time before me a table which I had formed of the variations between the quartos and the folio. By this laborious process not a single innovation, made either by the editor of the second folio, or any of the modern editors, could escape me. (I, xliv–xlv)

In common with many of his predecessors Malone regarded certain aspects of the text as being fully within his remit as an editor. Thus, for example, he observes that all "the stage-directions . . . throughout this work I have considered as wholly in my power, and have regulated them in the best manner I could" (I, lviii). He also continues the tradition of regularizing certain features of the text that do not square with the practice of his day, for instance, correcting disagreements in number between a subject and its verb. Simon Jarvis notes that he also "silently supplies missing accusatives to pronouns and silently brings the tenses of verbs into conformity, in each case in line with the Johnson and Steevens 1785 text" (which, of course, served as his base text) (1995: 187).

Malone's 1790 edition can be seen essentially as the culmination of the eighteenth-century editorial tradition (for a contrary view, however, see de Grazia 1991a). Like Capell, Malone certainly had a high respect for the earliest editions and he worked hard to trace the relationships among these texts. Though he failed to follow Capell's practice of literally creating his own text from scratch, he did, nevertheless, subject his base text to a rigorous process of collation with the earliest editions. His investment in the earliest texts notwithstanding, he was willing, where he felt it necessary, to incorporate the emendations of other editors into his own text. Following in the footsteps of his predecessors stretching back to Rowe, he was also prepared to invoke the principle that changes to certain aspects of the text lay wholly within the editor's province, even when he knew that this involved overriding forms of usage that were perfectly acceptable in Shakespeare's own time.

If Malone's edition can be seen as, essentially, a synthesis of the main aspects of editorial procedure that had emerged over the course of the eighteenth century, it can also be seen as pointing forward to the normative editorial practice of the nineteenth century (and even, to some extent, beyond). His text appeared in a second edition in 1821, brought to press by James Boswell the younger, Malone himself having died in 1812. This text, together with the final edition of the Johnson–Steevens–Reed sequence (published in 1803), dominated the textual landscape of the early nineteenth century. The impact of these two texts and of the editorial practice that they signaled can be traced clearly through the editions which succeeded them in the nineteenth century. Thus, Samuel Weller Singer observes in the preface to his 1826 edition that the "text of the present edition is formed upon those of Steevens and Malone, occasionally compared with the early editions" (I, xvii–xviii) and A. J. Valpy, in the "Advertisement" to his 1832–4 edition, tells his reader that the "text of Malone, as published in 1821, in twenty-one volumes, is scrupulously followed" in his edition (I, v).

The one early nineteenth-century editor to challenge the Malone and Steevens texts, and the principles which underlay them, was Charles Knight. We have seen that Malone, in common with Capell, placed a high premium on some of the earliest quartos, granting them more authority than their F1 equivalents. We have also seen Steevens argue against elevating F1 above all other editions. Knight, by contrast, sought to argue the case for the absolute and exclusive centrality of F1, proposing for it an authority that exceeded that of the earliest authoritative quartos. He acknowledged that these quartos were "entitled to a very high respect in the settlement of the author's text," but he argued that "they do not demand an exclusive respect," since F1 was printed from sources which, in his view, appeared to be "distinguished from the printed copies by verbal alterations, by additions, by omissions not arbitrarily made, by a more correct metrical arrangement." Knight argued that, in these changes we can see the minute but most effective touches of the skilful artist; and a careful examination of this matter in the plays where the alterations are most numerous is quite sufficient to satisfy us of the jealous care with which Shakspere watched over the more important of these productions, so as to leave with [those responsible for F1] more complete and accurate copies than had been preserved by the press. (I, xvi)

In Knight's view, then, the source texts for F1 were likely to have carried the imprint of authorial correction and amendment, thus possessing a higher authority than their quarto predecessors. On the basis of this speculative theory, Knight broke with the practice of constructing his text from a combination of quarto and F1 sources. Or, at least, he tried to do so. He could not escape the fact that the early quartos often contain material which is not to be found in the F1 text (as Rowe had realized, when, for instance, he discovered that the "How all occasions" speech and the dialogue which precedes it were missing from the folio text of *Hamlet*). For this reason, Knight was forced, in some measure, to compromise his intention to present a text wholly based on F1: "Where there are omissions in the folio of passages found in the quartos, such omissions not being superseded by an extended or a condensed passage of a similar character, we give them a place in the text; distinguishing them, however, by brackets" (I, xviii). While Knight's reading of the textual narrative of F1 has not been followed by other editors (or, at least, by the vast majority of editors), his separation of F1 and quarto textual elements on the page does strikingly anticipate the practice of some late twentieth-century textual scholars.

Knight was a publisher by profession; Malone, like Capell and Theobald, was a lawyer by training; Steevens was independently wealthy; Warburton was bishop of Gloucester; Rowe, Pope, and Johnson were professional writers. The signature characteristic of Shakespeare editing from the beginnings of the eighteenth century to the middle of the nineteenth century was that it was the arena of gentleman-amateurs. Some of them, to be sure, were formidable scholars who built up extensive libraries of primary and secondary materials, but none of them was formally attached to an institution of learning. A considerable change would come in the 1860s, when a group of scholars based at Trinity College Cambridge was commissioned to produce a new edition, to be jointly published by Macmillan and Cambridge University Press. This development signaled the professionalization of Shakespeare studies generally and of Shakespeare editing more particularly. Henceforth, most noteworthy editions of Shakespeare would be undertaken by university-based scholars.

Though the Cambridge text was enormously influential, in many respects it did not represent a radical break with the traditions we have seen emerge through the work of such editors as Capell and Malone. In the prospectus for the edition which was circulated in 1860 (and which included, as a sample text, Act I of *Richard II*), William George Clark and his earliest collaborator H. R. Luard observed that

> The plan we have adopted in our specimen is as follows: The text is generally formed on that of the first quarto, *every* variation in the second, third, and fourth quarto, and the first two folios being given. If the reading in the first quarto seemed satisfactory, and not in need of alteration, it has been always retained; when this text appeared faulty, it has been altered from the subsequent editions, the reading which has the greatest weight of authority being chosen. When none of the early editions give a reading that can stand, recourse has been had to the later ones; conjectural emendations have been rarely mentioned, and never admitted into the text except when they appeared in our judgment to carry certain conviction of their truth with them. (3)

The method of proceeding here is certainly more cautious than Capell's, but the fundamental principles are the same. The first quarto of *Richard II* is privileged as the base text, but where the editors feel the text needs corrections then emendations are drawn in from later quartos and folios and, where necessary, from still later texts within the editorial tradition. It should be no surprise, then, to discover that Falstaff babbles of green fields in the Cambridge edition too (IV, 520, line 16).

Paul Werstine discusses the Cambridge edition in further detail in the immediately following chapter in this volume. Moving beyond the Cambridge edition, he also discusses the radical attempts of those twentieth-century scholars who would find themselves styled the "New Bibliographers" to set the editing of Shakespeare on a more scientific track. What becomes clear, however, is that many of the fundamental paradigms evolved during the eighteenth century – and many of the problems and contradictions thrown up by those paradigms – persisted into the twentieth century and beyond. The New Bibliographers certainly offered new narratives for old histories. But, as Werstine indicates, what is less certain is whether they really offered new solutions to old problems.

Chapter 6

The Science of Editing

Paul Werstine

As Andrew Murphy has noted in chapter 5 of this volume, with the Cambridge edition of 1863–6, the editing of Shakespeare passes into the hands of professional academics (Clark et al.). Gifted amateurs of the sort who made up the earlier editorial tradition do not immediately exit but continue to publish well into the twentieth century. However, early in that century they are displaced by their professional successors. When these early twentieth-century scholars are celebrated in 1945 by F. P. Wilson, he fashions their work into a unified movement, the "New Bibliography." Unfortunately for subsequent scholarship, under Wilson's label disappear significant differences and open disagreements among the scholars of whom he writes – A. W. Pollard, J. Dover Wilson, R. B. McKerrow, and W. W. Greg. Gone through this mislabeling too is the awareness that twenty-first-century divisions in the Shakespeare editorial community reproduce to a significant extent those that fissure the New Bibliography. The label fails as well to distinguish between the research method developed by the New Bibliographers and the particular conclusions at which they as individuals arrived using their method. These conclusions remain open to further examination, revision, and outright rejection through the use of the very method established by the early New Bibliographers. This chapter will later provide a description of the method as well as of some of the most important and influential conclusions to which it initially led, and then will go on to provide accounts of the continuing scrutiny to which these conclusions have been subjected. In spite of the objections just raised about the label "New Bibliography," it is to be acknowledged that it has proved effective in commanding admiration from succeeding generations of professional scholars led, in America, by Fredson Bowers and C. J. K. Hinman, and, latterly in England, by E. A. J. Honigmann and Peter W. M. Blayney. Furthermore, Greg's "The Rationale of Copy-Text," published near midcentury in Bowers's annual *Studies in Bibliography*, established the orientation for a number of subsequent editions of Shakespeare. Although none of these editions precisely followed Greg's procedure for establishing the texts of the Shakespeare canon, nonetheless the "Rationale" made author-centered Shakespeare editing the norm for the later twentieth century, by the end of which the goals of the 1863–6 Cambridge editors seemed to belong, as they in fact do, to another century.

The three Cambridge editors, J. Glover (who worked on only the first volume of the nine), W. G. Clark, and W. A. Wright, were all officials at Trinity College Cambridge, at which they also trained. Clark planned the edition and, in doing so, turned his back on the variorum style that had been developed in an eighteenth-century tradition culminating in Malone and Boswell's 1821 edition. Instead of recording in their edition the notes of all the previous commentators and editors as in a variorum, the Cambridge editors focused almost exclusively on establishing a text of the *Works*. This they printed above notes recording without comment all the readings of the early printings and selected readings from the intervening editorial tradition. They relegated discursive notes to a few pages at the back of their volumes, most of these notes being concerned with textual questions. The text that they arrived at was widely reproduced (with some few alterations) in the Globe Edition (1864) and was the preferred "Shakespeare" until the rise of the New Bibliography after World War II; and, as Michael Best observes in his chapter in this volume, the Globe still serves as the basis for the most commonly available free internet texts of Shakespeare.

The Cambridge editors only rarely speculate about what kind of manuscript may lie directly behind an early printed Shakespeare play (I, 312; II, 234; V, 17; VI, 10, 15; VII, 7, 12). And only twice does this speculation, which is always frankly presented as such, take the form of the suggestion that Shakespeare's own manuscript served as printer's copy (II, 234; VII, 7). The objects of this speculation are the 1598 quarto of *Love's Labour's Lost* and the 1623 Folio *Julius Caesar* – the latter because "it is more correctly printed than any other play" and, in this regard, resembles the narrative poems that the Cambridge editors and many other scholars believe Shakespeare saw through the press. Yet the Cambridge editors' refusal to suggest that any but a couple of plays were printed from the author's manuscript certainly does not arise from indifference to the author, whom they invoke in exalted terms: "greatest of merely human men, . . . subtlest of thinkers[,] . . . most eloquent of poets." Instead their sense of their distance from Shakespeare arises from close acquaintance with the early printed texts of Shakespeare's plays, and with the profoundly disappointing "textual imperfections and uncertainties which stand between the author and his readers." They can only conclude that "Some ruder hand has effaced the touch of the master. And these blemishes cannot be entirely removed, even by the most brilliant conjectural criticism" (IX, xxi).

In spite of the new direction set by the Cambridge edition, in 1871 H. H. Furness, Sr., a lawyer, resurrected eighteenth-century editorial tradition with his New Variorum edition of *Romeo and Juliet*. Furness's purpose was "to provide a detailed history of critical commentary together with an exhaustive study of the text" (Knowles 2003: 1). Between them, Furness and his son were able to issue 19 volumes by 1928, and publication of the edition was taken over by the Modern Language Association of America (MLA) in 1932 (Shaaber 1935). Volumes continue to appear, the latest, *The Winter's Tale* in 2005, published both as a book and as an electronic edition. The output of the Furnesses far exceeded that of their academic successors, but their successors' volumes have been subjected to far more rigorous supervision by professional scholars appointed by MLA.

The great learning of the amateur Furnesses notwithstanding, the twentieth century was to belong to the professional scholars, who announced themselves only shortly after the turn of the century with an outstanding bibliographical discovery regarding the true dates of some Shakespeare quartos. These quartos, including one of *King Lear*, had been printed with the dates 1600 or 1608 (and some, including the *Lear*, were believed by the Cambridge editors and others to be first editions). Between 1908 and 1910 two of what would become the most prominent of the New Bibliographers, Pollard and Greg, together with the American scholar William J. Neidig, conclusively demonstrated, from a study of watermarks and the typography of title-pages, that these quartos were falsely dated and that they were actually printed in 1619; they thus belonged among the 1619 "Pavier" quartos, so called after the stationer responsible for their publication (for a summary of the discovery, see Greg 1949). The consequences for what succeeding generations of readers would be given by editors as "Shakespeare" were enormous.

This bibliographical discovery and its clarification of the Shakespeare textual situation may well have inspired in Pollard and Greg, and in their friends McKerrow and J. Dover Wilson, the confidence that they could discover much more about the nature of the texts in early printings of Shakespeare. In a 1912 paper read to the Bibliographical Society and subsequently published as "What is Bibliography?" Greg laid out in ambitious terms what continues to be the New Biblio-graphical research method: "the study of book-making and of the manufacture of the materials of which books are made, . . . a know-ledge of the conditions of transcription and reproduction, of the methods of printing and binding, of the practices of publication and bookselling – . . . the whole of typography and the whole of palaeo-graphy" (1966: 80). However, the narrow purpose to which this broad method was turned was the establishment with nearly scientific pre-cision of the relation of early printed and manuscript texts to Shake-speare himself so that editors could base their editions on, and draw their readings only from, the most authoritative sources, a practice eventually codified by Greg in his "Rationale." In pursuit of this goal, the New Bibliographers went on to announce one discovery after another that had apparently eluded generations of earlier editors, even those as meticulous as Furness and the Cambridge editors. By way of providing examples of their research, while also supplying some glimpses into the lively disputes among them, this chapter will attend to four of the discoveries they later announced: (1) Pollard's 1909 claim that the Shakespeare quartos could be divided into the "good" and the "bad"; (2) Greg's 1910 claim that the 1602 quarto text of *The Merry Wives of Windsor* is a memorial reconstruction; (3) the 1923 claim made by Pollard and a few others that three pages of the manuscript *The Booke of Sir Thomas Moore* could be identified as free composition by Shakespeare; (4) the 1927 claim made by Greg that dramatists routinely gave their plays to acting companies as "foul papers" and that the acting companies preserved and routinely pro-vided publishers such manuscripts to use as printers' copy, thereby granting us, through many of the early printed texts, the nearly immediate access to Shakespeare longed for by the Cambridge editors. Yet none of these four discoveries was so solidly convincing even within the small group who would later be yoked together by F. P. Wilson as the New Bibliographers as was the redating of the falsely dated Pavier quartos.

These four claims are highly diverse; they cannot be forged into a coherent body of knowledge – in spite of efforts to do so. As these claims were being advanced and disputed among the New Bibliographers, there was never any shared sense that the claims were mutually reinforcing or even compatible with each other. Instead, as will be shown below in detail, the New Bibliographers who made some of these four claims were energetically opposed by New Bibliographers who made others of the four. Only long after the last of these claims had been published could it be made to seem, in good faith, that there had emerged from this early twentieth-century research a unified theory of the Shakespeare editorial problem. This illusion of consensus is presented most comprehensively and very persuasively in Greg's 1955 *Shakespeare First Folio*. To judge from that book, the New Bibliography had initially been made possible by the first of the claims listed above, Pollard's division of the Shakespeare quartos into the "good" and "bad." According to Greg, from that crucial distinction arose in turn the other claims. The second claim, that the 1602 *Wives* prints a memorial reconstruction by an actor, showed that such "bad" quartos bore no transcriptional relation to Shakespeare's own manuscripts. By contrast, the fourth claim showed that the "good" quartos and some equally good Folio texts were printed directly from Shakespeare's "foul papers." Finally, the third claim, that *More* gives us a few pages in Shakespeare's own hand, means that the "foul papers" printer's copy for these "good" texts could be imaginatively reconstructed in detail. Editors who worked under the influence of Greg's *Shakespeare First Folio* could be confident that they were offering their readers what Shakespeare wrote if they based their editions squarely on the "good" texts and had as little as possible to do with the "bad" ones. However, these editors could sometimes improve the "good" texts by emending them in light of the knowledge they could glean from Shakespeare's *More* pages. Only by returning, now, to the occasions on which the four foundational claims were made is it possible to see how this apparently unified editorial theory is a deeply flawed construction. And those who enable us to see the flaws are the New Bibliographers themselves.

When in 1909 Pollard, working in very close conjunction with Greg, took up the matter of the Shakespeare quartos and folios, all these printed versions were shadowed by editorial suspicion like that voiced by the Cambridge editors. Suspicion of the quartos arose from the denigration of all previous printings of the Shakespeare plays by John Heminge and Henry Condell (Shakespeare's friends and colleagues while he lived) when they addressed "the great Variety of Readers" in a preface to the 1623 folio collection of the Shakespeare plays: "(before) you were abus'd with diuerse stolne, and surreptitious copies, maimed, and deformed by the frauds and stealthes of iniurious impostors, that expos'd them." Suspicion of the First Folio itself arose, in turn, from its well-known dependence for printer's copy for a number of its playtexts on the very quartos that Heminge and Condell had so reviled. Pollard attacked this suspicion by dividing the quartos into two mutually exclusive classes – the "good" and the "bad" – and then argued that Heminge and Condell's unqualified disparagement of the quartos must be read to have reference only to his "bad" quartos (1909: 64–80). In accord with what would become commendable New Bibliographical practice, Pollard sought to ground his distinction in documentary evidence, in this particular case, the *Stationers' Register* (in which the Stationers' Company recorded who owned the rights to publish particular books). Pollard discovered irregularities in the entrance for each of his five so-called "bad" quartos (*Romeo and Juliet* 1597, *Henry V* 1600, *The Merry Wives of Windsor* 1602, *Hamlet* 1603, and *Pericles* 1609) but found that his 14 "good" quartos had, at least for the most part, been properly entered (1909: 65). He concluded that the company refused the right to publish to those of its members responsible for the "bad" quartos because these stationers had failed to demonstrate that they had purchased play manuscripts for the "bad" quartos from the acting companies that owned the plays; instead, these stationers had acquired "stolne, and surreptitious" printer's copy. For Pollard, the illegal origins of the "bad" quartos were obvious in the poor quality of the texts printed in them. In contrast, the "good" quartos, properly entered in the *Register*, offered "good" texts based on manuscripts that publishers had legitimately purchased from the acting company that owned them. Pollard claimed that this account legitimated not only the "good" quartos, but also the Folio, which depended, he said, for its texts only on some of these "good" quartos and never on a "bad" one (1909: 121–2). In his preface to *Shakespeare Folios and Quartos*, he informed the "bibliographical pessimists" that they were in for a dose of "healthy and hardy optimism" (1909: v).

Greg quickly followed Pollard's announcement with one of his own concerning the 1602 "bad" quarto of *The Merry Wives of Windsor* and his discovery of the agency through which it had been surreptitiously stolen from Shakespeare's acting company. Greg claimed that the quality of its correlation with the Folio's dialogue varies markedly in connection with the entrances and exits of a single character in the play, the Host. Greg inferred that these variations indicate the creation of the "bad" quarto's text by the player who took the role of the Host. This player, according to Greg, was attempting to reconstruct the play's text from memory and was doing much better with his own dialogue and what he had heard while on-stage than he was with the rest: "Not only do we find the Host's part alone usually in more or less substantial agreement in the two versions, not only do we as a rule find the versions springing into substantial agreement when he enters and relapsing into paraphrase when he quits the stage, but when he disappears for good and all at the end of the fourth Act (and the actor very likely went home or to the tavern) we find what remains of the play in a more miserably garbled condition than any previous portion" (1910: xli). In the heat of new discovery, Greg exaggerates. His theory is most persuasive for the play's third scene and still has some bite on three of the Host's other eight appearances (2.1, 2.3, 4.5); in the four others the Host's entrance makes very little difference, except in the resemblance of his own speeches to their counterparts in the Folio, and only some of the time are his speeches better than their context (3.1, 3.2, 4.3, 4.6). At other times, as with Falstaff's entrance in the first scene, there is a striking improvement in the resemblance of the "bad" quarto and Folio texts that has no relation to the Host. In 1942 Greg, who must be credited with a nearly life-long searching skepticism about many of his theories, acknowledged the difficulties I have raised about the 1602 *Wives* quarto being entirely a memorial reconstruction by the Host (1942: 71).

In spite of his own reservations, Greg's story of the *Wives* "bad" quarto decades later became the paradigm for all Shakespeare "bad" quartos and many non-Shakespearean ones too. Before that happened, J. Dover Wilson joined Pollard in 1919 to announce that Greg's theory of the genesis of the 1602 *Wives* could not account for the complexity of that quarto's relation to the Folio's version. Nor, they argued, could Greg's hypothesis explain the fluctuations in quality to be found in Pollard's other "bad" quartos when they are compared to "good" texts of the same plays. (There is no "good" text of *Pericles*.) For Pollard and Wilson (1919), the complexity of the problems posed by the "bad" quartos called for a theory that mirrored their complexity. According to their hypothesis, the "bad" quartos started out as non-Shakespearean plays that Shakespeare later took up and extensively revised; they uncritically accepted Malone's view that such is precisely the initially non-Shakespearean state in which we find *The Second* and *The Third Part of Henry VI* when these were printed as *The First Part of the Contention betwixt the two famous Houses of Yorke and Lancaster* (1594) and *The True Tragedie of Richard Duke of Yorke* (1595, an octavo) before Shakespeare set about revising them. Pollard and Wilson's account of the typical Shakespeare "bad" quarto goes like this: after Shakespeare had begun revising a text of a play by an unknown author and had progressed most of the way through the first two acts, the partially revised script was then cut down for provincial performance; hence the much more impressive correlation of the text of the "bad" quarto with the "good" text in the first two acts. By the time the members of the company returned to London with their partially reworked and abridged script of the play, Shakespeare had finished his renovation of it, which was a great success on the London stage and was thirsted after by stationers unscrupulous enough to put it into print any way they could. A stationer found a rogue actor or actors who had played one or more parts in the fully revised London success to supplement the abridged provincial version with what they could remember of performance. From this manuscript (originally composed by a pre-Shakespearean author, partially revised by Shakespeare, first abridged, and then expanded by memory) the "bad" quarto was printed. Wilson and Pollard's narrative had all the complexity needed to mirror the complex variation between "good" and "bad" texts, and then some – not that their narrative could ever be validated.

On this occasion Greg chose not to argue with Wilson and Pollard, as he would later on other issues, but instead found a place for their hypothesis in his 1922 study of two obscure 1594 non-Shakespearean "bad" quartos – *The Battle of Alcazar* and *Orlando Furioso*. Since for Greg not every "bad" quarto was a memorial reconstruction, he could regard *Alcazar* as a "bad" quarto even though memory played no role in his story of its transmission into print. Rather he said that *Alcazar* was "a version drastically cut down by the omission and reduction of speeches, by the elimination and doubling of parts, and by the suppression of spectacular shows, for representation in a limited time, by a comparatively small cast, with the minimum of theatrical paraphernalia" (1922: 15), just the kind of playtext Wilson and Pollard had imagined an acting company taking with them when they were forced by the plague into the provinces. However, Greg did not altogether abandon his own theory; he regarded *Orlando* as a "bad" quarto "based almost throughout on reconstruction from memory" (1922: 134).

Soon, though, it would be Greg's theory of memorial reconstruction that would prevail over Wilson and Pollard's elaborate story of the "bad" quartos' origins. Paradoxically, Wilson and Pollard would find their account displaced by Peter Alexander, a scholar who, inspired by Pollard's 1909 identification of five Shakespeare "bad" quartos, extended the category to include *The First Part of the Contention* (1594) and *The True Tragedie* (1595). Before Alexander, these printings, as noted above, were understood to be pre-Shakespearean plays that Shakespeare later reworked to create the Folio plays entitled *The Second Part* and *The Third Part of Henry VI*. Indeed *The First Part of the Contention* and *The True Tragedie* constituted the primary evidence for Malone's influential belief that Shakespeare began his career as a dramatist by taking up and substantially rewriting plays already in his company's repertory – the very belief on which Pollard and Wilson had depended for their theory of the "bad" quartos' ultimate origins. When in 1929 Alexander showed that *The First Part of the Contention* and *The True Tragedie* could be regarded as deriving from, rather than preceding, Shakespeare's plays, just like Pollard's other "bad" quartos, then Pollard and Wilson's 1919 hypothesis was swept away. Into its place slipped Greg's theory of memorial reconstruction by particular actors, which, as Pollard's category of "bad" quartos continued to grow, would be extended to almost every early printed text gathered up as "bad" quarto, in spite of Greg's sometimes explicit reservations (see below). Forgotten by Greg's many followers would be the legitimate objections raised by Wilson and Pollard against the simplicity of Greg's account. This pattern of the ascendancy of one New Bibliographical theory as a consequence of the disappearance of its rival, rather than through the validation of the ascendant theory, was repeated over and over again. All too often, although not always, it was left to scholars at the end of the century to expose the lack of foundation in New Bibliographical hypotheses that had been allowed to harden into fact once their rivals had fallen away.

However much Greg assisted Pollard in arriving at the division of Shakespeare quartos into "bad" and "good" and no matter how popular with his juniors Greg's theory of memorial reconstruction was to become, Greg later stood out against the simplicity of Pollard's division and against the identification of all texts in the expanding class of "bad" quartos as memorial reconstructions. In 1942 in his *The Editorial Problem in Shakespeare*, he sought to preserve respect for the quartos' variety by opening up a third category called "doubtful" quartos. Into this intermediate class he sorted the 1597 quarto of *Richard III*, which D. L. Patrick had argued in 1936 was produced through memorial reconstruction by the play's whole cast, and the

1608 quarto of *King Lear*, which Greg could not believe, from his close analysis of its variation from the folio, could have the same origin as *Richard III* or as any of the "bad" quartos (1942: 77–101). Instead, Greg argued that *Lear*'s quarto text originated in a shorthand report of a performance, even though, unfortunately for Greg, there is virtually no good evidence to indicate the medium of shorthand (1933, 1936, 1940, 1942: 88–101). He would not prevail. Instead, when in 1949 G. I. Duthie proved persuasive in *Elizabethan Shorthand and the First Quarto of King Lear* with the contention that no shorthand system available in 1608 could have provided the quarto's text, memorial reconstruction won the day for quarto *Lear* not because the text could be demonstrated to be a memorial reconstruction, but because, in line with the pattern observed above, it could not be demonstrated according to its rival theory to be a shorthand report. Once the quarto *Lear* had been dislodged from Greg's intermediate category of "doubtful" quartos and filed among the "bad" quartos as a memorial reconstruction, not much stood any longer in the way of understanding as a "bad" quarto any printed play regarded to be somehow defective. Leo Kirschbaum had already included both quarto *Lear* and quarto *Richard III* in his "Census of Bad Quartos" (1938: 26–9). For Kirschbaum and Harry Hoppe, characteristics allegedly shared among some 23 early printed texts or part-texts, only 10 of them Shakespeare's, allowed for their reduction to and inclusion in a single class, the "bad" quartos (Kirschbaum 1938, 1945b; Hoppe 1946), and, as we will shortly see, the class continued to grow.

While Pollard's division of the quartos into "good" and "bad" won wide acceptance, his attempt to establish the authority of the Folio by showing that it employed only annotated "good" quartos as printer's copy, without ever having recourse to "bad" ones, was dealt a telling blow by a discovery by McKerrow in 1937 about *The Second Part* and *The Third Part of Henry VI*. By then *Contention* and *True Tragedie* had been accepted as "bad" texts of these *Henry VI* plays, and McKerrow demonstrated that these "bad" texts must have been consulted in the printing of the Folio, presumably when the printer was no longer able to follow manuscript copy. Observing the identity between Folio and "bad" texts in some passages, McKerrow refused Pollard's optimistic approach to textual problems and insisted on the possibility that Shakespeare's words may have been irrecoverably lost, in the process echoing Pope, Johnson, and the old Cambridge editors. "Where the *wording* is identical," McKerrow wrote, we must consider whether we have not merely a case of the "good" text here following the "bad," for if so we have only *one* text and not two independent texts, and that text one which may be no more than [a] quite inaccurate "report" [memorial reconstruction]. The verbal coincidence of the two texts may therefore mean not that the reading is almost certainly correct, but that it is actually more likely to be in error, being derived from a "bad" text, than other readings of the "good" text which have not the apparent support of the "bad" one. (1937: 72)

The failure of those responsible for the construction of the Folio texts consistently to observe Pollard's distinction between the "good" quartos, of which they could avail themselves, and the "bad," of which they must not, should have cast some doubt on the historical validity of Pollard's division. The grounds for this division that he had located in the *Stationers' Register* had already been shown to be worthless. In 1923 E. K. Chambers's wider consultation of the *Register* had shown that some "bad" quartos are properly entered there, some not; some "good" ones are, some not (1923: III, 186–7). Further twentieth-century research inspired by the New Bibliographers has not been favorable to Pollard's 1909 discovery or to the habit of regarding "bad" quartos as memorial reconstructions of texts cut down for provincial performance and then procured by shady London stationers looking for a "get-penny." Pollard's assumption that the acting companies would be recognized by the Stationers' Company as enjoying owner-ship of the rights to publish their plays has been exposed as baseless; copyright, in this period, belonged exclusively to the stationers who took the risk of publishing texts, however they acquired their manu-script copy (Kirschbaum 1955). It was left to Peter W. M. Blayney in 1997 to demolish the rest of Pollard's construction, especially the assumption that there was always a market for a printed Shakespeare play. Blayney pointed out how small a proportion of the market for printed books was occupied by plays, and thus showed how unlikely it would be for publishers to resort to extraordinary and unscrupulous means to acquire play manuscripts, when such publishers were not likely in their lifetimes to recover costs for putting plays into print. Challenges to Blayney's position have been successfully refuted by him; in "Alleged Popularity" (2005) he answers Farmer and Lesser's "Popularity of Playbooks" (2005a), and they attempt to answer him in "Structures of Popularity" (2005b). When in 1996 Laurie E. Maguire addressed the class of "bad" quartos with a view to testing the claims of various scholars who had, extending Greg's 1910 discovery about quarto *Wives*, associated them with memorial reconstruction, she had to deal with a category distended to include 41 printed books. Yet of those 41 she found only four, including the 1602 *Wives*, where there was some probability but no certainty that they are in part or in whole memorial reconstructions (1996: 232–322). Research conducted for the Records of Early English Drama (REED) has turned up evidence that among favorite and frequent stopping-places of London playing companies touring the provinces were the great houses of those who, when in London, went to the playhouses. Wilson and Pollard's 1919 assumption, therefore, that provincial audiences would be satisfied with "bad"-quarto performance texts when London audiences would accept only "good" texts on stage – an assumption picked up by Greg in 1922 and by so many after him – is exposed as prejudice against the provinces, because audiences there and in London included some of the same people (Werstine forthcoming). Despite Pollard's failure to reduce the textual variety of the quartos to two classes, the New Bibliography cannot be denied some success in identifying two of the Shakespeare quartos as, to some extent, memorial reconstructions (1602 *Wives*, 1603 *Hamlet*) and in identifying several more (including 1597 *Richard III* and *Romeo*, 1600 *Henry V*) as containing texts deriving in some other (yet unknown) ways from Shakespeare's plays.

Thus Pollard and Greg enjoyed greater success among their colleagues and successors with their theories of the so-called "bad" quartos than Pollard and Wilson would with their attempt to identify three pages in the manuscript *The Booke of Sir Thomas Moore* as free composition by Shakespeare. These are the pages that Greg, in his great 1911 edition of the manuscript, had assigned to the anonymous "Hand D" (fols. 8a–9a). For the 1923 book introduced by Pollard and entitled *Shakespeare's Hand in the Play of Sir Thomas More*, E. Maunde Thompson was responsible for adducing paleographical evidence for the identification of Shakespeare's hand, Wilson for spelling evidence linking the three pages to the "good" quartos, and R. W. Chambers for locating parallels in the expression of ideas between the three pages and the Shakespeare canon. Greg contributed a transcript of the three pages, an edition of some of the play's scenes, and an essay on the different hands in the play manuscript. Today's Shakespeare scholars are still divided about attribution of the three pages to Shakespeare, as should not surprise us, since the contributors to the 1923 book were themselves divided, with Pollard enthusiastically declaring his view "that in these three pages we have the tone and the temper of Shakespeare and of no other Elizabethan dramatist I have read"

(Pollard 1923: 31), while Greg could admit only that Pollard's view was not entirely impossible: "D *may perhaps* be the hand of Shakespeare" (Pollard 1923: 47, emphasis mine). In his review of the book, McKerrow found that the case for Shakespeare was far from conclusive: "I confess that in reading these chapters I have at times felt, even more than how much has been done, how much remains to do" (1924: 239). McKerrow never saw reason to alter his skepticism; in his last work, his *Prolegomena for the Oxford Shakespeare*, he classifies *More* among "doubtful plays in which some believe Shakespeare had a hand" (1939: 4 n.1).

The evidence adduced for Shakespeare as Hand D in the 1923 book has been endlessly cited, even though when the individual classes of that evidence are reassessed by advocates of the book's case, these have not stood up. By 1927 Greg was willing to endorse the case as a whole, but his opinion of the paleographical evidence was not high: "Setting S[hakespeare] aside, it can be shown that [Hand] D was not written by any dramatist of whose hand we have adequate knowledge" (1927: 908). While Greg may thereby seem to suggest that Hand D is Shakespeare's, he may instead be expecting us to take into account that we have lost far more plays from this period than have survived, an historical consideration that Scott McMillin emphasizes (1987: 135–59). In this light, the balance of probability tips heavily in favor of Hand D as "Anonymous." Another advocate of the book's case as a whole is MacDonald P. Jackson, who in the 1980s was forced to a reassessment of the worth of R. W. Chambers's evidence for the Shakespeare attribution. Chambers had argued that "Certain ideas were linked in Shakespeare's mind, and this coupling [of ideas] recurs with a curious similarity [in multiple plays]" (Pollard 1923: 156); Chambers then located resemblances between the coupling of ideas in the three Hand-D pages and in such Shakespeare plays as *Troilus and Cressida, Coriolanus, Hamlet, Richard III*, and *Julius Caesar* (Pollard 1923: 156–65). When Eric Sams, in 1985, used Chambers's method to argue for Shakespearean authorship of the early seventeenth-century manuscript play *Edmond Ironside*, Jackson was forced to conclude that Chambers's practice was of no worth: "The total absence of constraints on our search for resemblances renders the calculations meaningless" (Jackson 1988: 225).

No one before 1999 subjected Wilson's spelling evidence to such re-evaluation (Werstine and Snook 2000). Wilson provided nine pages of allegedly "abnormal" and therefore significant "spellings of the three pages, with parallels from the quartos," all the spellings listed supposed to be "abnormal" for the period and thus significant (Pollard 1923: 124, 133–41). In compiling this impressive list, Wilson made three crucial assumptions. First he assumed that if a writer spelled one word in a particular way, then the writer could be assumed to employ morphological consistency and therefore always to use the same form. For example, Hand D spelled *chidd* with a final double *d*, so Wilson assumed that Hand D would also have spelled *madd, redd, sadd*, all of which Wilson found in the Shakespeare "good" quartos. However, the Hand-D pages themselves indicate that although the writer spelled *chidd* with two *d*'s, he never doubled the final *d* in any other words, spelling "bid," "breed," "did," "dread," "god," "good," "had," and so on. In 1963, T. H. Howard-Hill pointed out from his exhaustive study of the scribe Ralph Crane that the principle of morphological consistency was invalid (Hill 1963: 11), as Wilson's own data, of course, show it to be. Therefore all of the words that Wilson found in the "good" quartos spelled only by analogy to Hand D's spellings of other words need to be eliminated from his list, which is thereby greatly shortened. Second, in collecting spellings from the early printed texts, Wilson also neglected to allow for another now well-known bibliographical fact: compositors made adjustments to spellings in long lines that stretched all the way across the page or the whole length of the compositor's stick in order to make the lines fit. This process of adjustment is called justification. Spellings in such lines have long been known to be unreliable indicators of the ways words were spelled in the compositor's manuscript copy (Reid 1974), but Wilson nonetheless assumed that he could mix spellings from long lines with those legitimately culled from short lines. Third – and Wilson can hardly be blamed for this limitation – he assumed that he could rely on the then newly published *OED* as an index of what constituted an abnormal spelling in Shakespeare's time. Now we have databases like Chadwyck-Healey's *Literature Online* (*LION*) to use to gauge the frequency of what appear to us to be abnormal spellings. Once Wilson's lists are lightened – of the spellings that are to be found frequently on *LION*, of spellings that occur only in justified lines in the "good" quartos, and of spellings that are only morphologically consistent, rather than identical – Wilson's nine pages of spellings shrink to just five examples, not nearly enough to be persuasive: "Taken singly coincidences like these prove nothing; they are at best negative evidence" (Pollard 1923: 117). McKerrow's repeated skepticism about the possibility that Hand D is Shakespeare seems to be consistent with the surviving evidence. Yet many Shakespeare editors have taken Hand D as a guide to their inferential reconstruction of Shakespeare's manuscripts of canonical plays.

Even more controversial was Greg's 1925 discovery that dramatists, presumably including Shakespeare, turned over to the acting companies "foul papers" of their plays (1926: 156), as well as his 1927 discovery of the nature of "foul papers" (n.d.). These discoveries came to be widely accepted in the Shakespeare editorial community in the latter half of the twentieth century, but their acceptance was grounded solely on the great authority commanded by Greg's work and name; he never published the essay in which he had worked out the meaning of "foul papers." The essay became available only when Grace Ioppolo found it at the Huntington Library, to which Greg's widow had donated it, and, in 1990, published a summary and excerpts. Now that it is available as one of the most important of so-called New Bibliographical documents, it is time to revisit the controversies that it generated. Greg discovered the words "foul papers" in a transcription of the dramatist John Fletcher's *Bonduca* made by Edward Knight, book-keeper of the King's Players, who joined the company in this capacity sometime between 1619 and 1624. Making a copy of a manuscript of *Bonduca* for a patron, Knight learned when he reached the final Act that his exemplar was missing more than two scenes that he recalled from seeing the play in production. He gave his patron the following explanation for the absence of these scenes (square brackets indicate erasure): *"the occasion. why these are wanting here. the booke where [it] by it was first Acted from is lost: and this hath beene transcrib'd from the fowle papers of the Authors w^h were found"* (fol. 23a).

With a view to discovering the nature of such "foul papers," Greg collated Knight's transcript with the version of *Bonduca* printed in the 1647 Beaumont and Fletcher First Folio. This printed text must have been based on a theatrical manuscript, either "the booke where by it was first Acted from" or a transcript of it, because we find in it the scenes Knight observed to be missing from the "foul papers." Knight's transcript of these papers, Greg learned, differed from the printed theatrical text in a most peculiar way. Lines, speeches, or sometimes longer passages of dialogue shifted positions, although they rarely differed very much in wording in their new locations. Here is the Folio's version of one passage (with what is moved or missing in Knight's transcript in bold face):

Car.   Go i'th' name of heaven **Boy.**
Hengo.   **Quick, quick, Uncle, I have it.** Oh. *Judas shoots Hengo.*

Car.	What ailest thou?
Hengo.	O my best Uncle, I am slain.
Car.	I see yee, **and** heaven direct my hand: destruction
	Caratach kils Judas with a stone from the Rock.
	go with thy coward soul. How dost thou Boy?
	Oh villain, pocky villain.
Hengo.	**O Uncle, Uncle,**
	oh **how** it pricks mee: **am I preserv'd for this?**
	extremely pricks me.
Car.	Coward, rascall Coward . . .
	(Hoy 1979: 5.3.124–31)

And here is Knight's transcription of the same passage:

Cara:	goe i'th name of heaven.
	Iudas steales nere him and shootes him: & startes back:
Hen:	oh. –
Cara:	what aylst thow.
Hen:	**quicke vncle. quicke. I have it.**
	o my best vncle I am slaine.
Cara:	I see ye.
	heaven direct my hand. – destruction –
	flings and tumbles him ouer: pulls him vp againe
	goe with thy coward soule. how dost thow boy.
	o villaine. pockye villaine. **am I preseru'd for this.**
Hen:	o it prickes me
	extreamely prickes me.
Cara:	coward rascall coward
	(Greg 1951b: 2502–13)

Discounting the possibility that variation in the lines' arrangement might be an effect of Knight's transcription, Greg sought to explain the shifts as arising from and thereby characterizing the kind of manuscript that Knight was copying – the "foul papers." According to Greg, at least two of the lines just quoted that got relocated in the transcript were "additional passages . . . written in the margin [of the 'foul papers' by Fletcher] with no clear indication as to how they were to be fitted into the text, and in each case the scribe bungled the operation" (n.d.: 15). From this interpretation of these variants, Greg arrived at his initial definition of "foul papers" as "at times illegible [as well as] full of deletions, corrections, and alterations" (1927: 4, 3). In his final summative work, Greg modified this early definition of "foul papers" to read "a copy representing the play more or less as the author intended it to stand, but not itself clear or tidy enough to serve as a promptbook" because of "loose ends and false starts and unresolved confusions" (1955: 106, 142). (By "promptbook," a word that did not enter the language until late in the eighteenth century, he meant a theatrical manuscript.) As early as 1931, Greg had extended his interpretation of *Bonduca*'s "foul papers" into a paradigm for dramatic composition in what he broadly defined as the "Elizabethan" period: "Most authors, when they set about composition, would probably produce a rough copy or mass of 'fowle papers' such as those upon which the scribe of *Bonduca* drew" (1931: 1195). Later he came to judge that about half the canonical Shakespeare plays had been printed for the first time from the dramatist's "foul papers," which, he believed, were deposited as a matter of course in the playhouse (1942: 183–7; 1955: 426–7). Although some of his followers have come to associate his conception of "foul papers" with the *Moore* manuscript, even though it is a theatrical copy of that play (Eccles's edition, 1980: 292–3; Taylor 1987: 9–10; Melchiori 2003: 17–30), for Greg, *Bonduca* alone exemplified this category of manuscript (1955: 109–10).

When Greg sent Pollard his 1927 manuscript essay about *Bonduca*'s "foul papers," Pollard raised problems with Greg's conception of "foul papers," problems to which it may be worth attending now that the editorial community is again split over "foul papers" (Mowat 2001: 23–5). In rejecting the essay for publication in the *Library*, Pollard gently pointed out that in such a long essay on *Bonduca*, Greg had failed to demonstrate any "wider applicability" of the peculiar case of this single manuscript (Greg n.d.: additional leaf). Pollard's observation is acute, especially if someone is attempting to apply the case of *Bonduca* to the canonical Shakespeare plays, as Greg did. *Bonduca* is remarkable for its several passages of the kind quoted above; in these passages lines occupy different locations in the *Bonduca* transcript and the play's printed text, and these particular variants are essential to Greg's characterization of Knight's exemplar, the "foul papers." However, in Shakespeare's plays, and especially in the ones for which, as with *Bonduca*, we have more than one text, it is hard to find more than a single instance in which a line, a speech, or a passage is misplaced in the way so often found in *Bonduca*. It would seem that rather than being paradigmatic, as Greg would later make *Bonduca*, it is rare – perhaps even unique. Pollard's objection, surviving only in a letter to Greg, necessarily went unheard by the many who took up Greg's conception of "foul papers" and attempted to apply it to Shakespeare.

Yet others close to Greg published equally cogent objections that have since been overlooked by Greg's followers. E. K. Chambers observed that although Greg inferred from Knight's note in *Bonduca* that the "foul papers" had been found in the playhouse, Knight did not say where he got them (1930: I, 125). The most vigorous objection came from McKerrow, upon whose essay "A Suggestion Regarding Shakespeare's Manuscripts" Greg depended heavily for the development of criteria for identifying "foul papers" immediately behind early printed Shakespeare plays (McKerrow 1935). Well aware of Greg's conception of "foul papers" as a holograph copy of a "play substantially in its final form" (Greg 1942: 32), McKerrow thought it "very doubtful whether, especially in the case of the earlier plays, there ever existed any written 'final form.'" Instead, in McKerrow's view, Shakespeare's "lines would be subject to modification in the light of actual performance, as well as to later revision . . . accepted [by Shakespeare] . . . as necessary [even if] . . . they introduced inconsistencies into what was originally conceived as a consistent whole" (1939: 6–7). For McKerrow, then, it is more probable that the inconsistencies in printed Shakespeare plays arise from playhouse intervention than from authorial uncertainty or carelessness in composition, as Greg would have it with his conception of "foul papers."

From this survey it would seem that the history and reception of the New Bibliography is a sad case of simplification (like the reduction of complex qualitative variation within and among the quartos to the "good" and the "bad"), and the extension of individual cases to cover dozens of others to which they have no demonstrable relevance – like Greg's own use of his inferential reconstruction of *Bonduca*'s "foul papers," or others' use of his demonstration of memorial reconstruction in parts of the 1602 *Wives* quarto. Consequently, many of today's Shakespeare editors no longer share the confidence of their later twentieth-century predecessors that we can identify with nearly scientific precision as "foul papers" or as memorial reconstructions manuscripts used as copy for early printings of Shakespeare's plays. Without such confidence many of today's editors do not claim to distinguish within early printed texts exactly what Shakespeare wrote. Instead such editors offer their readers editions of individual printed versions – an edition of the 1604–5 second quarto of *Hamlet*, an edition of the 1599 second quarto of *Romeo and Juliet* – rather than pretending to provide an edition of Shakespeare's *Hamlet* or of Shakespeare's

Romeo and Juliet that is in fact made up of an editor's own particular mix of readings ripped, according to New Bibliographical criteria, from the various early printed texts of the plays.

True as it may be to characterize the New Bibliography in part as simplifying the editorial problem in Shakespeare, simplification is far from the whole story. Those who would later be called the New Bibliographers also resisted each other's simplifications and over-generalizations in struggles with the Shakespeare texts that continue to be our struggles. Today's scholars who represent New Bibliographers as locked in perfect agreement regarding most if not all the issues raised in this chapter serve neither today's readers nor the New Bibliographers they hold up for admiration (Melchiori 2003; Honigmann 2004). Yet such admiration inspired later generations to massive efforts to display the differences that printing-house practices made to the Shakespeare texts, most notably Hinman's reconstruction of the manufacture of the 1623 folio, and Blayney's of the 1608 *Lear* quarto in the context of Nicholas Okes's printing house. Finally, to the New Bibliographer Pollard and his collaborators we also owe the 1926 *A Short-Title Catalogue of . . . Books . . . 1475–1640* and to the New Bibliographer Greg *A Bibliography of the English Printed Drama* (1939–59) that have provided the basis for so much later research. Beyond these most valuable particular resources, they also left us an invaluable research method by which their own claims continue to be tested.

Chapter 7

Editing Shakespeare in a Postmodern Age

Leah S. Marcus

> *Finally, it should be clear that it is not up to us to provide reality.*
> Jean-François Lyotard, *The Postmodern Explained*

If we accept the usual definitions of postmodernism, which, following Lyotard, associate it with pluralism, relativism, and recognition of incommensurable differences, with a rejection of grand narratives and totalizations of all kinds, then the title of this chapter presents an impossibility. Editing is by its nature a choosing among available alternatives, a setting of limits upon a range of possible forms and meanings. If by editing Shakespeare we mean the construction of a text that claims to offer readers an authoritative, reliable version of a Shakespearean play or poem – to provide readers with a "reality" of that Shakespearean text – then that construction will not be postmodern because it will have settled into a stability that is inimical to the restless kineticism we tend to associate with postmodernism. And yet, even in a "postmodern age," if Shakespeare is to continue to be read and performed, someone must provide readers, students, and actors with versions of the text that they can use productively and collectively. A digital edition that allows readers to play with a wide array of possible words, actions, and stage directions and construct their own, say, *Hamlet* can come fairly close to being a creditable postmodern edition, but it will perforce settle down into something more traditional the minute a given reader specifies his or her own preferred version of the play and communicates it to others as a stable text that a group can use collectively.

That is not to suggest, however, that Shakespearean editing cannot absorb elements of postmodernist thought, or at least attempt to revamp the Shakespearean text in ways that acknowledge elements of undecidability. Editing as a cultural practice is not now and never has been immune from the broader culture within which it is practiced. If we are presently situated in a "postmodern age" then we have no choice but to update our editing of Shakespeare if we wish Shakespeare to remain alive and compelling to today's readers and performers. The present chapter will not attempt to construct a (self-defeating) grand narrative of how this updating might be and is being accomplished, but will instead, in postmodernist style, confine itself to a series of local suggestions and particulars. At the end of the chapter, I will briefly readdress the problem of how and to what degree a Shakespearean edition in the "postmodern age" can reflect the art of "perpetual negation" that is part of the aesthetic of postmodernity.

Decentering the Author

Editors are beginning to distrust many of the author-centered narratives by which earlier editions have traditionally determined textual authority. Rather than justify an emendation on the (often circular) grounds that it is clearly what the author "intended," editors are now increasingly inclined to consider the broader cultural situation within which a text was produced and altered. About half of Shakespeare's plays exist in more than one early printed version. There are, notoriously, three very different early versions of *Hamlet* and two of *King Lear*, each of which has some claim to textual authority. Which did the author mean to put forth as his final word on the subject? Earlier editors would typically address this dismaying situation by assuming that Shakespeare created only one single intended text of a play. They would choose one early printed version as closer to "authorial" and attempt to suppress or denigrate the others as in some way unacceptably altered by institutional practices – especially corruption by the players who acted the play and by the printers who set type for the early editions.

Beginning in the 1980s, however, with Gary Taylor, Steven Urkowitz, and Michael Warren's groundbreaking contention that Shakespeare himself revised his work and created two distinct versions of *King Lear* (Taylor and Warren 1983; Urkowitz 1980), editors have been increasingly willing to consider the possibility that Shakespeare may

129

have had more than one intent for a play. He may have revised the play over time as he saw how it worked on stage; he may have constructed subtly altered versions for different audiences or occasions. Jill L. Levenson's recent single-volume Oxford World's Classic edition of *Romeo and Juliet* (2000) offers an edited version of both the early quarto versions of the play as separate texts, on the grounds that the text of the play is "mobile" rather than fixed. (See also Bevington and Rasmussen's edition of *Doctor Faustus* [1993], and Wells and Taylor's Oxford *Complete Works* of Shakespeare [1986].) Recent editors have been willing to press even further, arguing that elements of a Shakespeare play that are probably traceable to theatrical practice, censorship, or other pressures aside from authorial intent can still be considered "authoritative," part of the play as we wish to read and perform it today. We might consider the issue of censorship as a case in point. David Bevington's chapter in this volume notes that most editors, faced with an early Shakespearean text that shows signs of censorship of profanities in response to the 1606 act to curb obscenities on stage, would even now be inclined to offer a conjectural restoration of the lost profanities on the grounds that they were present in Shakespeare's original text, and that they help to characterize the speakers. But such a solution will not be easy for editors operating within a postmodern frame of reference: if the conjectural restoration of oaths accomplishes one set of interpretive goals, such as an illumination of character or of authorial intent, it may obscure others, such as an understanding the play as it was performed before audiences and made available to readers after 1606.

In poststructuralist thought generally, the concept of individual intentionality has been banished along with the autonomous subject. Editors now will still probably ask what Shakespeare may have intended, but their answers will likely be multiple and even mutually contradictory rather than single. And they will also ask in what ways the play may have been crucially shaped by pressures – from court, city authorities, actors and audiences in the playhouse, government or other forms of censorship, printing-house practices – outside authorial control. For example, might Shakespeare after 1606 have "intended" a different set of verbal patterns through the alteration of oaths than he had "intended" before the 1606 ordinance forbidding them on stage? Might not both intents have validity for modern readers? Following Foucault's witty formulation, the author can still be invited as a guest into the text, so long as he is not mistaken for its master. Along with the hegemonic narrative of authorial control, recent editorial practice has also begun to attenuate or abandon other familiar narratives that postmodernism has called into question, such as the traditional mapping of the development of Shakespeare's career and traditional assumptions about his inevitable "improvement" as an artist over time.

Embracing Contamination

A hallmark of nineteenth- and twentieth-century editing of Shakespeare was the attempt to recreate a "pure" text, which was assumed to be the text the poet intended. Beginning at least with the late eighteenth-century editor Edmond Malone, who announced that the editorial apparatus for his edition would protect Shakespeare against "modern sophistications and foreign admixtures" (cited in de Grazia 1991a: 10), editors have devised elaborate schemata for detecting elements of textual pollution, and have worked by various means to erase them as much as possible. Postmodernism, however, famously embraces contamination, hybridity, heterogeneity, and self-negation, and its celebration of these things is filtering into editorial practice. Some editors are beginning to feel less pressure than in the past to emend Shakespearean texts to make them self-consistent in terms of place, action, speech prefixes, stage directions, and other important details, on the grounds that inconsistency is often considerably more interesting and revealing than consistency. David Bevington's chapter in this volume discusses the matter at some length. Editors are also increasingly willing to allow verbal forms that sound ungrammatical to modern ears to remain in the edited Shakespearean text. As Margreta de Grazia has noted, Shakespearean texts are "prelexical" in the sense that they were produced before English grammar had been codified as it was during the eighteenth century. Although we now are taught not to use double superlatives or double negatives, or to combine a singular subject with a plural verb and vice versa, Shakespearean texts do all of these things routinely. Some of their grammatical "errors" are too blatant to be repaired, such as Anthony's "most unkindest cut of all" in *Julius Caesar* 3.2.182, but ordinary cases of failed verb–subject agreement are still routinely corrected even in some recent editions (fortunately, not in all), lest Shakespeare sound unacceptably uncouth.

Another element of the traditional fear of contamination has been an editorial unwillingness to see Shakespeare as a wholesale borrower from other writers, his wit posited as too sublime to sully itself by absorbing inferior material. This is an odd position to take, particularly given that one of the first accusations made against Shakespeare by his contemporaries was Robert Greene's accusation in the *Groatsworth of Wit* (1592) that he was an "upstart crow, beautified with our feathers," that is, an inveterate borrower of material from his more genteel contemporaries. Early twentieth-century editors were not afraid to point to Shakespearean borrowings – in fact some editors, like John Dover Wilson, considered "inferior" plays, like the *Henry VI* trilogy, to be pastiches of material largely by other playwrights. But even for Wilson, patches of genuine Shakespeare were by definition uncontaminated by admixtures from inferior writers. Other twentieth-century editors like W. W. Greg and his followers coped with the existence of infelicitous and unacceptably popular elements in the plays by positing such materials as contaminations introduced by pirates or other unauthorized agents – most likely renegade actors who attempted to reconstruct Shakespeare's plays from memory in order to sell them to printers, but who were too ignorant to reproduce their sophisticated artistry.

Such explanations are rapidly losing currency among editors, though few would deny Laurie Maguire's contention (1996) that a few early texts of Shakespeare show at least fleeting signs of having been reproduced from memory. In a postmodern aesthetic, the tables are turned on earlier editorial practice, in that patchwork, palimpsest, and textual hybridizations of various kinds are coming to be valued, even celebrated, rather than being regarded, in Greg's heavily fraught language, as the "blushing sins of the author" that beg for the redemptive hand of a correcting editor (1966: 252, n. 31). Now, increasingly, we are coming to see Shakespeare as an insatiable, omnivorous borrower; our perception of the Shakespearean text's inveterate assimilation and ventriloquism of a very wide range of heterogeneous cultural material helps to create our sense of Shakespeare's continuing value. In the sections that follow, I will look more closely at some particular instances of "contamination" and how they are beginning to be – or could profitably be – handled in new ways as we produce new editions of Shakespeare. Several of my examples will come from *The Merchant of Venice* because it is a play that I recently edited myself. Some will also come from a non-Shakespearean play, John Webster's *The Duchess of Malfi*, because it is a play I am presently editing.

Characters' Names and Speech Prefixes

Early printed texts of Shakespeare's plays do not, as a rule, offer lists of *dramatis personae*; those in modern editions have been editorially supplied. So our acquaintance with the characters' names in the early texts comes from within the plays – stage directions and speech prefixes – and these are notoriously unstable, as David Bevington's chapter below amply illustrates in a discussion of *I Henry VI*. *The Merchant of Venice* offers another case in point. In its earliest surviving quarto text (1600), Shylock is often identified merely as "Jew" in the speech prefixes. Launcelot the clown's name is most frequently spelled Launcelet, in the quarto, which suggests "little lance" rather than an echo of Arthurian legend (Andrews 2002), and he is frequently designated in speech prefixes as "Clowne" rather than either Launcelot or Launcelet. The names of Antonio and Bassanio's mysterious friends, who have been regularized to Salerio and Solanio in modern editions, are much more unstable in the early texts. The quarto identifies them on first appearance in 1.1 as Salaryno and Salanio, but when they exit the scene they are Salarino and Solanio. Later one of them becomes Salerio, or is this yet a third friend with a suspiciously similar name? At times, if there are only two of them, Salerio, Solanio, or Salarino is required to be in Venice and Belmont simultaneously. How many S-named friends do Bassanio and Antonio have, and who are they? Salerio, Salanio, Solanio, Salarino, Salaryno, Salario, Sal., Sol., Sola., Sala. – all of these forms occur in the first quarto version, and they are by no means used consistently.

In the case of Salerio/Solanio and Launcelot, my own choice as an editor was to follow the usual convention in naming, even though the possibility of reproducing the inconsistent nomenclature of the quarto version was extremely tempting. To do so would have created interesting games with identity that would alter our reading of the play, but I chose to concentrate on what appeared to me a more significant case of speech-prefix confusion, that between "Shylock" and "Jew." What happens when readers in a modern edition are forced to encounter the quarto inconsistency in naming this central character, which seems to concentrate the references to "Jew" around issues of anti-Semitism and blood libel, especially in the trial scene, but which does not alternate the two names with anything approaching predictable regularity? My choice to keep the inconsistent speech prefixes in my edition may have been based on a preference for quirkiness and self-contradiction derived from the current climate of postmodernism, but it will enable readings of the play that will link its instability in speech prefixes to broader social issues such as the status of Jews in Shakespeare's England and in *Merchant* in particular.

Similar questions about racial or genealogical stereotyping arise from other early speech prefixes. In both the quarto and First Folio texts of *King Lear*, Edmund, the bastard son of Gloucester, is referred to with remarkable consistency in the speech prefixes as "Bastard." The pattern is invariable in the quarto, slightly less so in the Folio, but in both cases, early readers were given a very different experience of the character than are readers of our modern editions, in which the speech prefixes for the almost nameless "Bastard" have been chastely regularized as "Edmund" (on other complex instances of the use of the speech prefix "Bastard" in Shakespeare, see McLeod 1997). As in the case of Shylock and "Jew," there are intriguing possible patterns to be found in the departures from the text's expected naming. In both early texts, the name "Edmund" emerges briefly in stage directions in Act IV when the "Bastard" emerges as Earl of Gloucester to accept his brother Edgar's challenge to single combat. But only in the Folio text does his given name bleed occasionally into the speech prefixes. In the quarto prefixes, Edmund, even as Earl of Gloucester, always remains "Bastard."

Similar language games take place in the speech prefixes and stage directions to *Titus Andronicus*, where Aaron is sometimes "Aron" and sometimes "Moore," with "Moore" predominating except at the point where Aaron acknowledges his "blackamoor child" in 4.2, when his identification suddenly and permanently switches in the speech prefixes to "Aron." Modern editions, by regularizing his name to "Aaron" throughout, lose the early texts' subtle interplay between racial and individual identification. By restoring these early speech prefixes in editions of Shakespeare, we can also communicate a creative tension between naming, racial or other stereotyping, and action, which runs through many of the plays. In marked contrast to Aaron, Othello, in both the quarto and Folio versions of *Othello*, is always referred to in stage directions and speech prefixes as "Othello" or "Oth." – never as "Moor." There is no stereotyping of Othello as a "Moor" in the formal nomenclature of the playtext; the chief character within the play to refer to Othello with any consistency as "Moor" is Iago, who can scarcely be considered a reliable guide to our or early audiences' responses to the title character. To what are we to attribute these interesting inconsistencies in the handling of names? The author? A playhouse scribe? Someone else in the acting company? A pirate? Compositors in the printing house? In the absence of manuscript evidence, it is impossible to know. But that does not mean that questions raised by these inconsistencies should be made unavailable to our study of Shakespeare because they have been normalized out of existence in the editions we use.

Asides

Another feature of edited texts which is beginning to change under the impact of postmodernism is the handling of asides. In Shakespeare and other dramatists of the period, it is quite common for a character on stage to make a comment or a full speech in the presence of other characters that has seemed, to modern readers at least, unlikely to be heard by them. One example from *The Merchant of Venice* occurs in 1.3.40–2, at the point where Antonio and Bassanio accost Shylock and ask him for a loan of three thousand ducats. Antonio enters, Bassanio says "This is Signior Antonio," and Shylock responds, "How like a fawning publican he looks! I hate him for he is a Christian," going on in the rest of his speech to complain about Antonio's hatred of the Jews and to articulate his desire for revenge. This speech is almost invariably labeled "Aside" in modern editions of the play, but not in the early printed texts. The modern editorial choice makes a certain amount of sense since at the end of Shylock's speech Bassanio says "Shylock, do you hear?" (l. 52), which implies that Shylock's thoughts had previously been elsewhere. But there are myriad other ways of understanding Bassanio's question: he may simply be bullying Shylock, or introducing the comments that follow.[1]

We need to consider what is accomplished through this and other labels of "Aside" for speeches that might, if not so labeled, complicate our understanding of dramatic character and of the relationship among characters on stage. Why is Shylock's denunciation of Antonio and his tribe assumed to be hidden while Antonio's later expression of hatred for Shylock – whom he states that he is likely to "spit on" and "spurn" in the future as he has in the past – is quite open? The dynamic of the scene changes considerably if the Jew's animosity toward the Christians is as visible to them as theirs toward him is to Shylock. Arguably, the designation of a speech as "Aside" functions to stabilize dramatic character: it clarifies motivation by distinguishing between public and private utterance; it simplifies and reduces the text by forestalling our (and other characters') recognition of inconsistencies and perceptual gaps.

A non-Shakespearean play in which the labeling of asides is particularly problematic on thematic as well as dramaturgic grounds is Webster's *The Duchess of Malfi*. Only once does the first quarto of this play give any typographic indication that part of a character's speech may be understood as an aside: in 2.3 Antonio, the clandestine husband of the Duchess, responds to probing questions by Bosola, the intelligencer who seeks information about the Duchess's possible marriage, by saying, "Bosola? / (This Moale do's vndermine me) heard you not / A noyce euen now?" (Sig. F1v). The phrase in parentheses appears to be marked as an aside, since Bosola is clearly the mole being referred to, but even this case is not certain, since the same punctuation is often used for descriptive phrases and direct address. *The Duchess of Malfi* is a play about suspicion, spying, overhearing, and mysterious echoes. Characters are constantly entering and exiting just at the point where key comments are made about them. Do they hear these comments, or not? The nervous uncertainty of audience and characters about who knows what and when is part of the mystery and power of the play.

To mark every seemingly private comment as an "Aside," as modern editors of *Duchess* have done, is to create a clear distinction between public and private that the play as a whole does not support. To leave characters' possible side-comments unmarked as "Asides" is to open the text to a paranoia and multiplicity of meaning that it loses in modern editions, with their careful sorting out of what is heard, and by whom. The same general principle applies to Shakespeare, though few of his plays are as steeped in suspicion as *The Duchess of Malfi*. By imposing an artificial clarity about what speech is an aside, uttered only to oneself and the audience, and what speech is a communication to another character, modern editors have simplified the psychology of characters and flattened out the complexity of dramatic interactions among them. As editors, by granting our readers (and ourselves) the comfort of the plainly marked "Aside" we can certainly clarify a scene's dramatic action; and clarity can be a virtue, particularly for younger and less experienced readers, who may be struggling to understand the language and action of the play at the most basic level. For more experienced readers, however, the "Aside" needs to be understood as a by-product of editorial faith in now discredited notions about autonomous subjectivity. The aside is a crutch we can well do without as we enter the labyrinth of Shakespearean character and motivation, which interests us in part *because* it is confusing and obscure.

Stage Directions

A hallmark of nineteenth- and twentieth-century editing of Shakespeare was the clarification of action on stage. Early Shakespearean editions are usually quite spare in the number and kind of stage directions they provide, and frequently leave characters' entrances and exits unmarked, even though from the characters' participation in the scene we know they must get on stage somehow. What is an editor's function in creating and emending stage directions? Is it to offer readers a clear, unproblematic sense of the pattern of action on stage so that they can visualize the play as they are reading it? Or is it to offer readers an array of possible scenarios for the action on stage with the goal of being suggestive rather than definitive, and with the expectation that users of the edited text may want to tackle problematic questions of staging for themselves? Of course, some readers and most actors and directors have always felt free to alter the action specified by any given modern edition, often by going back to the early quartos or Folio (which are readily available in facsimile editions and online) for themselves. Until quite recently, editors have taken it as part of their responsibility to readers to provide them with stage directions that communicate a scene's basic patterns unambiguously. Now, that traditional expectation is beginning to change. Over time, editorial specifications of the location and environment of a given scene have become increasingly brief and unobtrusive. While an early twentieth-century editor might specify a scene in *The Merchant of Venice* as taking place "In Belmont, on a terrace outside Portia's palace," a modern editor might be content with "Belmont," or no indication of place at all. The new preference for spareness is based in part on a desire to communicate some of the spareness of the Shakespearean stage, which used minimal props and scenery. But it is also at least to some extent a by-product of postmodernist taste, which tends to prefer fluidity and flexibility to specificity in the conceptualization of dramatic action.

In Shakespearean plays with more than one early printed text, the problem of stage directions becomes particularly acute, because different texts may offer contradictory or confusingly disparate statements about what is happening on stage. Some classic cases come from the graveyard scene in *Hamlet*. Does Hamlet actually pick up Yorick's skull in order to conduct his famous meditation on mortality? That action, so quintessential to many modern interpretations of the play, is not specified in any of the early printed texts. At most we can say that Hamlet gets close enough to the skull to smell it, since in all the early texts he reacts with some version of the speech, "And smelt so? Pah!" Should an editor indicate that Hamlet picks up the skull at the beginning of his musings, then throws it down in disgust on the word "Pah"? Or would it be better to prefer reticence, and leave the decision about Hamlet's likely actions to the reader, actor, or director?

Later in the scene, there is a yet more ambiguous case. Shortly after Ophelia's body is lowered into the grave, Hamlet and Laertes become locked in a verbal battle over who loved her more. Laertes vows to catch her "once more" in his arms and, according to most modern editions, leaps into the grave. Hamlet announces his presence, "This is I, / Hamlet the Dane!" and, according to most modern editions, leaps after Laertes into the grave, where they wrestle over Ophelia's body. The trouble with this scenario is that it is specified only in the first quarto of *Hamlet* (1603), which most editors otherwise disparage, considering it crude, overly melodramatic, and probably pirated rather than being "true Shakespeare." The second quarto (1604), which most editors consider a good text of the play, does not specify that either Hamlet or Laertes jumps into Ophelia's grave. The First Folio (1623) specifies only that Laertes "Leaps into the graue" (TLN 3444), leaving open the question of whether Hamlet follows suit. The image of the two rivals wrestling in the grave is stupendously theatrical, which is presumably why editors have tended to perpetuate it. But the fact that the "good" second quarto omits Hamlet's leap suggests that the gesture can also be understood as a precursor of the many flamboyantly overwrought gestures that Laertes makes in his quest for revenge toward the end of the play. In both the second quarto and the Folio texts (but not the first quarto), Hamlet has a speech that can be interpreted as critical of Laertes's gesture – a reaction that would go along with his earlier expression of distrust for "outward show": "What is he, whose griefes / Beares such an Emphasis? Whose phrase of Sorrow / Coniure the wandring Starres..." (TLN 3449–50). (Alert readers will note parenthetically that this citation in its Folio spelling, unemended by modern editors, contains not one but two cases of failed subject–verb agreement.) Clearly, much is at stake in the editorial decision whether or not to have Hamlet leap into Ophelia's grave after Laertes. Rather than offer a specificity that forecloses interpretive possibilities that two out of three early texts leave open, an editor working with a postmodern textual framework in mind would be likely to leave the matter undecided, weighing the differences among the early texts in a note.

The Duchess of Malfi offers even more opportunities for creative shaping of the mise-en-scène, since the earliest printed editions of the play do not specify when characters enter, but simply list all the characters who will eventually appear in a given scene at the head of it. We do not know why the play was printed in this frustrating (or liberating?) way – most likely the published version was based on a manuscript transcription by Ralph Crane, who had a penchant for massing characters at the beginning of the scene instead of marking their individual entrances. How is an editor to decide where to bring characters on stage? If they speak to other characters, we can usually presume they have entered, unless they can be understood as shouting from offstage. But the question of how and when they get on stage can lead to many opportunities for creative interpretation in stage directions. A case in point is the chilling moment in 3.2 after Antonio and Cariola have played a practical joke on the Duchess by secretly exiting her bedroom while she is still talking to them. As she banters with her husband Antonio, unaware of his departure, her murderous brother Ferdinand enters. The question is, how much of her speech does he hear?

Here is the Duchess's speech in my edited version, but with my added stage directions omitted:

DUCHESS
   Doth not the colour of my hair 'gin to change?
   When I wax gray I shall have all the court
   Powder their hair with arras to be like me.
   You have cause to love me. I entered you into my heart
   Before you would vouchsafe to call for the keys.
   We shall one day have my brothers take you napping.
   Methinks his presence, being now in court,
   Should make you keep your own bed. But you'll say
   Love mixed with fear is sweetest. I'll assure you
   You shall get no more children till my brothers
   Consent to be your gossips. Have you lost your tongue?
   'Tis welcome.
   For know, whether I am doomed to live or die,
   I can do both like a prince.
FERDINAND   Die then quickly!

The fourth quarto of the play (1708) and some modern editions have Ferdinand enter unseen after the fourth line of the Duchess's speech, "I entered you into my heart" – a line she thinks she is addressing to her husband Antonio; several other modern editors have Ferdinand enter after the next line, "call for the keys." The first choice makes it possible that Ferdinand has heard the Duchess say the words "I entered you into my heart" and mistakenly applies them to himself. Also, given the first choice, Ferdinand enters just as she has uttered the word "entered," which generates an ironic counterpoint between the stage action and the Duchess's meaning. The second choice, having Ferdinand enter after line four of the speech, makes it less likely that Ferdinand can misunderstand the Duchess as entering *him* in her heart. In my edition, if all goes according to plan, Ferdinand will enter after only the second line of the speech. I could not resist the impulse to have him hear all of his sister's declaration of love – and possibly apply it to himself. The play is so steeped in brother–sister incest motifs – particularly in the language of Ferdinand – that this choice made strong sense to me.

But my "sense" may be some readers' nonsense. And it certainly serves to create an element of consistency to Ferdinand's character that other readers may object to because it makes too much sense. In other words, depending on one's perspective, my intervention may be too postmodern, or not postmodern enough. I will include a note pointing out other editors' choices, and why the precise point of Ferdinand's entry matters so much to interpretation. Character entrances are usually more settled than this in the early printed texts of Shakespeare, but they are sometimes omitted; they are not necessarily consistent from one early text to another; and they are sometimes confusingly placed. Rather than specifying one possibility at the expense of others that may be equally fruitful and evocative, editors in our "postmodern age" are well advised to devise some way of keeping the scene in question open to more than one interpretation, and of acknowledging that the different options may well open different and conflicting interpretive possibilities for the rest of the play. Practically speaking, of course, such editorial openness can only be achieved within strict boundaries – no such inquiry can go on *ad infinitum* in print because publishers tend to become quite testy when editors exceed the prescribed word count for their editions. No printed edition can have the endless openness we like to associate with postmodernism, but a little suggestiveness can go a long way in encouraging readers to generate possibilities for themselves. Editors now are increasingly likely at least to gesture toward some of the games that the text invites us to play.

Explanatory Notes

In a Shakespearean edition geared toward readers in a "postmodern age," explanatory notes should perhaps be instead termed "exploratory," to emphasize their greater openness and diminished dogmatism by comparison with the notes in most previous editions. In practice, editors who write "exploratory" notes will, more frequently than in most editions at present, offer an array of plausible definitions for a word or phrase rather than only one. Insofar as it is possible, they will also avoid the hermeneutic traps that have sometimes caused editors to close off new inquiries into Shakespearean meaning because they have placed unquestioning trust in traditional scholarly resources. In *Unediting the Renaissance*, I used the editorial treatment of "blue-eyed" Sycorax in *The Tempest* to make this point at some length, arguing that modern editions unnecessarily closed off the possibility that Sycorax could be blue-eyed in the usual sense of the term because of cultural anxieties about gender, colonization, and race (1996: 5–17). Rather than repeat that argument here, I will briefly mention a few other examples. Why in *Othello* do most editors emend the early texts, in which Othello describes himself as having a name as "fresh as Dian's visage," to refer instead to Desdemona (3.3.386–7)? Why in Marlowe's *Tamburlaine* do editors usually not allow the Mongol conqueror to have limbs that are "snowy" or "snowy white," the readings in the early quartos, instead emending "snowy" to "sinewy," a more plausible but less startling and challenging epithet for an Asiatic warrior? In *The Duchess of Malfi* all editors emend Antonio's Ovidian line about Daphne's avoidance of Apollo "We read how Daphne for her peevish slight / Became a fruitless bay tree" to "peevish flight" on the grounds that the *OED* does not allow "slight" to mean "display of contemptuous indifference" until 1701. All the early quartos read "slight," which suggests that Webster's near contemporaries did not have difficulty with the word. The *OED*'s compilers may simply have missed Webster's early usage of "slight" in this sense – perhaps because in writing their *OED* entries they were using a printed edition of Webster in which "slight" had already been emended to "flight."

Creative anachronism is one of the bywords of postmodernism. By pursuing textual possibilities that appear anachronistic or simply erroneous, editors can often open new avenues for interpretation. In *The Duchess of Malfi*, Duke Ferdinand, who makes it abundantly clear through most of the play that he lusts after his sister, tells her in the quarto, "I'll instantly to bed, / For I am weary: I am to be be-speake / A husband for you." Assuming "be be-speake" to be a printing-house error, all modern editions and, for that matter, all early editions beginning with the second quarto, make sense of the line by altering it to "I am to bespeak." Why does the line require emendation? We have learned about parapraxis (a misuse of language that points toward some hidden meaning) from Sigmund Freud, but he did not invent the phenomenon. Would it be impossibly anachronistic to suggest that Webster was creating a parapraxis for Ferdinand, who wants to "be" the duchess's husband, not only "bespeak" her a husband? Similarly, in Shakespeare, unfamiliar usages are frequently emended when they could more fruitfully be explored through the use of creative anachronism. Here, as in my previous discussion of stage directions, a little ingenuity in suggesting non-traditional possibilities for meaning can go a long way toward breaking the authority of past editorial practice in favor of greater openness and multiplicity. My list of areas in which editorial practice is changing, or should change, to reflect postmodern tastes could easily extended to other areas of the art and craft of editing, but it is time instead to consider the limitations of the implicit master narrative I have offered here about the limitations of traditional editorial master narratives.

A Multitude of Shakespeares?

How can any single edition of a Shakespeare play encompass all of the suggestions for updating that I have offered here? The answer is that it can't. An edition that left everything open (if indeed that were possible) would be so formless as to be unusable in practice for all but the most sophisticated readers, its postmodernist art of "perpetual negation" working against the need of most readers to have something tangible to grasp as an identifiable text of Shakespeare. Rather than attempting to create a postmodern edition, we can create editions that stimulate readers to experience elements of undecidability in their reading of Shakespeare. Rather than expect an infinite array of textual and dramatic possibilities to be unfolded within a given edition, we should expect and encourage a greater range of editions than are presently available. The Shakespeare industry generates many new editions of plays each year, both in individual volumes and in collections. Many self-respecting Shakespeareans have by now edited at least one play, or are planning to edit one. But generally speaking, these editions are too uniform, too much alike, too often geared to the same audience rather than to disparate audiences. The amount and kind of editorial intervention we undertake will depend on the purpose of the edition. High-schoolers just encountering Shakespeare for the first time obviously need different texts than do advanced scholars who want to play elite games with indeterminacy. But perhaps urbanites and agriculturalists and men and women and gays and straights and right-wing Republicans and left-wing Democrats and Labourites and Conservatives and South Asians and Latin Americans and Europeans and North Africans also need, or could fruitfully use, different kinds of editions of Shakespeare.

That is not to suggest that we should abandon the idea that we can achieve broad common communication about Shakespeare across cultural differences. We are haunted, I think, by a fear of abandoning the Victorian dream of a standardized Shakespeare. Before the late nineteenth century, as Andrew Murphy details in chapter 5 of this volume, Shakespeare editing was largely the province of amateur scholars who worked in relative isolation and independence from each other. As Gary Taylor has shown in *Reinventing Shakespeare* (1990), however, and Paul Werstine further discusses in chapter 6 of this volume, university scholars gradually took over the creation of the major Shakespeare editions in the late nineteenth century. Shakespearean "experts" working in interlocking groups produced the highly influential Cambridge edition, which stabilized the text for many decades to come. The Cambridge editors of course had rifts and disagreements, but these editors were uniformly dedicated to the project of creating reliable, standardized texts of Shakespeare, with notes recording the readings of earlier editions, and numbered lines so that references could be instantly traced and the way would be cleared for additional scholarly endeavors based on the existence of a standardized text: concordances, the practice of critical close reading, grammars of Shakespearean English, dictionaries, even the *OED* itself, which was an outgrowth of the same codifying impulse (see Werstine's chapter above; Taylor 1990: 184–93). There are many flaws in this tremendous late nineteenth- and early twentieth-century edifice of codification, as I have suggested above, but the advantages of preserving some type of uniform Shakespearean text are obvious: without it, scholarly communication, the teaching of Shakespeare, and many other activities such as the simple checking of a quotation would become cumbersome. Readers will be quick to note that I have used standardized texts at various points in this chapter, and David Bevington's discussion of editorial standardization (chapter 9 below) shows that it is still considered desirable for many purposes.

Indeed, the previous codifications of Shakespeare shadow post-modernism at every turn – even as we argue for some purposes against the received standardized texts, they continue to occupy the periphery of our attention. They exert a shaping presence even when placed *sous rature*, under erasure. They are perhaps necessary to postmodern dispersals of them in that they stand as the form against which we define our various forms of difference. They are widely disseminated in libraries and personal collections and often conveniently available online. Editing Shakespeare in a "postmodern age" does not require us to suppress previous efforts through rigid rituals of avoidance and condemnations. It requires us only to provincialize them in Dipesh Chakrabarty's (2000) sense of the term – to recognize as much as possible their limitations, their unstated biases, their hidden agendas, while at the same time striving as much as possible to acknowledge and undo their profound influences on ourselves as we re-edit Shakespeare for our own times.

Note

1 Quotations from Shakespeare are taken from G. Blakemore Evans (ed.), *The Riverside Shakespeare* (Boston: Houghton Mifflin, 1974, second edition 1997), with the exception of *Merchant of Venice*, for which I have used my own edition (2006c).

Chapter 8

Shakespeare and the Electronic Text

Michael Best

Since the earliest days of hypertext, techno-scholars have enthused about the potential of the electronic medium. Even before the advent of the World Wide Web, there were some remarkable trailblazers, each giving some sense of the way that a hypertextual, multimedia environment could enhance our reading experience of Shakespeare's texts: the *Shakespeare Project* spearheaded by Larry Friedlander (1984; see Friedlander 1991) and Voyager's *Macbeth*, released for the Macintosh platform in 1994, for example. The exponential expansion of the World Wide Web has put Shakespeare-related materials on the monitors of computers around the world, in impressive variety: witness the extensive links to resources listed in major "gateways" or "portals" dedicated to Shakespearean materials (Gray; *Internet Shakespeare Editions*, "Links," for example). It comes therefore as something of a surprise that two decades later, with the medium expanding at a speed only the most visionary would have anticipated, the potential of a Shakespearean text wholly designed for the electronic medium is not yet fully realized. There are no obvious theoretical constraints. In the early days of the medium, there were perceptive theoretical discussions of the potential of the electronic text, led by George Landow (1992, 1994) and Jay David Bolter (1991); in the field of English literary studies hypertext as a medium received an early imprimatur from Jerome J. McGann, whose "Rationale of Hypertext" (1995) took his earlier discussions of the "social" text as a basis for establishing the academic credibility – even desirability – of an electronic edition.

Indeed, as Leah S. Marcus indicates in her chapter in this volume, the emphasis in recent years has been on editorial theories that stress the richness of multiplicity in texts rather than the search for a single, elusive (or illusionary) reconstruction of an ideal; this approach should make for a climate where the capacity of the computer to present variable versions simultaneously would be seen as a perfect reflection of textual variation. Michael Warren's *The Parallel King Lear* (1989) pushed the print medium to what must be close to its limit, with its unbound pages waiting for different readers to assemble them according to taste. No wonder that Bernice Kliman turned to the web to create a more usable version of her and Paul Bertram's *Three-Text Hamlet* (2003), a book that in print is awkward in size, and full of blank spaces where only one of the texts has anything to say. On the screen, alternative readings become much clearer, and the user has more control over the layout.

With this kind of critical momentum behind the creation of electronic texts, it may seem the more puzzling that the medium has not been more fully exploited. But the reasons why electronic texts are only beginning to achieve maturity are many: economic, political, technical, academic, legal, political-academic, economic-political-academic, and, no doubt, economic-political-technical-legal-academic. In this discussion, I will begin with a brief history of the development of early electronic Shakespeares, then discuss some more recent advances, concluding with an exploration of some of the new directions that are being explored, by both commercial and non-profit enterprises.

Early Texts on Disk: Economic-Academic Challenges

Early electronic editions of Shakespeare can be divided into two kinds: those that adapted print to the new medium, using disks (first floppies, then the CD-ROM) as the method of distribution, and, once the World Wide Web had become a reality, those that scrambled to disseminate copyright-free texts to a growing community of readers looking for free access to downloadable texts (see Bolton 1990 for more detail on early electronic Shakespeare).

Though it seldom registers in discussions about editing Shakespeare, the driving force behind the production of Shakespearean texts is economic. Shakespeare sells; and for that reason there are a perhaps surprising number of competing editions, even for similar markets.

Most notably, the audience for full scholarly editions is well served by three major series: the long-established Arden, published by a commercial press (or conglomerate), and the Cambridge and Oxford series, published by university presses, which, though non-profit, still have to be aware of the bottom line. The economic reward for editors is less obvious, since even Shakespeare brings little in the way of royalties, but publication by one of these series provides editors reward in the currency of the profession – prestige and advancement. So significant is this in-kind payment that most editors relinquish copyright of the completed text to the publisher.

The earliest machine-readable texts of Shakespeare were published on disk, a medium that offers the same kind of physical presence as a book and can therefore be marketed through the same channels. These texts took advantage of the electronic medium by providing tools for the textual analysis of Shakespeare's work. An early, still useful, edition of the plays was created in the 1960s by Trevor Howard-Hill as the first step in the process of creating old-spelling concordances of the plays for Oxford University Press (Oxford Text Archive); these texts were never put online, though they were eventually made available to scholars on floppy disk for a modest fee, and can now be freely downloaded. The *Riverside Shakespeare* (ed. Blakemore Evans, 1974) was released in 1988 as part of a software package that included the textual analysis program *WordCruncher*; the texts were accessible only through the program, however, so it was impossible for anyone but a hacker to extract them in a simple format for use in a word processor. In the same year, the text of the new *Oxford Complete Works* was also released on CD-ROM.

By the 1990s, advances in the hardware and software of personal computers made genuinely multimedia editions possible. With remarkable prescience, Philip Brockbank, in 1991, imagined the delight and power of a "mobile text" made possible by the computer; three years later, the Voyager *Macbeth* (1994), based on the Cambridge text edited by A. R. Braunmuller (1997a), was the first real attempt to fulfill this vision. The Voyager edition was graphically attractive, and more fully interactive than the earlier CD-ROMs; it also provided some video footage, and a complete audio performance. The disadvantage of the edition was that it was released for the Macintosh platform only, since at the time Macintosh's *HyperCard* was the only generally available software that could handle the combination of hypertext and multimedia. Priced for individuals in an anticipated educational market, the edition did not succeed well enough to encourage further titles. Since the Voyager *Macbeth*, there have been a number of educational CD-ROMs of individual plays, but the medium has been rapidly superseded in popularity by the World Wide Web as browsers have become sophisticated enough to display multimedia materials.

Nonetheless, major publishers continued to promote works on CD-ROM. As well as being marketable through traditional means, a CD-ROM offered its publisher a modest assurance that copyright would be respected on the works published. The Modern Language Association (MLA) published a powerful text analysis program, *TACT*, with texts of Shakespeare (including a three-text version of *Hamlet* contributed by Ian Lancashire) in 1996. The following year, Thomas Nelson published *The Arden Shakespeare*; this CD-ROM was for its time innovative in its comprehensiveness, as it contained electronic versions of the second Arden series, together with some useful additional resources – facsimiles, sources, glossary, and so on – and it permitted extensive searching on the texts. Thus the CD-ROM established a basic tendency for the electronic edition to become a reference archive, above and beyond the capabilities of print. It included, however, a significant number of texts that had already been made obsolete by the third Arden series. A later publication on CD-ROM was *The Cambridge King Lear CD-ROM: Text and Performance Archive*, edited by Jackie Bratton and Christie Carson for Cambridge University Press. The subtitle of this work proclaimed its scope as an archive rather than an edition. It included three modern texts, quarto, folio, and conflated (the "finder" text), together with major adaptations, and an extensive gallery of graphics of performance. Both these CD-ROMs were, however, very expensive, and were clearly aimed at libraries rather than individuals.

Two early projects took advantage of the capability of the computer to display both text and multimedia. Larry Friedlander's *Shakespeare Project* (1984) combined laserdisc technology with Macintosh's *HyperCard* to develop an interactive workspace that interlinked film segments of selected plays with the text, and with other resources. As a study tool, students could create their own essays, quoting segments of film to support their arguments. Eight years later, Peter Donaldson headed a team at MIT in the development of the *Shakespeare Electronic Archive*. Their aim was to create an archive, "eventually networked and available throughout the world, in which documents of all kinds – films, sound recordings, texts, digital facsimiles – would be linked in electronic form to one another and to the lines of text to which they refer or which they enact" (Donaldson 1997: 173). Like Friedlander in the *Shakespeare Project*, Donaldson sidestepped the immense problem of obtaining copyright for the use of film by accessing it on laserdisc, for which performance rights could be purchased for a limited audience of students. The custom-built software also linked film and text with high-quality digital facsimiles of selected folios from the collection at the Folger Shakespeare Library. This project solved many of the technical problems of hyperlinking disparate digital documents (video, facsimile, text), but has been used only at MIT and the Folger, again for copyright reasons. A subset of the project is available on the web as *Hamlet on the Ramparts*.

Free Websites: Technical-Legal Challenges

The anticipated audience for the early CD-ROMs was, with the notable exception of the Voyager *Macbeth*, the scholar, and the cost of putting together what amounted to a library of information using complex programming meant that the only purchasers would be libraries. In contrast, the culture of the web has led to an expectation that content will be free. No one expects a print volume to be free, but the resistance to subscription sites on the web has been strong; the initial online version of the Arden texts, *ArdenOnline*, failed through lack of support for its subscription-only site. (I will discuss below the recently launched site by Thomson-Gale, *The Shakespeare Collection*, which again uses the Arden texts.) In the early days of the web, most sites were developed by enthusiasts rather than scholars; they sought a usable, rather than scholarly, text, one that was free from copyright restriction.

The first freely available electronic text of the plays, still almost ubiquitous on the web, was the Moby Shakespeare. This edition appears to have been extracted by Grady Ward from a CD-ROM that claimed to use the Stratford Town modern-spelling edition of 1911, edited by Arthur Bullen; however, it is more likely to be a transcription, not wholly accurate, of the Globe text published in the 1860s (see Lancashire, "Public-Domain Shakespeare"). This is the text that is still used on two sites that made Shakespeare readily available in the early days of the web. Matty Farrow's site *The Works of the Bard* provides a powerful, if somewhat arcane, search engine, and Jeremy Hylton's site at MIT is still frequently cited as a recommended source for the texts. It is typical of the casual nature of these sites that Farrow remarks, "I picked these up some time ago from a server in England"; Hylton provides the slightly more helpful citation, "The original electronic source for this server is the Complete Moby(tm) Shakespeare," but the embedded link is no longer functional, so provides no more precise bibliographical information. The Moby text is ubiquitous for two reasons: it is in the public domain, and it is good enough for general readers looking for a downloadable text or a quotation – arguably the most common activities of web users.

Some Theoretical Issues: Legal-Technical-Academic-Political

The almost-universal use on the web of the Globe edition, some 150 years old, highlights a major challenge for those who wish to publish Shakespeare on the web: copyright. Texts must be old enough to be out of copyright – in which case they will be well past their "use-by" date for scholars – or they must be re-edited specifically for the edition. No current publisher would be willing to license their texts for free distribution, for obvious economic reasons. Copyright problems are not limited to the texts themselves, however, since many of the added attractions of a multimedia edition require permission to publish as well: images, passages from current critical discussions, music, and, ideally, video clips of performance. Fortunately, there are many institutions that have a mandate to make their works available to the general public, and there are often ways of acquiring permission to use restricted materials so long as there is no profit motive. Graphic and other materials can be published on the web in such a way that illicit duplication will be limited or ineffective – graphics that display well on a screen will look coarse when printed, video clips can be streamed rather than downloaded, and so on.

A second major issue is the preservation of scholarly work in a medium that is still subject to rapid change and development, in both hardware and software. Some of the early CD-ROMs are instructive illustrations of these dangers, even those that took pains to create texts in standard format. Both the Arden Shakespeare and the Cambridge *King Lear in Performance* CD-ROMs used texts encoded in SGML (Standard Generalized Markup Language), accessed through the proprietary software *DynaText*. SGML has been largely superseded by the more flexible and powerful XML (eXtensible Markup Language), and *DynaText* is no longer supported. Peter Donaldson's *Shakespeare Electronic Archive* was initially based on the technology of the laserdisc, but, as DVD took over, his programmers had to rewrite the software to interact with the new technology; recent developments in this technology again threaten the still-new DVD with obsolescence.

It is thus for very good reason that the academic community will be conservative in its response to the new medium. Academic standards are set by peer review, and it is inevitable that many academics will be skeptical of the quality of publication on the web: the happy proliferation of amateur sites – like some of those listed above – can be read as a signal that publication on the web is untried and untested by appropriate standards. Thus a further challenge to the development of scholarly editions on the web is that scholars working on them may lack adequate recognition in the currency of the profession. This problem will no doubt become less acute over time, as web publication becomes more widespread (but see Siemens et al., *Credibility*). A number of electronic journals and scholarly sites have begun to set standards of peer review in the field; typically they involve oversight by an editorial board of senior scholars in the field, and mechanisms of peer review which are at least as rigorous as those employed by print publishers.

It is a sign of the increasing acceptance of publishing in the electronic medium that the MLA has included electronic editions in its "Guidelines for Editors of Scholarly Editions." The "Guidelines" stress the importance of adherence to accepted standards in encoding and file types, the provision of careful archiving, and the necessity for full documentation of the underlying technology that the electronic edition uses. It is worth looking in more detail at the rationales and implications of these requirements.

Encoding Shakespeare: Technical-Academic Standards

Standards in encoding (the "Guidelines" single out XML and SGML) are vital in ensuring stability as the medium changes. Files encoded in XML are converted into web format by "stylesheets" that can be modified as new browsers become available; thus the stylesheets may need to be updated, but the underlying scholarly data remain unchanged and stable. Early sites created texts of the plays much as they are recorded in a word processor, with each page a single file, formatted in HTML (HyperText Markup Language) for web browsers. More recent sites create the texts from XML, a more sophisticated format that provides the additional information the computer needs both to display the text and to search it intelligently. The XML can then be stored in a database that makes it possible to display varying views of a play on demand: as individual scenes, as a whole, or as a concordance, for example.

A valuable feature of XML as an encoding language is that it is self-describing: each file is associated with a "schema" or "Document Type Definition" (DTD) that fully defines what each item of the encoding means; a related stylesheet indicates how each item is to be displayed. Thus the encoding, or "tagging," for a stage direction might be Exit; the stylesheet might cause the browser to display the stage direction on a separate line, right aligned, and in italics. Tagging a text in this manner may seem rather more like programming than editing, but the truth is that we already do this kind of encoding using typographical signals. As we read (or edit) a text, we immediately recognize the difference between the word "Hamlet" as an indication of the speaker, as an instruction in a stage direction (*"Enter Hamlet"*), or as a mention of his name by another character; the process of tagging in an electronic text makes this kind of recognition more formal and machine-readable. The ideal result of effective encoding is to create intelligent texts: those that describe themselves and the functions of their constituent parts. Once such a text has been created, it becomes possible to search it in creative ways: to test whether Romeo or Juliet uses the word "love" more often, for example, or to limit a search to any one or combination of the three kinds of references to "Hamlet" I have listed.

Computer languages expect an ordered world. Humanities texts, however, are fractal and fractious, reveling in ambiguity and multiplicity, and they resist reduction to the orderly structures computer languages expect. Nonetheless, there has been a great deal of work done in developing a standard for the encoding of the kinds of texts we work with, notably by the Text Encoding Initiative (TEI). There remain, however, some teasing gaps between computer and human language, even in so basic a matter as the structure of a text. In a modern-spelling edition, Shakespeare's plays fall into an orderly array of acts and scenes (though different editors may put the act and scene breaks in different places, or even dispense with acts altogether). If, however, an editor wishes to re-create in electronic form a quarto text, the imposition of act and scene breaks can be seen as an anachronism. Scholars interested in the early texts are acutely conscious of the importance of the physical book as it influences form and meaning; for such readers, a structure of pages, columns (in the Folio), and lines would more faithfully represent the original. The question here is not trivial. An electronic text that attempts to transcribe an early modern original must make the choice between displaying the text by its conceptual units – acts and scenes – or physical units – pages – or as a single long file. The single long file is arguably the closest to the conceptual structure of a quarto text, but scrolling through a long file is the most awkward possible way to view a work (it is no accident that the codex so completely replaced the scroll). The best solution is to use the medium to offer a choice between different displays; unfortunately, XML cannot elegantly represent overlapping structures of this kind. While there are several projects that are finding ways of working around this problem (see TEI, "SIG: Overlap," for example), it is fair to say that at the moment there is no single standard that has been accepted. Electronic editions that are working in this area are therefore in the adventurous, but potentially risky, role of pioneers.

Since electronic editions can include multimedia – graphic images, sound files, and video files – standards are also important in the storage and display of these digital artifacts. These formats are all far more demanding of disk space and download time than text. A single page of the Folio scanned at the relatively low resolution of 600 dots per inch will take up over 100 megabytes of disk space if stored in a "lossless" format (TIFF). The same image, however, can be compressed intelligently in the standard "lossy" JPEG format to download at a readable 72 dots per inch in a file of one hundredth of the size. Both formats are important, since the uncompressed file will be needed for archiving purposes. There is a tradeoff between readability and file size; as a file is compressed further, the algorithm averages values in larger areas, so colors become less vivid, and edges (important in recording print works) become more blurred. Similar tradeoffs are needed in working with video files, though the standard compression algorithm for sound files, MP3, is now universally accepted.

Archiving and Documentation

The MLA "Guidelines" are salutary in their concern for long-term archiving and accessibility in a medium that is likely to evolve rapidly in the next few years. A book will go out of print, and its contents will be superseded by more recent scholarship, but it will last in a library for hundreds of years. The safeguard for scholars, who, reasonably enough, do not want to see their work on electronic editions become obsolete, is to ensure both that multiple backups of all work are maintained in separate locations, and that all data are stored in fully standard formats to ensure conversion to a format that will work with any future hardware and software. But an electronic edition is not just a compilation of data: what makes it function as an edition is the software that drives it, and this software will change as new versions are released. The important safeguard here is full documentation. The MLA "Guidelines" recommend (27.3) that any software developed uniquely for an electronic edition make its source code "available and documented." Documentation is one thing, but the eminently desirable requirement of making the source code available is easier for a publicly funded enterprise than for one that is for profit. Paradoxically, the long-term viability of an electronic edition, for this reason, may be more achievable on publicly funded free websites than on commercially driven ones.

New Insights: Academic-Technical Opportunities

The MLA "Guidelines" do not attempt to deal with the most interesting issues facing those developing electronic editions: the possibility that the medium is capable of changing the way we read and understand Shakespeare. Some CD-ROMs pointed toward new ways of representing Shakespeare on the computer screen in their hypertextual combination of text and facsimile, or text and performance; a more fundamental evolution employs the capacity of the computer for revisualizing the plays as the result of queries to a database. The success of the Google search engine in the recent past has radically changed the way that most people interact with large bodies of data. They expect to be able to enter simple queries into a text box, and to select from the resulting list of "hits" that the computer returns; if the list is unhelpful they will refine their search until they find what they are looking for. Increasingly, computer users are reading computer data in a fundamentally different way from the way they read a book. They seek specific information, consult or download it, then move on – it is a case of hit-and-run rather than the more sustained journey that a book encourages. Despite the announcement that Sony has released an e-book that uses electronic paper rather than a screen, it is likely that for the foreseeable future an electronic Shakespeare edition will be treated more as an archive for searching than as a way of reading the plays from beginning to end. It is also clear that the brief day of the CD-ROM as a means of distributing electronic editions is effectively over, and that future work will use the web, either to publish freely accessible sites, or to generate sites available by subscription. The one exception to this trend may be the splendid Octavo facsimiles of the plays. These beautifully produced CD-ROMs provide superior digital facsimiles, fully searchable, and are priced very reasonably for the individual purchaser.

With the fading of the CD-ROM as a medium, it is no surprise to discover that recent electronic Shakespeares have been published on the web; they have also made a concerted effort to ensure greater scholarly credibility. Two recent projects attempt in different ways to overcome the limitations of sites based on the Moby Shakespeare: the *Open Source Shakespeare*, created by Eric Johnson; and *The Nameless Shakespeare*, edited by Craig Berry, Martin Mueller, and Clifford Wulfman. Both sites aim to provide tools of textual analysis rather than scholarly texts of the plays, and both provide some powerful tools for those interested in Shakespeare, from the enthusiast to the scholar. The *Open Source Shakespeare* takes its inspiration from the Open Source movement in software development, a movement that has as its most notable success the increasingly impressive and popular operating system Linux (see Raymond, "Cathedral," and Rasch, "Brief History,"for discussions of its aims and procedures). Johnson's site provides a thorough discussion of the origin of the text he uses as a starting point – again the venerable Cambridge Globe edition – and his hope is that contributors to the site will collaboratively improve its accuracy. The main difficulty in adapting the Open Source concept to Shakespeare's texts is that a "bug-free" text of Shakespeare is a logical impossibility, since there is now general agreement that the texts are ineluctably multiple, and that in many cruces there can be no final "accurate" version (see the chapters by Leah S. Marcus and David Bevington in this volume for more discussion of this question). The site is more useful in its impressive array of alternative ways of searching and viewing the text.

If the *Open Source Shakespeare* provides powerful tools for arranging, printing, and searching the plays, its major limitation is the dated nature of the texts it uses. The creators of *The Nameless Shakespeare* have taken a different approach. They have modified the "good enough" criterion that led to the widespread use of the Moby text by adopting a somewhat more scholarly method; although they started with the Globe text, they undertook "a systematic comparison with the University of Victoria's digital transcriptions of the quarto and folio editions . . . to produce a modern text that observes as closely as possible the morphological and prosodic practices of the earliest editions" (*Nameless Shakespeare*, Home Page). As the language of this passage suggests, the editors' main interest, like so many of the earlier sites, is in textual analysis, but they have provided significantly more advanced tools, and have parsed and lemmatized the texts to enable sophisticated searches on groups of related words. The texts are not, however, in the public domain, since copyright is held by the universities where they have been developed, and are thus unlikely to supplant the Moby edition. They have been developed as a part of a larger philological project, Word Hoard, a project which seeks to make possible "the empirical and computer-assisted study of large bodies of written texts or transcribed speech." The larger project includes texts from early Greek epic, Chaucer, Shakespeare, and Spenser, and is still under construction.

A third site points toward a very different way of structuring an edition in the electronic medium. *The Enfolded Hamlet*, edited by Bernice Kliman, moves well beyond the limitations imposed by print in her and Bertram's earlier book *The Three-Text Hamlet*. Using various brackets and colors, the text provides either a compound ("enfolded") view of the three early texts (Quartos 1 and 2, and the Folio), or separate views of the source texts. The result, while appearing somewhat arcane, is far more intuitively comprehensible than the earlier use of various brackets in such texts as the New Folger Library series (see their text of *Othello*, for example). The site is expanding as some additional materials derived from editing the electronic New Variorum electronic *Hamlet* are being added. Other New Variorum Shakespeare editions are also contributing in a potentially interesting way to the use of the electronic medium. A variorum is a very specific kind of edition, much closer to an exhaustive database of all editorial emendation and commentary on a given play than is found in even a scholarly edition. One contributor, Alan Galey, has begun to realize the potential of an electronic version, especially when it comes to plotting changes in readings that have occurred over time, and that can be retrieved automatically from the detailed collations that a variorum provides. He is able, for example, to create color-coded tables that show when readings were adopted, how long they remained accepted, and when (if at all) they were abandoned; in a single visual spreadsheet it is possible to track changes in editorial style and fashion in a manner that would never be clearly demonstrable using anecdotal information (Galey 2005). The proposed method for publication of these electronic texts will be on the web, with access by subscription.

These four projects employ advanced computer technologies for the display, and particularly the searching, of Shakespeare's texts, but they are aimed at significantly different audiences. The *Open Source Shakespeare* continues the tradition of sites that aim at a very general reader, while *The Nameless Shakespeare* is specifically designed for a very select group of users who are interested in exploring patterns of Shakespeare's use of language; both the *Enfolded Hamlet* and the electronic New Variorum Shakespeare editions are aimed at textual scholars. The target audience is similarly formative in the final two major sites I wish to discuss: *The Shakespeare Collection* and the *Internet Shakespeare Editions*. Both sites, in very different ways, attempt to provide a comprehensive archive and edition of the plays.

A Major Economic-Academic Initiative

At the center of *The Shakespeare Collection* is a third electronic version of the Arden Shakespeare. Learning from the early Arden CD-ROM, and the failed *ArdenOnline* website, Thomson-Gale have assembled an impressive and extensive library of resources for the study of Shakespeare. As a major commercial publisher, they have copyright access not only to the Arden editions themselves, but to extensive repositories of critical articles from journals that specialize in Shakespeare, and to general introductions to Shakespeare and the Renaissance (from their Scribners arm). They have also obtained permission to use facsimiles from the Folger, prompt books from a wide range of libraries, and reproductions of the sources Shakespeare used. The overall archive makes materials available for a variety of approaches to Shakespeare, and is of value not only to the student, but to the scholar. The designers of *The Shakespeare Collection* have clearly learned from earlier failures in the medium. The various resources are interlinked by a powerful and comprehensive search engine that allows the user to generate connections between the text and the other resources, and to move readily from one to the other. As with any advanced computer application, it takes some practice to become familiar with the tools, but there is no doubt that the collection provides a comprehensive research environment for the study of Shakespeare's work.

As an electronic edition of the plays themselves, however, *The Shakespeare Collection* adds very little that is new. The powerful search engine permits users to create their own paths through the archival materials associated with the edition – an admirable advance – but the Arden texts remain stubbornly wedded to print, and inevitably fail to take advantage of the kinds of explorations that are being undertaken by sites discussed in the previous section.

A Fully Electronic Edition: A Technical-Academic Marriage

Editors and publishers in the new medium have an opportunity to illuminate Shakespeare as never before. Like a medieval illuminated manuscript, the screen can reward the user both in its aesthetic and in its wealth of information. The development of editions genuinely native to the electronic medium will require time, money, and a tenacious combination of experiment and imagination. Time will select functions and features that are genuinely useful, though the emergence of the practice of undertaking "usability studies" with representative subjects will help to weed out the least effective and the most eccentric.

An ideal edition will include a combination of hard hypertext links created by the editor, whose understanding of the text and its context will be invaluable in providing pathways through the potentially bewildering range of information, and the dynamic links generated by user queries (Lancashire 1989; Siemens, "Disparate Structures"). At this point I must declare my personal interest: in 1996, soon after the birth of the web, I founded the *Internet Shakespeare Editions* (ISE) as a non-profit site published at the University of Victoria, BC, in an attempt to create online editions that were freely available, academically rigorous, and at the same time capable of exploiting the capacity of the new medium for interlinked, multimedia, searchable texts. The *Internet Shakespeare Editions* have as an objective the creation of texts completely re-edited for the electronic medium. The texts are freely available on the web, and the level of scholarly collation and annotation is equivalent to the major print editions (Arden, Oxford, Cambridge). Such an undertaking is clearly a long-term project, since the re-editing of a single play will take a scholar anything up to five years; the first fully edited texts are being published on the site as I write this chapter. ISE texts include painstakingly accurate diplomatic transcriptions of the original documents, including the markup of all early modern type-forms; the transcription makes possible searches on graphic facsimiles, and automatic linking between all related versions of the text (transcription, facsimile, modern-spelling version, collation). Since the texts are marked up in XML, all the tools of searching now available through the Open Source movement can be applied to them. The University of Victoria is fortunate in being one of six institutions involved in a project to develop and apply precisely these kinds of software (see TAPoR). This kind of dynamic linking can be treated as an extension of the concept of annotation, since each version of the play comments upon its siblings.

The editorial process becomes far more open and accountable as readings and the accompanying collations can immediately be seen in context. In some particularly complex texts – those of plays like *Lear* or *Othello*, where there are multiple texts of some authority – the user will be able to choose to highlight by color the origins of different readings and passages. Since collations are stored in XML files, it is possible to list readings chronologically, in the standard fashion, or by source text, with each reading linked to its original. Editorial choices can also be signaled more transparently: one feature of the medium that might be used, again by the user's choice, is animation to demonstrate visually either the alternatives available from different source documents ("Indian" or "Iudean" in *Othello* 5.2.407), or the semantic field of meaning available from an original, ambiguous spelling ("weyard"/"weird"/"wayward" in *Macbeth* 3.1.2; see Best, "Standing in Rich Place"). Similarly, the many ambiguous entrances and exits in the plays could be signaled by the use of either arrows, question marks (*"Enter Hamlet?"*) grey type, or animation (Best, "Forswearing Thin Potations").

Editors are also presented with a potentially far larger canvas for their work: annotations have in effect no theoretical limit, since storage on disk has become so inexpensive in modern computers. Practical limitations, however, are important; readers still expect editors to make choices and to limit annotation to what can be seen as genuinely useful. Ranganathan's fourth law of library science still holds: "Save the time of the reader" (Ranganathan 1931: 287). Indeed, Ranganathan's law might well be adapted to become the first law of hypertext: a click must link to something worth reaching. For this reason, ISE annotation comes in three levels. The first level is a simple gloss or explanatory phrase; the second is a full annotation to the level of an edition like the Arden; and the third is reserved for full discussions of an important point, of the kind that might become an appendix in a print edition. The second level of annotation is the most interesting, since from it the editor can invoke further links to illustrate the text: to relevant passages in texts that form part of the supplementary materials provided as part of the edition, or to stable sites elsewhere on the web, for example. Notable in this second category will be the growing list of scholarly resources being developed around the world: Ian Lancashire's *Early Modern Dictionaries Database*, Richard Bear's *Renascence Editions*, articles in *Early Modern Literary Studies* or *Renaissance Forum*, Harry Rusche's *Shakespeare Illustrated*, and others. All these are available free of charge, so can be accessed without restriction. Annotations at this level can also involve the creative use of graphic materials. Illustrations tend to be associated with teaching rather than scholarly editions, but since the web reaches a wide audience, it is an attractive option for an editor to provide, for example, a graphic illustration of a crossbow in explicating Lady Macbeth's injunction to Macbeth to "screw [his] courage to the sticking place" (1.7.61). And while it may puzzle GPS (Global Positioning System) software to find Illyria, or the isle on which *The Tempest* takes place, it will certainly be possible to provide interactive maps of the movements of characters and armies in the histories, and perhaps to link directly to a resource like Google Earth.

A particularly productive use of the larger space an electronic edition provides would be to link passages of the play to moments of performance, on stage or film. This is quite a different kind of bridge between performance and text from Donaldson's *Shakespeare Electronic Archive*, which makes continuous connection between film and text, and it would be less detailed and specialized than *The Cambridge King Lear CD-ROM*; the aim would be to expand the current editorial summary of the reception of Shakespeare in performance, such that second-level annotations would link to illustrative, and often contrasting, performances of specific moments in the play. Toward this end, the ISE has created a database of Shakespeare in performance. The usual problems of copyright limit the kinds of artifacts that can be stored in the database, but already it includes full information about Shakespeare and film, thanks to the generous donation by Kenneth Rothwell of his comprehensive listing in *Shakespeare on Screen* (1990). In addition, the database contains an increasingly representative range of digitized materials from stage performances, focusing initially on productions in Canada and the US, with the intention of adding international performances in the future. Performance is, of course, evanescent by its nature, but performance critics are adept at reconstituting the principal qualities of a production from the shards of evidence left behind: prompt books, directors' notes, costume and set designs, program notes, and so on. All are digitized and, archived at high quality. Editors will thus be able to access the database in their annotations, and the metadata stored with each digital artifact permit searching and the automatic linking of a given scene to any relevant items.

Perhaps the feature of the electronic medium that differentiates it most profoundly from print is that published materials can be maintained after publication. As additional scholarship becomes available, the editor can modify annotation, or even the text itself; thus the next generation of Shakespeare editions will be in the best sense dynamic, responding to their audience and to advances in both scholarship and the technology. The task in the next decade will be to consolidate economic models, both commercial and grant-funded, and to continue the combination of imagination and scholarship that is re-creating Shakespeare's texts for a new generation of online users.

Part III

Practicalities

Chapter 9

Working with the Text: Editing in Practice

David Bevington

This volume has been concerned heretofore with theories of editing, including its history as it emerges from the birth of the editor in the eighteenth century, through the New Bibliography of Alfred Hart, A. W. Pollard, W. W. Greg, and Fredson Bowers, to the postmodern editorial theory of Paul Werstine, Randall McLeod, and many others, and then into the age of electronic editing. The purpose of this chapter is to examine some practicalities and to look at ways in which theory – indeed, a grasp of the whole history of textual theory – can inform the detailed choices an editor must make on a daily basis.

The gap between theory and practice can seem dauntingly large. Let me illustrate autobiographically, if I may. My first editing assignment came along in the early 1960s, when Alfred Harbage, my mentor at Harvard, was assembling a team of editors for the Penguin Shakespeare of that era. Having nailed down lots of big names for the big plays, he came eventually to *1 Henry VI* and decided to be generous to a cub scholar whose work he had directed, namely, me. I was about to head off to a beginning assistant professorship at the University of Virginia, working under Fredson Bowers, who had just been named chair of the English Department. Wonderful! I said to myself, I can study textual theory with him, and thus learn what I need to know in editing *1 Henry VI*. It was an important factor in my deciding to go to Virginia. (We had choices in those palmy days.) I had not studied textual scholarship at Harvard; the department officially looked down its critical nose at the field as technical and non-literary. Fredson Bowers would be my teacher.

I sat in on several graduate seminars with Bowers, and he was terrific, of course. I read McKerrow, Greg, Nosworthy, Sisson, Hinman, etc., and worked through sample problems. I learned, for example, that one could look for evidence of crowding or "leading" in columns of the First Folio, or some other text, on the entirely plausible theory that the compositors, having been given a fixed stint of cast-off copy to set up into type in a single gathering, might well discover toward the end of any given stint that they had too much copy or too little. If the former, they would resort to abbreviations, crowded lines, ends of lines turned up into space in the previous lines, etc. If faced with too much space and not enough copy, the compositor would then be likely to pad out spaces with extra lead. Such evidence could well provide the editor with information as how to assess the purpose of abbreviations or extra spacing. Well, what about *1 Henry VI*? Nary a single instance of either crowding or leading was to be found.

Ah, well. Back to class. I learned about the complexities of plays with two texts, like *Hamlet* or *King Lear* or *Doctor Faustus*, and how the New Bibliography provided guidelines for how one could reconstruct the process through which one text seemingly evolved into the other, and how one could look for irreversible pieces of evidence that would definitively identify which early text preceded and influenced the other. But *1 Henry VI* has only one text, and a puzzling one at that.

Perhaps then one should concentrate on evidence in the early printed text of *1 Henry VI* as to whether it seems to have been based on authorial "foul papers" (the term then in use) or a fair copy or a theatrical "prompt book," the first presumably to be identified by variations in the speech heading and other inconsistencies that a prompt copy made for use in the theater would find impractical and would therefore weed out. To be sure, these New Bibliographical stigmata have more recently been shown, by Paul Werstine and William Long among others, to be highly problematic when one starts looking a concrete examples (a supposed "foul paper" text like *The Comedy of Errors*, for instance, incorporates features that certainly look performance-oriented), but a fledgling editor in the 1960s would not have encountered this bracing challenge to the Establishment ideology (Werstine 1988a, 1988b, 1990; Long 1985). What I found was that the printed text of *1 Henry VI* in the First Folio (no quarto having been printed, so far as is known) is somewhat similar to the textually puzzling situations described by Werstine in that its manifest confusions bearing witness to an authorial draft coexist cheek by jowl with what look like theatrical annotations and signs of recopying. The neat distinctions between authorial and prompt copy postulated by the New Bibliography did not seem to apply in this case.

What I discovered, in short, is that the text of *1 Henry VI* is an extraordinarily difficult one, but not in ways that lend themselves to New Bibliographical solutions. This text remains highly controversial, not least of all in Gary Taylor's editing of the play for the Oxford edition of the *Complete Works* published in 1986, for which Taylor freely emended some passages that were admittedly problematic in the Folio text (see also the Arden 3 edition by Edward Burns). The text is laden with readings that simply look wrong. Proper names appear to be mangled: Reignier is *"Reynold"* at one point (TLN 105) and *"Reignard"* at another (TLN 2091); Duke Humphrey is *"Vmpheir"* (TLN 393); Joan of Arc (if that is what the author intended) is *"Ioane of Acre"* at one moment (TLN 791) and *"Ione of Aire"* at another (TLN 2689) as well as *"Puzel"* and *"Pucelle"* (see below); the Countess of Auvergne turns into "Ouergne" (TLN 810); Burgundy is sometimes *"Burgundy"* (TLN 683) or *"Burgundie"* (TLN 771) but at other times *"Burgonie"* (TLN 1471, 1474); Coeur de Lion's (in the possessive) is rendered *"Cordelions"* (TLN 1519); Machiavel is "Macheuile" (TLN 2714).[1] Lord Talbot's title of "Goodrich" comes out as *"Goodrig"* (TLN 2298). Should one regularize all these on the basis of Holinshed, or of historical convention? What about place names and titles, like "Wexford" (today's spelling) for the Folio's *"Washford"* (TLN 2297)? Is it proper to modernize thus in a modern-spelling edition? If the name is French, like *"Santrayle"* (TLN 494) for today's "Santrailles," does that make a difference, given the tendency in some of Shakespeare's texts to render French phonetically and even comically? Is the fact that the name of Sir William Glasdale (as recorded in the chronicles) is rendered twice as *"Glansdale"* (TLN 531, 536, the latter in a speech heading) persuasive evidence that the author preferred this spelling, and if so does an editor follow it or the historically recognized form? What does one do with the speech headings of the character who is variously *"Puzel"* (TLN 267, etc.) and *"Ioane"* (TLN 739, 758), and who appears in stage directions sometimes as *"Ioane Puzel"* (TLN 264) and *"Pucell"* (TLN 1422, 1471, 2640, etc.)? Should the Folio's recurrent *"Dolph."* (for *"Dolphin"*) be retained or changed to the recognizably modern *"Dauphin,"* acknowledging that one is losing a play on words in Talbot's derisive *"Puzel or Pussel, Dolphin or Dog-fish"* (TLN 581)? What of the fact that this same character is first introduced as *"Charles,"* in stage direction and speech heading (TLN 193–234), before he then suddenly becomes

"Dolph." (TLN 247 ff.)? He is also *"Charles"* in 3.3 (TLN 1584 ff., for example). None of these difficulties is illuminated by textual theorizing as to which compositor or compositors seem to have set *1 Henry VI*, or what watermarks emerge on the printing paper, or in what order the formes were printed, or the like.

Changing titles of aristocrats and churchmen present problems that again are not very receptive to theory. A case in point is the character who is identified in his entering stage direction as *"Richard Plantagenet"* (TLN 926) and then is immediately named *"Yorke"* and occasionally *"York"* (TLN 991) in the speech prefixes of the scene of confrontation between the Yorkist and Lancastrian factions in the Temple Garden. He is called *"Richard"* throughout his scene with the dying Mortimer (TLN 1103 ff.), then generally *"Yorke"* in the rest of the play. The situation is complicated by the fact that, as Somerset charges in the Temple Garden scene, Richard's father the Earl of Cambridge was executed for treason in the time of Henry V, as a result of which Richard was "exempt from ancient Gentry" (TLN 1023). Somerset and Richard quarrel as to whether the Earl of Cambridge was "attainted" or simply "attached," i.e., arrested (TLN 1027), and the chronicles do indeed seem to confirm that Cambridge had been arrested and summarily executed without a proper bill of attainder, but the upshot in any case is that Richard is not legally entitled to be called "York" until he is "restored to his Blood" by King Henry VI in 3.1 (TLN 1376). Should the editor then call him "Plantagenet" or perhaps "Richard" down to 3.1 and then "York" thereafter? A good question, and one to which textual theory has little to contribute. If one does change from "Plantagenet" to "York" in the speech headings, will readers be confused? It is like the situation in *Richard II*, where the son of John of Gaunt, Duke of Lancaster, is, legally speaking, Henry Bolingbroke, Earl of Hereford, in the first act; then the Duke of Lancaster when his father dies; then the Earl of Hereford again just moments later when King Richard demotes him by seizing into royal possession "The plate, coine, reuennewes, and moueables, / Whereof our Vncle *Gaunt* did stand possesst" (TLN 807–8); then Duke of Lancaster once more in the opinion of his supporters like Northumberland (TLN 873–6) but Hereford still to those who, like the Bishop of Carlisle, remain loyal to King Richard (TLN 2054); and finally King Henry IV to his followers when he mounts the English throne. These incessant shifts create a puzzle for the editor as to what names to use when there are two kings in contention. How many speech headings does the editor want to impose on the reader to follow this chase?

Another difficulty in naming characters is illustrated in the man who is historically identified as Henry Beaufort, illegitimate son of John of Gaunt and hence great-uncle of King Henry VI. In his first appearance, as he enters with his men to forbid access to the Tower of London to the Duke of Gloucester and his followers, this man is *"Winchester"* in both stage direction and speech heading (TLN 391 ff.); he is also referred to as "The Cardinall of Winchester" (TLN 381). The upshot of the encounter is that *"Glosters men beat out the Cardinalls men"* (TLN 425). The rank of Cardinal is insisted upon: "Ile canuas thee in thy broad Cardinalls Hat," Gloucester taunts him, further threatening to desecrate his "scarlet robes" and to stamp his "cardinall's Hat" underfoot (TLN 402–16). The Mayor agrees that the churchman is chiefly to blame for this disturbance: "This Cardinall's more haughtie then the Deuill" (TLN 455). Yet much later in the play the Duke of Exeter expresses dismay on learning that "my Lord of *Winchester*" is about to be "call'd vnto a Cardinalls degree," recalling a prophecy of the now-dead Henry V that "If once he come to be a Cardinall, / Hee'l make his cap coequall with the Crowne" (TLN 2364–8). A powerful "Piel'd Priest" (TLN 395) such as this could of course hold two important church offices at once, as historically Beaufort did, but the play seems genuinely confused as to when he was installed as cardinal. For most of the play after 1.3 he is specifically referred to as a bishop. "I, see the Bishop be not ouer-borne" (TLN 1260), says Warwick sarcastically of him in the big Parliament scene of 3.1. "The Bishops men" are twice blamed for the uproar erupting at the very doors of the Parliament (TLN 1285, 1290; see also 1347). Later, in 4.1, the "Bishop" is on hand to crown King Henry in Paris (TLN 1746). Even after we learn that he has been called to the Cardinal's degree, he is still referred to as "Winchester" and "The Bishop," Gloucester's most dangerous enemy (TLN 2391–5).

Gary Taylor, in the *Oxford Shakespeare*, irons out these inconsistencies by emending "The Cardinall" to "My lord," "Cardinalls Hat" to "bishop's mitre," etc. in 1.3 (at TLN 381 and 402). But should an editor do that? The repeated error surely is not the work of some copyist or compositor. To be sure, the word "Bishop" (or "Bishops") is used more often in *1 Henry VI* than in any other play in the canon. The inconsistency continues in *2 Henry VI*, where the King's great-uncle is variously *"Beauford," "Winchester,"* and *"the haughtie Cardinall"* in scene i, with speech headings shifting from *"Win."* to *"Car.,"* then generally "the Cardinal" until he dies in 3.3. Does one clean up inconsistencies that the dramatist seems to have overlooked? If one does that here, where does one stop in other instances? My own preference, at any rate, is to leave the text as it is and explain in the commentary.

Probably the most fascinating character in *1 Henry VI* from a textual point of view is the "Sir *Iohn Falstaffe*" who is described in scene i as having "played the coward" by fleeing from the French in battle when he was under orders to relieve the English soldiers ahead of him in the vanguard, resulting in the capture of Lord Talbot by the French (TLN 143–51). The name is spelled "*Falstaffe*" with notable consistency throughout the Folio text, suggesting that it was spelled this way in the compositors' copy. Holinshed, on the other hand, refers to the historical figure as "Sir Iohn Falstolfe," and a number of editors follow suit, including W. G. Clark, J. Glover, and W. A. Wright in their nine-volume Cambridge edition of the works, and, more recently, George Walton Williams (Holinshed 1587; Williams 1979). In the 1598 quarto of *1 Henry IV*, the usual spelling is "Falstalffe" for the name that Shakespeare evidently substituted for "Oldcastle" when Lord Cobham and other Puritan-leaning reformers took offense at the seeming lack of respect for a revered "saint" in Foxe's *Book of Martyrs*. The editor is thus faced with a number of choices, between "Falstaff" and "Fastolfe" in *1 Henry VI* and between "Falstaff" or "Falstalffe" and "Oldcastle" in *1 Henry IV*. Again these choices are not ones for which textual theory offers much guidance, though one certainly wants a knowledge of the early texts and the history of the Lord Chamberlain's Office. (Cobham was lord chamberlain from July of 1596 until he died in March of 1597, during which time Shakespeare's acting company took the name of Lord Hunsdon's Men; they resumed the title of the Lord Chamberlain's Men when Cobham died and George Carey, Lord Hunsdon, was given the chamberlain's title previously held by his father.) I faced the choice of Falstaff vs. Oldcastle when I was editing *1 Henry IV* for the new separate-volume Oxford *Shakespeare* at the same time that Stanley Wells, Gary Taylor, John Jowett, and William Montgomery were preparing the single-volume *Complete Works* that appeared in 1986. We had agreed that the two editions of *1 Henry IV* being prepared simultaneously for the Oxford University Press, though independently edited, would avoid differences as much as possible. Yet ultimately we decided to part ways on Falstaff/Oldcastle. Since I have written about this matter elsewhere, and since the issue is by now familiar, I need not go into it again (Bevington 1987; Taylor 1985). My point is that it is a question that textual theory is not well prepared to resolve, and is one on which editors still disagree. *The*

Norton Shakespeare adopts the Oxford edition texts generally but refuses to go along with "Oldcastle."

Hoping that I have sufficiently demonstrated that many of the problems an editor must face are not very amenable to theoretical analysis, let me now turn to two texts where textual analysis is indeed crucial. I do not mean to sound hostile to textual theory; my own view is quite the opposite. I've simply been making the point that many editorial tasks, including the modernization of spelling, punctuation, and capitalization, the writing of commentary notes, the studying of Shakespeare's sources, the writing of critical introductions, and much more, are often scholarly in the inclusive sense rather than technically bibliographical.

Othello is an especially interesting case because the quarto text of 1622 and that of the Folio in the following year differ in multitudinous details of wording, and yet without substantial changes in the speeches, for the most part. The names of the speakers, the numbers of lines, and the metrical pattern remain pretty constant from quarto to Folio, and yet many individual words or short phrases, even some sequences of several lines, are rephrased without altering the essential meaning. Sometimes the changes seem relatively inconsequential, with a synonym inserted in the Folio in place of the quarto. For example, when in scene i of the Folio text Iago complains that "Preferment goes by Letter, and affection, / And not by old gradation" (TLN 39–40), the quarto reads "Not by the" instead of "And not by." The meter is undisturbed, one flows about as well as the other, and the meaning is hardly changed at all. Sometimes the change is material in meaning, but from one acceptable reading to another, as when the Duke says to Brabantio, at 1.3.68–70 in the Folio, "the bloodie booke of Law, / You shall your selfe read, in the bitter letter, / After your owne sense" (TLN 404–6); the quarto's "its" for "your" in the last phrase is perfectly intelligible as referring to the "booke of Law" rather than to Brabantio's own sensibility. Single-word substitutions are often synonymous, as when "worthy" in the Folio at TLN 1848 is substituted for the quarto's "trusty." This sampling could be extended very extensively. The question becomes, how are we to account for such numerous changes?

Compositorial interference seems the least likely hypothesis; compositors may well impose their own spellings and capitalization and punctuation, but are hardly likely to venture on wholesale rewriting of this sort. Copyists too would be totally out of line to take such liberties with their material. To be sure, a scribal transcript may indeed stand somewhere between Shakespeare's working manuscript and the Folio printed text; E. A. J. Honigmann has proposed that Ralph Crane prepared a transcript to be given to the Folio compositors, and, though not all scholars agree that Crane's distinctive copying habits are to be observed here, there is something like agreement that a transcription by some copyist was prepared for that purpose. Honigmann also posits another transcription of a different authorial manuscript as the basis for the quarto (Honigmann 1996). But what is the relationship between the two? It is seemingly not one in which a copy of the quarto was annotated (like *Richard II*) and then supplemented with manuscript material (as in the case of *King Lear*), even though some quarto readings may have made their way into the Folio text by way of consultation. The Folio copy for *Othello* seems to have been derived (via an intermediate transcript) from a revision of Shakespeare's original manuscript, copied over by himself. Why he would have done so is not clear; perhaps it was to prepare an updated acting version for his company. At any rate it gave him the opportunity to rewrite as he went along, substituting new words or phrases, adding new material (some 160 lines, mostly in scattered small additions), making a few deletions as well. Shakespeare was, by all accounts, a fluent writer, and he might well have taken the opportunity to polish a successful play. The resulting manuscript eventually became, under the editorship of Heminges and Condell, the basis for the Folio text. Those colleagues of Shakespeare had access to his papers and evidently felt that this version represented the play that they wanted to publish. Whether this version may have served as a playbook is a matter of dispute.

The evidence for this scenario is hypothetical and deductive. We have the data, in the multitudinous changes from quarto to Folio. What other plausible explanation is there, other than that Shakespeare rewrote his own play, and with a view not to change the plot or dialogue or cast of characters in any substantive way but rather to render its language a little more graceful? The consequence for an editor is what concerns us here. Such a scenario privileges the Folio as the text of choice for a modern edition. At the same time, the scenario posits a number of other interventions in the Folio version, the results of which might not be desirable. Scribes and compositors might misread their copy, or they might undertake to regularize or "sophisticate" certain usages in the interests of consistency or their own sense of style. They would not change the purport of the dialogue, presumably, but they could do some of the things that a house editor or copy editor might do today for a publisher. In addition, there is the question of censorship, either by the direct intervention of the Master of the Revels, who had authority to censor plays for performance, or, more often, by a removing of profanity in response either to the 1606 Act to Restrain Abuses of Players or to public taste, or to both (Mowat 2003). *Othello* was first performed in 1603 or 1604 or perhaps slightly earlier; it was not published until 1622. Might the Folio version, based seemingly as it was on the playbook, reflect a need to excise profanity in performance? The Act itself was directed chiefly at the speaking of the name of God on stage.

Many verbal changes from quarto to Folio in *Othello* do indeed excise profanity. In line 4 of the opening scene, Iago's "'Sblood" in the quarto is removed, leaving "But you'l not heare me" (TLN 7). But then Iago's opening utterance, "Tush," is also gone, suggesting a more general wish to clean up such utterances than simply meeting the requirements of the Act, which presumably would never object to "Tush." More in line with legal requirement, perhaps, is Iago's conclusion of his first long speech in the Folio with "And I (blesse the marke) his Mooreships Auntient" (TLN 35), thereby deleting "God" in the quarto's "God blesse" and in the process maiming the scansion of the verse line. At the same time, one could argue that the alteration in line 4, already quoted, regularizes the meter: "But you'l not heare me: If euer I did dream." To precede this line with "'Sblood" makes for a rush of unaccented syllables: "'Sblóod, but you'll not héar me. If éver Í did dréam." Effective, but unorthodox.

Iago's "Sir, y'are rob'd, for shame put on your Gowne" (TLN 94) in the Folio leaves out "Zounds," a strong profanity presumably forbidden by the 1606 Act since it means "By God's wounds." The Folio line scans tidily enough, though without the rough vigor of the quarto's "Zounds, sir, y'are robbed, for shame put on your gown." Another "Zounds," at TLN 121, is at the head of a prose speech by Iago and hence the deletion does not have the same metrical effect. Montano's "Pray Heauens he be" in the Folio (said of Othello in 2.1, TLN 790) replaces the quarto "Pray heauen it be," presumably because "heauens" has a more generalizing effect. The Herald's "Heauen blesse the isle of Cyprus" in the quarto, 2.2, loses "Heauen" in the Folio version (TLN 1108). Cassio's swaggering "'Fore God" as he is getting drunk twice becomes "'Fore heauen" (TLN 1178, 1187), somewhat anomalously, as Barbara Mowat observes, in light of the earlier emendation of "heauen" to "Heauens" at TLN 790. And so it goes. Some inoffensive expletives are removed ("By my troth" is changed to "Trust me" at TLN 2629, "Faith" to "Why" or "Yes" at TLN 2510 and 2550, "By this hand" to

"Nay" at ᴛʟɴ 2910), and some profanity remains in the Folio (such as "by Heauen" at ᴛʟɴ 2544), but we should not expect the clean-up to be completely consistent or thorough, especially if it was done in response to a gradual shift of preferences among audiences rather than as a legalistic maneuver mandated by the 1606 Act.

What is the modern editor to do? Virtually all take the position, as do I, that Shakespeare wrote the play prior to 1606 with profanities that help to characterize the speakers (they are especially plentiful as Cassio gets drunk), and that an editor should restore the original. Whether the Act itself was chiefly instrumental, or indeed whether the excising of oaths actually took place after 1606, is hard to determine and really doesn't matter editorially. The oaths are Shakespeare's, and he should be allowed to say what he wants to say.

An editor also wants to be wary of sophistications in a text like the Folio of *Othello*. Having passed through stages of rewriting, recopying, and press composition, the text may have picked up features of those processes that were not Shakespeare's. For example, when Othello says to Montano, in the wake of the riot on watch, "Worthy *Montano*, you were wont to be ciuill" (Folio, ᴛʟɴ 1309), we might well suspect that the quarto's "wont be ciuill" is the authentic reading and that somewhere along the line a copyist or compositor has added "to" to clarify the grammar, albeit at the expense of the meter. Cassio's "Dost thou heare me, mine honest Friend?" in the Folio (ᴛʟɴ 1539), addressed to a musician, adds a "me" that is absent in the quarto's "Dost thou heare, mine honest friend" in a move that could easily be a sophistication, even though authorial rewriting is not out of the question. Some of these instances might seem like small matters, but they are integral to the process of being as accurate with the text as one can by tempering one's reliance on the Folio with informed guesses about textual history.

When the Folio reading looks wrong, adoption of the quarto original is of course highly desirable, though one wants to reason in each case as to how the error may have occurred. Some are obvious and easily explained. When Iago says in soliloquy, as he watches Cassio pay courtly attentions to Desdemona, "I will gyue thee in thine own courtship" (the quarto reading), we can see how easy it would be for some copyist or compositor to turn "gyue" into "giue," as happens in the Folio text at ᴛʟɴ 944. The quarto's "conster" in Iago's reflections on how Othello's jealousy "must conster / Poor Cassio's smiles" may have been misread as "conserue" in the Folio (ᴛʟɴ 2486); "conserve" makes sense, and "conster" is perhaps a more difficult metaphor, but all the more reason to preserve it. When Iago's "Come hither" to Roderigo becomes "Come thither" in the Folio (TLN 998), the latter is outwardly plausible and even conceivably right, since Iago has just said "Do thou meet me presently at the Harbour," and "thither" could mean "at the Harbour." Yet "hither" makes such good sense, and has an earlier authority on its side, so that one suspects an easy copying or compositorial error from "hither" to "thither." Handwriting difficulties obviously add to the likelihood of occasional error all along the line.[2]

Personal pronouns and accompanying verbs are always a problem. Should one retain Roderigo's "I take it much vnkindly / That you (*Iago*) who has had my purse" in the quarto, scene i, in place of the Folio's "I take it much vnkindly / That thou (*Iago*) who hast had my purse" (TLN 4–5)? Perhaps not, in view of the fact that "you . . . has" is unidiomatic, and that the quarto and Folio alike use "thine," "Thou," and "thy" in what Roderigo next says to Iago. (Iago for his part addresses Roderigo as "you" at TLN 7, 45, 62, 159, 172, etc., rejecting, it would seem, the plea for intimacy in Roderigo's use of the familiar form, though later Iago does reciprocate by addressing Roderigo as "thou" when he has need of him, at TLN 655 ff.) But how far does one carry consistency? When Iago says to Roderigo of Cassio that he "has all the requisites in him that folly and green minds look after," in the quarto reading, should one follow the Folio "hath" (TLN 1028) for "has," which could be a sophistication? Similarly, why not the quarto's "does demonstrate" for the Folio's "doth demonstrate" at TLN 67? Or the quarto's "My cause . . . has no lesse reason" for the Folio's "hath no lesse reason" (TLN 717–18)? Or "He has a person" for "He hath a person" at TLN 743? There are enough of these to make one wonder.

Contractions pose a problem, especially in prose, where the meter cannot come to the editor's assistance. When Cassio says of Desdemona, as he converses in prose with Iago, that "She's a most exquisite lady" and "she's a most fresh and delicate creature," as recorded in the Folio version (TLN 1130, 1132), should one prefer the quarto's uncontracted "She is," especially in view of Cassio's emphatic conclusion a moment later in the Folio text, "She is indeed perfection" (TLN 1139)? (The quarto here reads "It is indeed perfection.") Most editors, including myself, prefer "She's" in the first two instances, but one is hard pressed by such instances where sophistication could be at work.

Meter can help make a choice, even though one must be wary of too much polishing and regularizing. Brabantio's "Take hold on me. For my perticular griefe" in the Folio reads better than the quarto's

"Take any hold of me. For my perticular griefe" (TLN 389). Conversely, Desdemona's "That I did loue the Moore, to liue with him" in the quarto is more convincing than the Folio's "That I loue the Moore, to liue with him"; the omission of "did" in the Folio TLN 598) looks like a simple error. The line in the Folio divided between Desdemona and Othello, "What is the matter (Deere)?" "All's well, Sweeting" (TLN 1375–6) moves more assuredly in the quarto's version with the word "now" supplied after "well."

Most of the omissions of quarto material from the Folio look like unintended oversight (Chambers 1930). The leaving out of Iago's "And, in conclusion" at TLN 19 leaves a lacuna in the sense. Iago's counseling to Desdemona about Othello's bizarre behavior, "And he does chide with you," missing in the Folio at TLN 2880, completes the thought of the preceding two lines. Both of these, and several others, are readily accounted for by their being on separate lines, easily overlooked by a copyist or compositor. On the other hand, the Folio additions frequently have the character of new material. They total some 160 lines in all, and contain, among other matters, Roderigo's urging Brabantio to verify the story of Desdemona's elopement (TLN 134–50), her famous willow song (TLN 3000–22, 3024–6, 3030–4, 3545–7), and Emilia's feisty observations on marital fidelity (TLN 3059–76) (Honigmann's *Othello*: 352). Clearly, as a principle, and while examining each case on its individual merits, the editor will want to keep both the Folio additions and the short quarto-only passages, not as a "composite" or "conflated" text (though the effect is like that) but on solid bibliographical grounds. Individual choices will vary from editor to editor on occasion, but in general today's modern editions of *Othello*, including Honigmann's Arden 3, the *Oxford Shakespeare* (edited in this instance by Stanley Wells), the *Riverside Shakespeare*, and my own fifth edition, are in substantial agreement.

Even more than *Othello*, *Troilus and Cressida* is an anomalous play in every sense: in its genre as historical-comical-tragical, in its radical experimentation with dramatic form, in its seeming failure as a stage play, in its bizarre placement in the First Folio between the histories and the tragedies without listing in the "Catalogue" or table of contents and with a specially devised system of page signatures unlike any other in the book, and in its text.[3] The first printing of the quarto of 1609 (the only quarto; there was insufficient demand for a second) was rapidly replaced by a second "state" of printing, with a new title-page and a publisher's blurb touting *"a new play, neuer stal'd with the Stage, neuer clapper-clawd with the palmes of the vulger, and yet passing full of the palme comicall."* The Folio text of 1623 varies from that of the quarto in ways that resemble those of *Othello*: the two texts are roughly of a length, covering the same ground with the same cast of characters and by and large assigning the same speeches to those characters, and yet with a great number of verbal alterations pointing to authorial revision. In these matters, the two-text situations in *Troilus* and *Othello* are not like those of *King Lear*, where substantial passages and even whole scenes appear in one version that are not found in the other, or *Henry V* and *A Midsummer Night's Dream*, in each of which the Folio reassigns passages to different speakers and replaces characters in certain scenes. In this important sense, *Troilus* and *Othello* are significantly alike. The big difference is that in the case of *Troilus*, editors have disagreed fundamentally during the last century or so as to whether the quarto or the Folio text was derived, with changes, from the other.

The editor's first big task, then, is to sort out the matter of precedence between quarto and Folio, since much will depend on that decision as to what to use as a copy text and, in individual instances, what words or phrases to adopt in preference to the alternative presented by the other text. Early editors, beginning with Pope, were content with the proposition that a major reason for collating all the variants between quarto and Folio was to give the editor free choice of whatever readings that editor regarded as most felicitously "Shakespearean." Once this way of proceeding was perceived to be too eclectic and idiosyncratically indefensible on textual grounds, nineteenth-century and early twentieth-century editors such as F. J. Furnivall and John Munro tended to the commonsense view that the quarto must be the earlier version, since it appeared in print first, and that the Folio was a revision (Furnivall and Munro edition; Williams 1949–50, 1950–1). Then the New Bibliography of the twentieth century, on the basis of detailed textual evidence, challenged that complacent assumption, albeit arriving at a preference for the quarto as the authorial revision that more recent textual analysis has challenged in turn as inadequate.

A major difficulty is that nearly all the many variants in *Troilus* are reversible. When Agamemnon talks about Fortune's "lowd and powrefull fan" (Folio text, TLN 482) that separates the wise from the foolish like wheat from chaff, did the quarto's "broad" come first in the place of "lowd," or is "broad" the later reading and arguably the author's revised choice? Or might "lowd" be later but a corruption? Or, to take another example, when Aeneas, in the same scene, responding to Nestor's offer to meet any Greek warrior in personal combat, declares, "Now heauens forbid such scarsitie of youth" (TLN 766), should the editor endorse this Folio reading or choose the quarto's "forfend" in place of "forbid"? The words are essentially identical in meaning, and of a comparable metrical value. The choice seems almost indifferent, and in that sense might seem not to matter a great deal, but of course it does matter in terms of determining which came first. On their surface, these two twinned words offer no guidance. And so it is with "worthy" (the quarto reading) and "Noble" (the Folio) in Troilus' remark that Paris brought home from Greece, in Helen, a "worthy/Noble" prize (TLN 1071). See also "such like/so forth" (TLN 411), "sillie/aukward" (TLN 609), "right/iust" (TLN 624), "men/youth" (TLN 766), "Shall/Must" (TLN 1399), "*Cressid/Cressida*" (TLN 1515, in a prose speech), "deserues/merits" (TLN 2228), "flowing ore/swelling ore" (TLN 2468), "lou'd/desir'd" (TLN 3575, in prose), and others. Longer variants, particularly the passages in the Folio not found in the quarto, can be explained either as Folio additions or as the quarto's intentional or inadvertent omission of material in its copy; and the reverse is true of the two two-line passages in the quarto and not in the Folio, at TLN 886 and 1959. Subjective grounds of choice as to which readings seem preferable are not reliable; both texts make sense as they stand, and are essentially alike.

The fact that so many variants are reversible as to which came first motivated a search, in the New Bibliographical method, for an instance in which the wordings could be argued to be not reversible. E. K. Chambers, in 1930, announced that he had found two. His argument, anticipated to a significant extent by Peter Alexander in 1928–9, was that the Folio text of *Troilus* had been set from a copy of the quarto that had been annotated with reference to the original authorial manuscript, whereas the quarto itself derived from a transcript of Shakespeare's papers that contained in them some authorial revisions (Chambers 1930: I, 438–9; Alexander 1928–9). Chambers' Exhibits A and B were two passages.

The first is at 2657–70, when, as Hector and Ajax enter the lists for their abortive encounter, Ulysses gives to Agamemnon a character sketch of the sad-looking Troilus, who is hanging back (having been deprived of his Cressida by her being exchanged for Antenor) from joining in the social pleasantries between the two sides. Ulysses' speech repeats, in the Folio text, the phrase "they call him *Troylus*" (TLN 2658, 2670), whereas the quarto gives the phrase only once. Chambers argued that the duplication in the Folio was a "first shot and second thought" phenomenon, a case of authorial rewriting with the traces of that rewriting still visible in the text, whereupon the quarto version, as the later version, provided an opportunity to delete the repetition. The first occurrence of the phrase in the Folio, moreover, introduces a metrical irregularity: "*Vlis*. The yongest Sonne of *Priam*; / A true Knight; they call him *Troylus*." The quarto version of this is regular: "*Vlis*. The yongest sonne of *Priam*, a true knight." The second occurrence of the phrase, at TLN 2670, is metrical in both texts, and thus looks like what the author wrote as a revision, perhaps marking the first with a deletion mark which the compositor failed to observe. But is the evidence really irreversible? Might not a copyist or compositor have introduced "they call him *Troylus*" into the Folio text by misreading what may well have been a confusing copy? As Honigmann says, Shakespeare's handwriting was difficult to decipher. The matter is hard to judge, but in any event looks now like an uncertain piece of evidence on which to base a claim for the whole of the Folio text having been prior to the quarto (see my edition of *Troilus and Cressida*).

Chambers's second instance purportedly demonstrating the earlier state of the Folio is at the end of the play. Both Folio and quarto bring on Pandarus in 5.10 for one last encounter with Troilus, who bitterly denounces his former friend and leaves the stage to Pandarus for a concluding smarmy epilogue addressed to the audience as "Brethren and sisters of the hold-dore trade," i.e., frequenters of brothels (TLN 3587). The last exchange of Pandarus and Troilus is similar in the two texts: Pandarus, entering, pleads, "But heare you? heare you?" to which Troilus replies, "Hence broker, lackie, ignomy, and shame / Pursue thy life, and liue aye with thy name" (Folio version, TLN 3569–71; the quarto reads, less satisfactorily, "ignomyny" in place of the Folio's "Ignomy and"). Folio and quarto differ, however, in that the Folio introduces this same exchange earlier in the fifth Act, at 3328–30, with slight verbal variation ("Why, but heare you?" in the first line instead of "But hear you? heare you?" and "brother" in the second line in place of "broker"). Chambers sees this as another instance of first shot and second thought; Shakespeare first planned to dismiss Pandarus from the play with this brief dialogue at the end of the sequence in which Pandarus brings a letter from Cressida to Troilus, only to learn that Troilus is determined to have nothing more to do with Cressida or her uncle, but then Shakespeare reconsidered and decided to bring on Pandarus for an epilogue. Again, the supposition is that the compositor failed to observe the author's deletion marks for the first shot.

Is the repetition nothing more, however, than a first attempt and then an authorial revision of these short lines? As early as 1860, the editor W. S. Walker proposed that Shakespeare introduced Troilus' curt dismissal of Pandarus in Act V, scene iii (at TLN 3328–30), so that the play could end without Pandarus. A number of editors, including H. N. Hudson and J. M. Nosworthy, have agreed, and Honigmann concurs that the dismissal was "first written for act 5, scene 3" (Walker 1860; Nosworthy 1965; Honigmann 1985: 45). Perhaps the quarto and Folio then represent two quite different conceptions of the play, and for different venues: one a more satiric-ending version (the quarto) possibly designed for sophisticated audiences at the Inns of Court, the other (the Folio) a more tragic version for public performance that would have left off Pandarus' gloating epilogue entirely (even though it is printed in the Folio text), ending instead with Troilus' call for a relentless continuation of the war in a "Hope of reuenge" to "hide our inward woe" (TLN 3567). The lack of duplication of the brief interchange between Troilus and Pandarus in the quarto version would then signify that in this script the intent was to save Pandarus' last conversation with Troilus for the very end, followed by Pandarus' epilogue; the Folio duplication conversely would point to an intent to end Pandarus' involvement in the play at the end of 5.3, although (according to this scenario) the Folio text then mistakenly added the epilogue after all, owing to a failure on the part of the compositor or some copyist to observe the deletion marks.

Richard Dutton has put forward the intriguing argument that the two "states" of the quarto, and the variant title-pages of those two states, similarly point to a duality of purpose. The original title-page offers the play to the reader *"As it was acted by the Kings Maiesties* seruants at the Globe," whereas the second-state title-page makes no mention of public performance, touting the play instead as "THE Famous Historie of Troylus *and* Cresseid. *Excellently expressing the beginning* of their loues, with the conceited wooing of *Pandarus* Prince of *Licia*." As we have seen, this second state, moreover, declares in an added publisher's blurb that the reader is here presented with *"a new play, neuer stal'd with the Stage, neuer clapper-clawd with the palmes of the vulger."* Why this contradiction? The allegation of never having been acted seems implausible, but it is of a piece with the publisher's insistence that he is offering the reader a literary work rather than a stage play, a book for the appreciator of fine style. Perhaps then this version is close to the play as it was acted for sophisticated audiences in an indoor theater charging high prices, as distinguished from the more public version acted at the Globe (Dutton 1996). To be sure, both states of the quarto end the play identically, but the variants in the front matter might still point to a dual conception in the play as it sought to find its most receptive audience.

Gary Taylor argues persuasively, at all events, that Chambers's first-shot-second-thought "proof" of the quarto's being the corrected and hence the later text is reversible as evidence. Taylor urges that the duplicate passage at 5.3 in the Folio can be viewed not as a first shot but as a revision enabling the play to end tragically without Pandarus' abortive encounter with Troilus and the subsequent epilogue (Taylor 1982). He finds this an attractive alternative ending, so much so that the Oxford edition of 1986 took the bold step of printing the epilogue as Additional Passage B, not a part of the playtext, though subsequently the Oxford editors have reconsidered that decision and issued a retraction (Wells and Taylor 1990). This was a sensible decision, for it acknowledges that what we may have in *Troilus* is a genuine two-text play, with the epilogue playing to audiences in one version and not in the other. Phebe Jensen has argued for the theatrical viability of both endings, thereby emphasizing the play's generic indeterminacy (Jensen 1995). Taylor admits that his hypothesis contains elements that are subjective and literary, but does so as a way of showing that Chambers's arguments also rely on subjective judgments.

Where does this leave the editor with the choice of the quarto or the Folio as the preferred text to follow? Jensen, while she is critical of some of Taylor's claims, agrees with him that the manuscript used to correct the quarto in order to produce copy for the Folio text was a theatrical script, and quite possibly the playbook itself. Honigmann does not concur, but Jensen's argument, to the extent that it is convincing, does invite the editor to give the Folio text serious weight. Her formulation of editorial choice is perhaps as sane and balanced as can be reached at this point: the substantial authority granted to the Folio "allows editors a reasonable basis either for using F as the control text or for correcting corrupt passages in Q with the help of F if the former is used as control" (Jensen 1995: 415 and 417).

In practical terms, this still leaves the editor having to grapple with each textual variant on a case-by-case basis, much as in dealing with *Othello*. When the wording varies in extended phrases, textual theory as presented here favors the Folio reading. When Ulysses proposes in the Greek council of war, for example, that they not allow Achilles to challenge Hector, he argues as follows:

Vlys. Giue pardon to my speech:
    Therefore 'tis meet, *Achilles* meet not *Hector*:
    Let vs (like Merchants) shew our fowlest Wares,
    And thinke perchance they'l sell: If not,
    The luster of the better yet to shew,
    Shall shew the better.
    (TLN 824–9)

The quarto has the following:

Vlys. Giue pardon to my speech: Therefore 'tis meete,
    Achilles meet not *Hector*: Let vs, like Marchants,
    First shew foule wares, and thinke perchance they'l sell;
    If not, the luster of the better shall exceed,
    By shewing the worse first.

Each version is entirely acceptable, so much so that a comparison ends up being indeterminate as to poetic value; the quarto passage fills out the full iambic pattern of the first line, but the Folio version uses the line breaks coherently to group grammatical units in each line, so that one could imagine Shakespeare moving to this rhythm. Or the reverse. The main point here is that the rewriting, in whichever direction it took place, stuck to a central idea and refashioned it stylistically. And so, an editor could choose the Folio on the more general hypothesis that it incorporates the revised version.

Inversions are common, and leave the editor with no certainty as to priority other than by resorting to a more general hypothesis. Nestor, in the speech preceding Ulysses' above, worries what will happen if a challenger chosen to meet Hector should happen to fail. "What heart from hence receyues the conqu'ring part," says Nestor, "To steele a strong opinion to themselues" (TLN 819–20). The quarto reads "What heart receiues from hence a conqu'ring part" in the first line here. Either seems fine. Or take Cressida's uncertainty about surrendering to Troilus in 3.2: "Where is my wit? / I would be gone: I speake I know not what" (TLN 1781–2), which, in the quarto, reads, "I would be gone: / Where is my wit? I know not what I speake." Presumably Shakespeare liked the sound of one of these better than the other when he had occasion to copy out and rewrite the whole play, though on what basis he made this choice, or indeed in what order, is very hard to say.

The Folio has many short passages not found in the quarto. Editorial policy is very likely to favor their inclusion generally in the text, whether one hypothesizes that Shakespeare had more to say at this point or that the text was cut for some reason in preparation of the quarto; in the latter scenario, one might well imagine that the cuts were made to accommodate a shorter length of performance, or for some other reason not entirely congenial to the author, in which case one might consider it an editor's duty to restore what might otherwise be lost. Yet arguments will persist as to whether any particular excision may in fact have been deliberate. As Fredson Bowers used to say in situations of indeterminacy like this, "You pays your money and you takes your choice."[4]

Other particular editorial choices could be examined here, but I hope that the pattern of my argument is clear. In practice, *Troilus* is much like *Othello*, and that means that textual principles need to be applied individually at every instance. Some things will appear clear in context, as when Pandarus says to the lovers that he has taken "such paines to bring you together" (TLN 1834); the quarto's "such paine" seems unidiomatic, and is a mistake easily made in copying or typesetting. When Aeneas says of his fellow Trojans that "their Fame, in peace" is to enjoy a reputation for generosity and a debonair spirit (TLN 696), the quarto's "same" for "fame" in some copies is obviously an error and may indeed be nothing more than a confusion of "f" with tall "s." Others instances are problematic. Many matters of textual choice in Shakespeare's plays, as we have seen, do not lend themselves to textual theory. The route from textual theory is an eventful and essential one, and it is thorny – nowhere more vividly so than in *Troilus*. As Alice Walker observed in her *Textual Problems of the First Folio*, "Editorially *Troilus and Cressida* presents, I think, more problems than any other play" (Walker 1953: 68).

Notes

1   Quotations from the First Folio are from the *Norton Facsimile*, ed. Charlton Hinman (New York: W. W. Norton, 1996, second edition). When quoting in modern spelling, I used *The Complete Works of Shakespeare*, ed. David Bevington (New York: Longman, 2003, 5th edn.).

2   Honigmann, *Othello*, argues from a careful analysis of QF variants that "Shakespeare's hand was often illegible, much more so than in the three pages of *Sir Thomas More*, which were probably written eight or nine years earlier" (355).

3   *Troilus and Cressida* was originally to have followed *Romeo and Juliet* in the First Folio, but the printing of the play at that point got no further than

the first leaf, and had to be put off till the end, presumably because of copyright difficulties. See Greg (1951a).

4   Bowers's students and colleagues heard him say this countless times in class and in conversation at the University of Virginia in the 1960s. I do not know that he ever set it down in print.

Chapter 10

Working with the Texts: Differential Readings

Sonia Massai

Differential readings in early modern printed texts stem from a variety of material instabilities. Even texts that were printed only once or survive in a single edition are inherently plural because proof corrections were carried out while the press work was in progress. As a result, copies of the same edition preserve randomly variant sequences of corrected and uncorrected formes. Stephen Orgel has usefully pointed out that early modern printers could probably have spared the time to proof each forme before printing it, and that their failure to do so is symptomatic of the fact that "the [Renaissance] book was a fluid text, not the final correct authorized version of the work" (1999: 117).

Differential readings are even more significant in early modern printed texts which survive in multiple editions. The status of differential readings in early modern play texts is often difficult to establish because playwrights were not always directly involved in the printing of their own works and editors can only speculate about the nature of the printer's copy from which the printed text was set, as Thomas L. Berger and Paul Werstine have explained in their chapters in this volume. Sixteen of Shakespeare's plays were first published in the Folio edition of 1623. Some of the remaining 20 plays included in F1, and most prominently *Hamlet*, *Othello*, *Troilus and Cressida*, and *King Lear*, had already been published in quarto editions which differ in a variety of significant ways from the text preserved in F1. The first quarto of *King Lear*, for example, which was first printed by Nicholas

Okes for Nathaniel Butter in 1608, includes roughly three hundred lines which do not appear in F1, lacks roughly one hundred lines which appear only in F1, and preserves a large number of local variants, which affect speech prefixes, stage directions, and dialogue. *King Lear* is a very good example of a plural, unstable text, whose editorial history has been determined by how subsequent generations of editors have interpreted the differential readings offered by Q1 and F1.

This chapter explores the evolution of the texts of *King Lear* from the seventeenth century to the present, in order to show how the editorial process itself, far from neutralizing the material instabilities in the early editions, endlessly transforms and reproduces an already unstable and multiple text. While the "theoretical underpinnings" of the editorial tradition are explored elsewhere in this volume (in Andrew Murphy's chapter 5), my own particular focus is on the practical impact that different editorial theories and changing assumptions about the editorial task have had on the evolution of the text of *King Lear* in a number of significant editions. It is also worth stressing that although this chapter considers a selection of editions of *King Lear* in chronological order its purpose is not to highlight a teleological development in the editorial tradition. While showing how different editors have fashioned their own *King Lear* out of the early editions and the work of their predecessors, this chapter does not mean to highlight a gradual progression toward a definitive edition or toward an exhaustive and uncontroversial understanding of the nature of the printer's copy underlying Q1 and F1. In fact, the editorial history of *King Lear* is fascinating exactly because it shows interesting revivals of theories, editorial strategies, and controversies which have haunted several generations of editors over the last three hundred or so years.

The theory of authorial revision, for example, which led to the revolutionary decision to publish Q1 and F1 as two separate texts in the 1986 Oxford edition of *The Complete Works*, was far from new. Commenting on a verbal variant in the opening scene of the play – in Q1 Kent urges King Lear to "Reuerse thy doome" (B3r 4), in F1 to "reserue thy state" (Qq2v, 65) – Samuel Johnson explains his views on the relative authority of these two readings as follows: "I am inclined to think that *reuerse thy doom* was *Shakespeare*'s first reading, as more apposite to the present occasion, and that he changed it afterwards to *reserue thy state*, which conduces more to the progress of the action" (V, 10). According to Johnson, Shakespeare himself revised the play as it first appeared in Q1 and, as a result, F1 is by and large a better text than Q1. However, while satisfied that some of the cuts in F1 improved the quality of the dramatic action, he memorably criticized other abridgments as "carelessly and hastily performed" (V, 99).

Johnson's views on the differences between Q1 and F1 anticipate some of the arguments used by the supporters and the detractors of the theory of authorial revision, which was vigorously debated throughout the 1980s. In a groundbreaking article, Michael Warren had argued that some of the differences between Q1 and F1 signal a "substantial recasting" of the characters of Albany and Edgar (1978: 99). More generally, Steven Urkowitz argued that all the major changes introduced in F1 were done "to bring the text into accord with important theatrical values – concision, contrast, and surprise" (1980: 44) and that the "dramatic boldness, sensitivity, and power demonstrated by [such changes] declare that only a masterful playwright is at work" (1980: 147). Another pattern of apparently interrelated changes, aimed at removing from F1 direct references to the arrival of Cordelia's army as a foreign invasion, was interpreted by Gary Taylor (1980) as a concerted attempt to neutralize any patriotic sentiments which might contribute to alleviating the shattering impact of Lear and Cordelia's defeat in the war. In fact, all variants except for obvious typographical mistakes in F1 were deemed to stem from authorial revision by the contributors to a seminal collection of essays called *The Division of the Kingdom: Shakespeare's Two Versions of "King Lear"* (Taylor and Warren 1983), which represents the strongest collective endorsement of the theory of authorial revision to date. Like Johnson, though, some late twentieth-century scholars felt unimpressed by the quality of the variants introduced in F1 and attributed them to non-authorial revision. P. W. K. Stone, for example, argued that the reviser was not Shakespeare, because F1 variants are "not poor certainly, and not even perhaps merely mediocre," but they are "never particularly distinctive . . . [or] beyond the competence of several of Shakespeare's contemporaries" (1980: 81).

The re-emergence of the theory of authorial revision in the 1980s was rightly hailed as a radical break from a traditional understanding of Q1 and F1 as two imperfect textual witnesses of the lost manuscript original. In some ways, though, the fact that the same theory had already gathered support among eighteenth-century editors like Johnson would seem to corroborate the latter's pessimistic assessment of the viability of the editorial tradition itself as a sound intellectual pursuit: "The opinions prevalent in one age, as truths above the reach of controversy, are confuted and rejected in another, and rise again to reception in remoter times. Thus the human mind is kept in motion without progress" (I, D3v). While Johnson's pessimism sounds a salutary cautionary note against a teleological understanding of the evolution of the texts of *King Lear*, genuine and significant changes have indeed occurred, which radically affect our understanding not only of individual variants but also of Q1 and F1 as a whole and how these two texts should be re-presented to the modern reader. One crucial difference which distinguishes Johnson and other eighteenth-century editors from twentieth-century supporters of the theory of revision is indeed the latter's belief that Q1 and F1 should not be conflated into a single text but edited and published as two independent and self-standing plays. Stanley Wells effectively sums up the extent to which the revisionists challenged the traditional practice of conflating Q1 and F1:

> Until recently . . . the general opinion has been that Shakespeare wrote one play about *King Lear*; that this play is imperfectly represented in both the Quarto and the Folio texts; that each of these texts contains genuinely Shakespearian passages which are missing from and should have been present in the other; that comparison of the variant readings of the two texts must form the most important basis for the correction of errors of transmission; and that conflation of the two texts, along with such correction, will bring us as close as we can hope to get to the lost archetype which each is supposed imperfectly to represent. This is the position to which the [supporters of the theory of authorial revision] are opposed. (Taylor and Warren 1983: 8–9)

Wells's polemical stance toward the popular and long-lived practice of conflating Q1 and F1 highlights what may look like a glaring inconsistency in Johnson's editorial treatment of quarto and folio variants in his edition of 1765. A note appended to the opening scene in Act III warns Johnson's readers that the last eight lines in the Gentleman's speech quoted below do not appear in F1:

Gent. Contending with the fretfull element,
       Bids the wind blow the earth into the sea,
       Or swell the curled waters boue the maine
       That things might change or cease, teares his white haire,
       Which the impetuous blasts with eyles rage
       Catch in their furie, and make nothing of,
       Striues in his little world of man to outscorne,
       The too and fro conflicting wind and raine,
       This night wherin the cub-drawne Beare would couch,
       The Lyon, and the belly pinched Wolfe

> Keepe their surre dry, vnbonneted he runnes,
> And bids what will take all.
> (Q1, F3r, 32–8; F3v, 1–5)

Johnson's note also advertises the editor's preference for the shorter version of this speech as it appears in F1: "The first folio ends the speech at *change, or cease*, and begins again with *Kent's* question, *but who is with him?* The whole speech is forcible, but too long for the occasion, and properly retrenched" (V, 77). Interestingly, Johnson's preference for the shorter version preserved in F1 and his belief that the absence of quarto-only lines from this speech was not the result of accidental omission but of intentional authorial abridgment did not stop him from including the whole speech in his edition of 1765.

If authorial revision was teleologically taken to represent the most advanced stage in the editorial history of *King Lear*, then Johnson's treatment of this speech could be dismissed as ultimately flawed. However, it is worth stressing that even recent editors who accept the theory that Shakespeare is the most likely agent responsible for the changes introduced in F1 do not necessarily believe that Q1 and F1 should be regarded as two different plays and that they should be presented to the reader as separate texts. For example, R. A. Foakes, the editor of the Arden 3 *King Lear*, defends his decision to integrate quarto- and folio-only passages within a single text by pointing out that supporters of the theory of authorial revision in the 1980s "may well have been right to argue that Shakespeare could have been involved in reworking the play, but less justified in their over-confident assertion that the Quarto and Folio texts of the play 'are distinct' . . . and that new editions should attempt 'to restore each text to an authentic, independent state'" (Foakes 1997b: 128–9). Foakes, like Johnson, retains the Gentleman's speech in its entirety, although, also like Johnson, he regards the shorter version in F1 as an improvement on Q1: "These lines seem to have been neatly excised from F so as to maintain the metre; in Q in effect they repeat [the first four lines], do not advance the action, and describe what we can see Lear do in 3.2" (259). In suggesting that "the image of Lear hatless and tearing his white hair has been suggestive for actors" (259), Foakes, like Johnson, values the authority accrued by the received text and the theatrical tradition associated with it over the integrity of the two versions of the play preserved in Q1 and F1. Besides, like Johnson, Foakes finds that quarto-only lines add strength to Shakespeare's dramatization of Lear's madness: "the idea of his 'little world of man' as a microcosm or epitome of the external world establishes the link between the storm in nature and the storm in Lear's mind that is dramatized in the next scene" (259–60).

The similarities in Johnson's and Foakes's views on the relative authorities of the differential readings in Q1 and F1 *King Lear* are obviously qualified by the vastly more sophisticated bibliographical resources, the increased accessibility to the original documents, and the growing body of information about theatrical and print cultures in the early modern period which are available to the modern editor. While it would therefore be foolish to deny that the two-hundred-year period of scholarly investigation which separates Johnson's and Foakes's editions of *King Lear* has produced a genuine advancement in the field of Shakespeare textual studies, to regard Johnson's editorial approach as benighted and impressionistic and Foakes's as beyond controversy would be equally misleading. In fact, what the rest of this chapter will show is that the editorial tradition of *King Lear* is best understood not as an evolutionary progression toward the recovery of Shakespeare's lost original but as a highly contested cultural field, within which fundamental ideas about authorship, authenticity, and the ideological currency of Shakespeare's work are constantly appropriated, reviewed, and adjusted in the process of re-presenting his texts to different constituencies of readers.

The tremendously influential assumptions queried by the supporters of the theory of authorial revision in the 1980s were first formulated by Nicholas Rowe in the biographical essay prefaced to his edition of 1709. Q1 and F1 were reprinted as separate texts throughout the seventeenth century: Q1 was reprinted twice, in 1619 by William Jaggard for Thomas Pavier, although the title-page bears a fake imprint suggesting that this edition, like Q1, was printed in 1608 for Nathaniel Butter, and in 1655 by Jane Bell; F1 was also reprinted independently of the quarto three times in subsequent folio editions in 1632, 1663–4, and 1685. As Andrew Murphy has indicated in chapter 5 in this volume, Nicholas Rowe was responsible for establishing the long-held belief that "his plays were surrepticiously [*sic*] and lamely Printed in his lifetime" (I, x) and that the best strategy to "redeem him from the Injuries of former Impressions" was "to compare the several Editions, and give the true Reading . . . from thence" (I, A2r–A2v). Paradoxically, having originated such an influential set of ideas – the inherent corruption of Shakespeare's texts and the editor's arduous task of recovering "the true Reading" by collating and conflating the early editions – Rowe based his edition of *King Lear* on the text of the play as it appeared in the last of the four seventeenth-century folios. Lewis Theobald, a later eighteenth-century editor, remarked on this peculiar discrepancy between Rowe's programmatic intentions and his actual editorial approach to *King Lear*: "The mangled Condition of *Shakespeare* has been acknowledg'd by Mr. *Rowe*, who publish'd him indeed, but neither corrected his Text, nor collated the old Copies" (I, xxxiv). His edition makes indeed no effort to signal the presence of Q1 and the ways in which it differs from F4. As a result, Rowe's *King Lear* lacks an entire scene (normally marked as 4.3 in modern editions), which appears only in Q1. This scene includes the Gentleman's emblematic description of Cordelia's passionate response to the heavy news about her father's decline – "you haue seene, / Sun shine and raine at once, her smiles and teares, / Were like a better way" (H4v 34–6) – which modern readers would immediately recognize as belonging to Shakespeare's *King Lear*.

Despite being criticized by his successors for failing to carry out a thorough collation of the old editions, Rowe's text proved as influential as the strategy of conflation which he had briefly outlined in his "Account of the Life, &c. of Mr. William Shakespear." Since most eighteenth-century editors used the edition prepared by their immediate predecessors as a base text for their own, they directly or indirectly endorsed Rowe's preference for the text preserved in the folios over its alternative in the quartos, as well as several of Rowe's silent emendations, his lists of *dramatis personae*, and his use of scene locators. The last two features of Rowe's edition have had a tremendous impact on the editorial tradition. As Barbara Mowat has observed, Rowe's lists of *dramatis personae*, which "place the names of the male characters first, in descending social order, then the names of the female characters, . . . present . . . a depiction of a radically hierarchized world (and thus a statement about class and gender) that few of us would want to defend" (Mowat 1994: 314). And yet Rowe's lists have been adopted by editors into the twentieth and twenty-first centuries. Similarly, as Mowat continues, Rowe's scene locators "encourage readers of the plays to read them novelistically or to imagine them within a proscenium arch on a stage filled with backdrops and furniture" (1994: 318). Still according to Mowat, the influence of Rowe's scene locators on the editorial reception of *King Lear* has been particularly problematic: "Rowe's decision to place much of act 3 of *Lear* on 'a Heath' has created a series of 'heath scenes' in that play, much to the consternation of scholars who argue that there is no mention of a heath anywhere in the play, but who have been unable to dislodge Rowe's 'heath' from scholarly writing about *King Lear*" (1994: 318). Rowe's choice of setting may actually signal an interesting instance of cross-fertilization between scholarly and performance editions, which during the eighteenth century and during the first quarter of the nineteenth century were based on Nahum Tate's 1681 adaptation. It was Tate rather than Rowe who first set Act III on a "Desert Heath" (Tate 1681: 24). Nicholas Rowe, who, like Tate, was a professional dramatist, was probably affected by his familiarity with the play as performed on the Restoration stage, which, unlike Shakespeare's stage, did have "backdrops and furniture."

In the next edition of Shakespeare's dramatic works, Alexander Pope retained Rowe's scene locators, despite his low opinion of the influence which the stage had on Shakespeare's literary achievements. In fact, Pope blamed both the printers *and* the actors for the poor state in which Shakespeare's texts had been preserved. Pope's appraisal of the professional skills of the printers are quite bleak: "their ignorance shines through almost in every page; nothing is more common than *Actus Tertia, Exit Omnes, Enter three Witches solus*; their French is as bad as their Latin, both in construction and spelling: their very Welsh is false" (I, xii). Pope's views on the deleterious effects that Shakespeare's association with the commercial theater had on his writing is even worse: "Most of our author's faults are less to be ascribed to his wrong judgment as a poet, than to his right judgment as a player. But I think the two disadvantages which I have mentioned (to be obliged to please the lowest of people [his audience], and to keep the worst of company [his fellow actors]) . . . will appear sufficient to mis-lead and depress the greatest genius upon earth" (I, vii). The fall of Shakespeare's genius into print and performance made the editor's task a daunting one: according to Pope, "had Shakespear published his works himself (especially in his latter time, and after his retreat from the stage) we should find . . . the errors lessened by some thousands" (I, xvii).

Given Pope's pessimistic evaluation of the scale of corruption in Shakespeare's early editions, he surprisingly professes moderation and restraint in his approach to the editorial task: "I have discharg'd the dull duty of an editor, to my best judgment, with more labour than I expect thanks, with a religious abhorrence of all innovation, and without any indulgences to my private sense or conjecture. . . . [The readings] I have prefer'd into the text are constantly *ex fide Codicum*, upon authority" (I, xix–xx). Paradoxically, the distinctive feature of Pope's edition is the extent to which he felt entitled to emend Shakespeare's text conjecturally, that is, *without* relying on either of the early editions. Before leaving the English court for France, Pope's Cordelia commits her father to her sisters' "professing bosoms," rather than "professed bosoms" as in Q1 and F1. At least on this occasion Pope warns his readers that "professing" represents a departure from the early editions by appending a note at the bottom of the page (III, 14). In the opening scene, though, Lear announces his plan to divide the kingdom among his three daughters by saying "'tis our intent / To shake all cares and business from our age" (III, 6). Once again Pope follows neither Q1 nor F1, where Lear's intent is qualified as either "first" (Q1) or "fast" (F1). This time, though, Pope emends silently, thus failing to give his readers a chance to evaluate the viability of his editorial intervention against the variant versions preserved in the early editions. Although conjectural and silent, some of Pope's emendations were prompted by genuine cruces and were indisputably enlightened. All modern editions, for example, adopt Pope's emendation of the first line of the Gentleman's description of Cordelia, which, as mentioned above, occurs only in the quarto. All quarto editions preserve the nonsensical lines, "patience and sorow streme, / Who should expresse her goodliest" (Q1, H4v 33–4), which Pope normalized by replacing "streme" with "strove."

Unlike Rowe, Pope consulted Q1 and included some quarto-only passages in his edition, possibly because, as he observed in his preface, F1 "was published by two players, Heming and Condell" and most Folio-only lines represented "trifling and bombast passages" added by the actors (I, xiv). Pope's use of Q1, though, was bizarrely selective. While some Q1 passages are admitted into the main text, some are "degraded to the bottom of the page" (I, xx). In his preface, Pope explains that such punitive treatment is reserved to "suspected passages which are excessively bad," while "some of the most shining passages are distinguish'd by comma's in the margin." "Bad" and "shining" in this context have a clearly aesthetic connotation, as confirmed by the third and last convention – "a star . . . prefix'd to the scene" – which Pope uses when "the *beauty* lay not in particulars but in the whole" (I, xx; emphasis mine). Pope also restores quarto-only lines when he feels that they reinforce the dramatic structure of the play. For example, the exchange including the Gentleman's description of Cordelia mentioned above was deemed both "necessary to continue the story of Cordelia" and "most beautifully painted," and therefore readmitted into Pope's main text (III, 86). Pope also retains Albany's arraignment of Goneril and her sister Regan, which includes the memorable epithet "Tigers not daughters," because Pope finds it "necessary to explain the reasons of the detestation which [he] expresses here to his wife" (III, 84). Interestingly, while Pope allows Albany to vent his disapproval of his wife's actions at great length, following Q1, he fails to include the quarto-only lines in Goneril's rebuttal of Albany's arguments, which, following Pope's own rationale, may have been deemed useful to explain the reasons of the detestation which *she* expresses here to her husband. However, Goneril's quarto-only lines are not even appended in a note at the bottom of the page. Similarly, Pope does not restore Albany's final speech in this scene as it appears in Q1, possibly because the noble Albany suddenly plunges from the heights of his moral outrage into the depths of barely repressed (sexual) aggression: "wer't my fitnes / To let these hands obay my bloud," Albany admits in Q1, "They are apt enough to dislecate and teare / Thy flesh and bones."

Pope's editorial approach to the texts of *King Lear* may not have struck him as inconsistent with his explicit rejection of "all innovation" and "conjecture." Given his pessimistic evaluation of the quality of the texts preserved in the early editions, he may well have felt that he was merely correcting genuine mistakes accumulated by Shakespeare's text on the stage and in the printing house. Simon Jarvis has usefully outlined this risk:

> Many commentators have remarked on the gaps between Pope's theory of editing and his practice – such as his failure to record emendatory departures from the received text in the margin – without noticing the important analogies between the contradictions in Pope's editorial theory and those of his editorial practice. Pope's prefatory account of editing argues, aprioristically, that most of the linguistic and stylistic infelicities of the text as we now have it cannot be Shakespeare's but must be the result of the corruption of his texts by near-illiterates, yet admits that contemporary editors are rarely in possession of the materials necessary to remedy this situation. (1995: 62–3)

Pope may indeed have regarded his conjectural emendations as imperative editorial intervention justified by the poor state of the early editions and by the limited bibliographical and documentary resources available to him to rectify it. It is nevertheless worth stressing that the discrepancy between his editorial principles and his editorial practice did not go unnoticed among his contemporaries. Lewis Theobald was one of his most vocal critics. Referring to Pope's interventionist approach, Theobald observed: "[Pope] has attack'd [Shakespeare] like an unhandy *Slaughterman*; and not lopp'd off the *Errors*, but the *Poet*" (I, xxxv).

In open opposition to Pope's approach, Theobald argued that since Shakespeare's works had started to be regarded as modern classics, they also deserved to be edited with the same level of systematic and rigorous attention accorded to the ancient classics. Theobald felt confident that by applying the method used to emend ancient Greek and Roman texts to Shakespeare he could "restor[e] to the Publick their greatest Poet in his Original Purity" (I, xxxix). Theobald's approach did represent an important point of departure from the editorial practices of his predecessors. His method included "a diligent and laborious Collation . . . of all the older Copies" (I, xlii), and a thorough consultation of Shakespeare's canon as a whole and of his main sources to emend corrupt passages for which the early editions provided no viable alternatives. Theobald was convinced that the conjectural emendations were not only unscholarly but also morally unacceptable because they obscured the author's original text and therefore undermined the primary objective of the editorial task, which was to *restore* rather than to *correct* it. Thanks to the systematic quality of his method, Theobald felt confident that his emendations were instead "establish'd with a very high Degree of moral Certainty" (I, xlii). Even the editor's emendation of the punctuation (or "pointing") in the early edition is described as a moral undertaking: "In reforming an infinite Number of Passages in the *Pointing*, where the Sense was before quite lost, I have frequently subjoin'd Notes to shew the *deprav'd*, and to prove the *reform'd*, Pointing" (I, xliv). Theobald defended his use of lengthy textual notes in similarly loaded terms: "Without such Notes, these Passages in subsequent Editions would be liable . . . to fall into the old Confusion: Whereas, a Note on every one hinders all possible Return to Depravity." The length of Theobald's notes devoted even to the most minute of his text's features and the self-congratulatory rhetoric of his editorial manifesto attracted Johnson's cutting sarcasm: "I have sometimes adopted [Theobald's] restoration of a comma," he mockingly grants in the preface to his edition of 1765, but, he adds, "without inserting the panegyrick in which he celebrated himself for his achievement" (I, D1v 16–19).

Despite Theobald's bold editorial agenda, his *King Lear* shows significant continuities with past editions. He restores more quarto-only passages than Pope, but his use of Q1 is still far from systematic. Theobald is the first editor to retain both quarto and folio versions of the Gentleman's account of France's involvement in British affairs at the beginning of Act III. However, he silently ignores Edmund's quarto-only reference to a prediction of impending familial discord and civil unrest, while retaining Gloucester's folio-only allusion to the same prediction in the same exchange in 1.2. Like Pope, Theobald evaluates quarto- and folio-only lines on an individual basis and his selection is once again informed by his own sense of aesthetic decorum and dramatic coherence. When, for example, he decides to restore the last two speeches in Kent and Gloucester's exchange and Edgar's soliloquy at the end of 3.6 from Q1, he does so because he believes Edgar's lines to be "extremely fine." "Besides," he adds, "how absurd would it look for a character of [Edgar's] Importance to quit the Scene without one Word said, or at least an Intimation what we are to expect from him?" Theobald's selection of quarto-only passages on aesthetic and dramatic grounds is not flawed or unjustified *per se*. Interestingly, late twentieth-century detractors of the theory of authorial revision attacked its supporters for using "interpretation as textual evidence" (Trousdale 1986: 220). Theobald's rationale is similarly interpretive, although the extent of his collations allowed him to make better-informed decisions than his predecessors. What has changed since Theobald's time, besides the vast amount of bibliographical information which in turn makes modern editors much better informed than Theobald, are the values – aesthetic, dramatic, or ideological – which affect the editor's assessment of those quarto and folio variants that cannot be attributed to compositorial, scribal, or memorial contamination.

Johnson, like Theobald and many of his successors, was concerned about the extent to which interpretation inevitably affects the editorial process, and, like Theobald, he attacked Pope for relying too freely on conjectural emendation. According to Johnson, Pope "rejected whatever he disliked, and thought more of amputation than of cure" (I, C8r 28–9). As a reaction against Pope's editorial approach, Johnson decided to "confin[e] [his] imagination to the margin," that is, to relegate his own conjectures to the notes. Johnson, for example, prefers Q1's version of Lear's curse against Regan at F1r 27–8 – "You Fen suckt fogs, drawne by the powrefull Sunne, / To fall and blast her pride" – to the alternative preserved in F1, which replaces "blast" with "blister." Despite his preference for Q1's reading, Johnson suspects compositorial corruption but instead of changing the text, he adds the following note at the bottom of the page: "I think there is still a fault, which may be easily mended by changing a letter . . . 'Do, fall, and blast her pride'" (V, 69).

Also as a reaction against Pope, Johnson, like Theobald, stressed the need for editors to collate the early editions as thoroughly as possible.

However, Johnson took his distance from Theobald too. Theobald openly congratulates himself on carrying out thorough collations and compiling lengthy notes even on the minutest features of the text of his edition. Johnson is, by contrast, self-deprecatory in the extreme when he describes the editorial task, although his remarks about the amount of acrimony generated by editorial controversies are clearly ironic: "Perhaps the lightness of the matter may conduce to the vehemence of the agency; when the truth to be investigated is so near to inexistence, as to escape attention, its bulk is to be enlarged by rage and exclamation" (I, D6r 7–11). Johnson actually starts to sound extremely earnest when he moves from the mocking tone of the previous remark to admitting that "to an editor nothing is a trifle by which his authour is obscured" (I, D7r 17–18). Johnson was indeed outraged by his predecessors' uncritical endorsement of the received text: by collating the early editions he claimed to have "found that the late publishers [i.e. editors], with all their boasts of diligence, suffered many passages to stand unauthorized, and contented themselves with Rowe's regulation of the text, even where they knew it to be arbitrary" (I, D8v 1–5). Johnson was indeed careful enough to dis-emend his edition on several occasions: his Goneril, for example, urges Albany "Never to afflict [himself] to know more of it," "it" being Lear's blind rage at Goneril's suggestion that he should reduce the number of his "insolent retinue" (V, 42). In doing so, Johnson's Goneril speaks a Folio line, whose counterpart in Q1 reads "the cause" instead of "more of it." This line had been silently modified by Rowe, and his emendation – "Never afflict your self to know of it" (V, 2489) – was then silently endorsed by Pope and Theobald. "These corruptions I have often silently rectified," Johnson explains, "for the history of our language, and the true force of our words, can only be preserved, by keeping the text of authours free from adulteration" (I, D8v 9–13). Despite Johnson's efforts to un-edit the received text of *King Lear*, his edition was still visibly affected by it. For example, he assigns the final four lines of the play to Albany, as in Q1, rather than to Edgar, as in F1, although he relies on F1 for all the other local variants in the sequence of Lear's death in the final scene. Johnson was here simply following the received text, as indicated by the fact that he merely reports Theobald's note to justify the reassignment of the last speech to Albany: "This Speech from the Authority of the Old 4to is rightly plac'd to *Albany*: in the Edition by the Players it is given to *Edgar*, by whom, I doubt not, it was of Custom spoken. And the Case was this: He who play'd *Edgar*, being a more favourite Actor, than he who personated *Albany*; in Spight of Decorum, it was thought proper he should have the last Word" (V, 158). Given their pro-claimed abhorrence of conjectural emendation, one can only wonder how Theobald could possibly speculate so wildly about the casting of the roles of Edgar and Albany while the play was being staged by the King's Men, and how Johnson could possibly endorse Theobald's views, having memorably pointed out that "conjectural criticism demands more than humanity possesses" (I, C8v 28–9).

More significant departures from the received text of *King Lear* occurred toward the end of the eighteenth century, when editors like Edward Capell and Edmond Malone tackled the problem of the origin of the printer's copy underlying Q1 and F1. Malone, for example, clearly spelled out the need to establish the relative authority of each extant early edition of Shakespeare's plays: "till it be established which of the ancient copies is entitled to preference, we have no criterion by which the text can be ascertained" (I, xii). So far as *King Lear* is concerned, Malone, like Capell, believed that the pre-eminence accorded to F1 by their predecessors was unwarranted, because, as Malone put it, "the first folio . . . labours under the disadvantage of being at least a second, and in some cases a third, edition of [the] quartos, . . . [which] are entitled to our particular attention and examination as *first* editions" (I, xiii). Recent scholars have disagreed as to whether Capell or Malone should be regarded as the first editor to depart from the received text of *King Lear* and to anticipate New Bibliographical methods through their advocacy for a systematic bibliographical investigation of the early editions. Although Capell's and Malone's approaches to Shakespeare's text did represent an important development in the editorial tradition, both their editions of *King Lear* were still squarely placed within it. They restored quarto-only passages more often than their predecessors, alerted their readers to the presence of press variants in Q1, and relied on both Q1 and Q2 to emend their texts, but they both assigned the last four lines in the play to Albany, while following F1 for all the other variants immediately preceding and following Lear's death in the final scene, as other eighteenth-century editors had done since Pope.

The influence of eighteenth-century editors stretched well into the nineteenth century. As Andrew Murphy has observed, "most of the editions produced for the popular market over the course of the 1800s were highly derivative, with a great number of them . . . being based on the later Johnson-Steevens-Reed and Malone texts" (2003: 188). A genuine break from the received text established in the eighteenth century occurred when the first woman editor of Shakespeare published a selection of the plays in 1807. Although by 1809 her brother Thomas Bowdler had attached his own name to this edition, Henrietta Maria Bowdler was responsible for producing the first officially expurgated edition of Shakespeare's works. Her objective was to offer young readers and "those who value every literary production in proportion to the effect which it may produce in a religious and moral point of view . . . the various beauties of the writer, unmixed with anything that can raise a blush on the cheek of modesty" (I, v–vii). In order to fulfill her task, she did not hesitate to omit several lines, occasionally entire scenes, which she regarded as vulgar and offensive. The text of her edition of *King Lear* departed from the received text in predictable ways by excising Gloucester's references to the circumstances of Edmund's conception from 1.1 ("there was good sport at his making"), Edmund's description of legitimate children as "a whole tribe of fops / Got 'tween a sleep and wake" from his soliloquy in 1.2, and Edgar-as-Poor-Tom's raving recollection of a time when he had "served the lust of [his] mistress' heart and did the act of darkness with her" from 3.4. She also predictably ignored Edgar's description of the five fiends who possessed Poor Tom, which appears only in Q1, presumably because one of the five fiends has the indelicate habit of "possess[ing] chambermaids / And waiting women" (H3 17–18). Less predictably, she excised the Fool's prophecy at the end of 3.2, which appears only in F1. The Fool's topsy-turvy vision of "the realm of Albion" evidently was deemed to cause as much offense as sexually explicit passages, possibly because at least two lines in it ("When priests are more in word than matter" and "When . . . bawds and whores do churches build") point an accusatory finger at the religious establishment.

Henrietta Maria's edition was expanded by her brother in 1818 and proved almost incredibly popular during the nineteenth century, when it was made available to the reading public in at least 20 different editions (Murphy 2003: 171). Although the Bowdlers became synonymous with nineteenth-century prudery rather than scholarly editing, their approach to Shakespeare's texts was not altogether new. None of their eighteenth-century predecessors had explicitly advertised their intention to purge Shakespeare's text of indelicate and morally offensive lines, and yet some of the passages which Henrietta Maria had found objectionable and had excised from her edition had already been ousted from the received text. The following passage is a good example:

Reg. Tell me but truly, but then speake the truth,
      Doe you not loue my sister?
Bast. I, honor'd loue.
Reg. But haue you neuer found my brothers way,
      To the forfended place?
Bast. That thought abuses you.
Reg. I am doubtfull that you haue beene coniunct and bosom'd
      with hir, as far as we call hirs.
Bast. No by mine honour Madam.
Reg. I neuer shall indure hir, deere my Lord bee not familiar with
      her.
      (Q1, K3r 11–18)

This passage is already shorter in F1, where Regan's suspicion that
Edmund and Goneril may have been "coniunct and bosom'd" with
each other is removed, but her allusion to her sister's "forfended
place" survives:

Reg. Tell me but truly, but then speake the truth,
      Do you not loue my Sister?
Bast. In honor'd Loue.
Reg. But haue you neuer found my Brothers way,
      To the fore-fended place?
Bast. No by mine honour, Madam.
Reg. I neuer shall endure hir, deere my Lord
      Be not familiar with her.
      (F1, ff1v 2–9)

Rowe included none of Q1's extra lines, but even Pope and Theobald,
who included an increasing number of Q1 passages in their editions,
failed to restore the quarto-only lines in this exchange. Uncharac-
teristically, Johnson's edition fails to follow either Q1 or F1 by reducing
the length of this exchange even further:

Reg. – Tell me – but truly – but then speak the truth,
      Do you not love my sister?
Edm. In honor'd love.
Reg. I never shall endure her. Dear my Lord,
      Be not familiar with her.
      (V, 140)

Steevens and Malone restored both the invariant lines omitted by Johnson and the quarto-only lines ignored by Pope and Theobald. Predictably Henrietta Maria opted for the same version of this exchange which Johnson offered his readers in 1765. Interestingly, though, unlike Henrietta Maria, Johnson is not generally perceived as a "bowdlerizing" editor.

The popularity enjoyed by the Bowdlers' editions continued to grow during the nineteenth century alongside an increasing scholarly investment in the thorough survey of the bibliographical evidence preserved in Q1 and F1, which culminated in the publication of the influential Cambridge edition prepared by William George Clark, John Glover, and William Aldis Wright between 1863 and 1866. The notes in this edition are purely textual and their conventional, abbreviated format is meant to give the reader "a complete view of the existing materials" at a glance (I, ix). The sparse, almost algebraic, look of these notes suggests that the editorial method was fully systematic and transparent and the resulting text an objective and unmediated reconstruction of Shakespeare's "true Reading." Accordingly, the editors place a great deal of emphasis on their uncompromising avoidance of conjectural emendations: "We look upon it as no part of our task to improve the poet's grammar or correct his oversight: even errors, . . . because we thought them to be Shakespeare's own blunders, have been allowed to stand" (I, xiii). Once again, though, their systematic investigation of the bibliographical evidence and their conservative approach toward speculative emendation did not lead to a clean break from the editorial tradition first established at the beginning of the eighteenth century. Among the many legacies of that tradition was the editors' decision to privilege F1 over Q1, unless the former was openly corrupt, to select local variant and verbal substitutions eclectically from both Q1 and F1, and even to go against their best editorial instinct in order to preserve the received text. This is, for example, how they commented on their decision to include Edgar's soliloquy at the end of 3.6, which, as mentioned above, occurs only in Q1: "Every editor from Theobald downwards, except Hanmer, has reprinted this speech from the Quartos. In deference to this consensus of authority we have retained it, though, as it seems to us, internal evidence is conclusive against the supposition that the lines were written by Shakespeare" (VIII, 433).

The influence of the Cambridge Shakespeare on both the popular and the scholarly market for Shakespeare publishing can hardly be overestimated. Its text was republished in the single-volume Globe edition of 1864, which, in turn, "dominated the textual world for many decades after its original publication" (Murphy 2003: 205). The scholarly editing of Shakespeare was also indebted to this edition. W. J. Craig, the editor of the first Arden Shakespeare text of *King Lear*, which was published in 1901, openly "acknowledg[ed] his obligations to the *Cambridge Shakespeare*" (viii) and to the editorial tradition as a whole:

> In this course [the practice of conflating Q1 and F1] I do but follow the example of my predecessors, and my readers must therefore not expect to find in my text any very noticeable differences from that generally received; the ground has been too exhaustively worked by preceding editors to admit of any new discoveries of importance. (xv)

Craig's acknowledgment of his indebtedness to the editorial tradition is tinged with a sense of intellectual exhaustion. The old theory of conflation first formulated by Rowe in 1709 had produced a long sequence of editions, whose texts were gradually modified thanks to a growing familiarity with the bibliographical make-up of the early editions. However, the fundamental principle according to which Q1 and F1 should be eclectically conflated to recover Shakespeare's "true Reading" had never been challenged. Craig's intimation that this principle reflected the past rather than the future of the editorial tradition was prophetic, although the first real break with the practice of conflating Q1 and F1 *Lear* only occurred toward the end of the twentieth century.

Parallel editions of Shakespeare's *King Lear* are the most recent development in its long editorial tradition, but certainly will not be the last. Interestingly, this approach to the complex web of differential readings in Q1 and F1 takes us back to the seventeenth century, when Q1 and F1 were reprinted several times as separate texts. It is possibly counterintuitive but not altogether misleading to point out that the arguments used by the revisionists to support this editorial practice may be less in keeping with the current sociological understanding of a printed text, that is, as the product of the collective efforts of several agents whose contributions cannot be disentangled, than the reasons underlying the publication of Q1 and F1 as separate texts in the seventeenth century. The sociological approach to the printed text promoted by recent textual scholars like Don McKenzie, Jerome McGann, and Roger Chartier challenges the revisionists' assumption that "we are justified, first, in attaching to any particular group of lines a particular dramatic effect, or, second, in attaching that effect to authorial intent" (Trousdale 1986: 219). Paradoxically, the fact that Q1 and F1 were reprinted several times in the seventeenth century as separate texts of *King Lear* may have little to do with the fact that they were seen as two authorial versions of the same play (or as two plays by the same author), since Shakespeare's status as a dramatic author was not as prominent then as it was to become from the eighteenth century onward. Maybe Q1 and F1 were reprinted as separate texts not because of their differential readings and their possible origin but because of their different size, of their being a single-text as opposed to a collected edition, or because the copyright for Q1 and F1 belonged to different stationers. In other words, although Q1 and F1 have started to be re-presented to the modern reader as separate texts, the assumptions which inform seventeenth- and late twentieth-century ideas about what constitutes an authoritative text, or an authorized text, or an authorial text, and which led to the publication of Q1 and F1 as different texts, are radically different. Rephrasing Johnson, one could therefore argue that the absence of (linear) progress in the history of the editorial treatment of Q1 and F1, far from making the motions of the editorial mind worthless, lends interesting insights into the wider cultural context within which the editing of Shakespeare's texts is inevitably embedded.

Chapter 11

Mapping Shakespeare's Contexts: Doing Things with Databases

Neil Rhodes

During the 1970s and 1980s the idea of getting students on under-graduate Shakespeare courses to undertake exercises in bibliography and textual criticism would have seemed perverse, antiquated, and unimaginative. In the 1970s, when the principle of literary value was still paramount, the aesthetic, moral, and emotional aspects of the text were what really counted; for many people, an interest in its material conditions was little more than trainspotting. In the 1980s, the coming of theory shifted teaching in large areas of English away from its traditional concerns toward a more political, historical, and culturally contextualized approach to literary study. Again, this seemed more exciting than the differences between quartos and folios. The 1980s, however, was also the period when much pioneering work on Shakespeare's text was produced: the view of the Shakespearean canon as something stable and unitary – a view deriving ultimately from Romantic ideas of authorship – came under challenge; studies of *King Lear* in particular presented a Shakespeare who seemed actually to have revised his work for publication, and in 1986 the landmark new Oxford edition of the *Complete Works* appeared. And even if these developments appeared to be operating at some remove from the prevailing excitements of literary theory, the political agenda of theory inevitably made English more receptive to material and materialist issues.

But what really enabled textual studies to come in from the cold was the computer and IT revolution of the 1990s. The drab and dusty subject of bibliography reinvented itself as the History of the Book, since the new and competing digital technology had made the printed page a medium worthy of study in its own right. At the same time, the technology itself was able to transform textual studies both through the development of electronic hypertext and through the creation of vast literary and bibliographical databases, available initially on CD-ROM and then, more usually, online. It was now much easier to compare multiple variants of a given literary text, to search and analyze bibliographical data about them, and to study the language of texts through word searches. From the point of view of both student and teacher this opened up interesting possibilities. On the other hand, intellectual questions about the status of the literary text, which had been discussed in theoretical terms in the 1980s, could now more easily be discussed in specifically material contexts. Questions about the media of representation were highlighted by the parallel worlds of print and digital technology in addition to the existing parallel worlds of stage and screen. At the same time, the new electronic search engines, which could identify all the instances of a specific word or name within a designated group of texts, enabled the kind of close reading favored during the 1970s and earlier, though now with much greater historical and philological precision. In every case, the new technology gave students the opportunity to undertake research exercises that would previously have required many years of study to perform, while providing teachers with the challenge of constructing exercises that would produce intellectual value.

The purpose of the present chapter is to describe some of the things that can be attempted in this way. Most of the examples come from courses taught at the University of St. Andrews in the ten years from 1995, when we first bought the *Chadwyck-Healey Full-Text English Poetry Database* on CD-ROM (now *LION*), so what follows is in part the reflection of a pedagogical response to the first decade of large digitization projects in literary studies. The Chadwyck-Healey CD-ROM quickly went online and was supplemented by individual databases, including *Editions and Adaptations of Shakespeare* and *Literary Theory*, which includes a good deal of Renaissance rhetoric and criticism. More recently the *English Short-Title Catalogue* (*ESTC*) became available, now taking the bibliographical record of printing in the British Isles through to 1800, and then *Early English Books Online* (*EEBO*), which provides access to full-text facsimiles of every title published in the period. There are, of course, other digital resources available for Renaissance studies, but these are the ones that we have chosen to use. Together they have enormously widened the possibilities for research not just at postgraduate but at undergraduate level, by offering access to searchable text (*LION*), the primary sources themselves (*EEBO*), and the material conditions of their production (*ESTC*).

I shall begin by outlining a number of different kinds of assignment on Shakespeare and/or other Renaissance texts that can be undertaken using online databases, and then describe in more detail a specific project on Shakespeare's publishers and printers. This development from literary text to publishing context in turn reflects the historical development of the databases themselves. There are perhaps two things to bear in mind here. The first (and this is part of the object of my introductory remarks) is to underline the point that the field "Shakespeare and the Text" has developed in tandem with and as a result of the massive shift in our view of text, and of the media more generally, brought about by electronic technology. The field does therefore ramify beyond those issues that are related specifically to the material production of books in early modern England. Second, as a caution to the first point, it is nonetheless important that we do not fetishize IT resources and imagine that printed research tools have been superseded. Most of the projects I am going to describe can best be done using print as well as digital resources.

Literature Online

Our original database projects at St. Andrews were designed for Renaissance rather than specifically Shakespearean courses (Rhodes 1998). They have been modified and varied from time to time, but they can be summarized as follows:

1   How did Renaissance poets view their contemporaries? Choose one writer of the period (not necessarily a poet) and discuss the way she or he is represented in poetry. You should identify the kinds of poem in which the author is named, e.g. prefatory verses, satire, elegy.
2   Discuss the various significances of any one mythological figure in Renaissance poetry or drama. In each case you should comment on the context in which the figure appears. (Ovid's *Metamorphoses* would provide you with a useful starting point.)
3   Prepare an annotated edition of a poem, or a group of poems on a similar subject (50–100 lines), which you consider to be of particular

verbal complexity. You should write a short critical introduction to the poem(s) and elucidate the meaning of significant words or phrases by comparing similar usages in other poems of the period.
4 Write an essay on some aspect of literary theory and criticism using the *Literary Theory* database on *LION*. Topics to consider might include attacks on and defenses of the theater; the function of rhetoric; the relationship of art and nature; the principles of creative imitation; the barbarism or otherwise of English as a literary language. What application does the theory of the period have to any particular literary texts?

The most popular of these topics has been the mythological figure, partly because in this case it is obvious what you are searching for. But it is important to choose the sort of figure who will yield productive results. Where the project has been done badly, a large amount of undifferentiated information has been produced without regard to the significance of the representations. On the other hand, we have had excellent work on Io, the Sirens, Echo, Flora, and many others, where the figures have yielded a manageable number of hits but of sufficient variety to show how the myths can be interpreted in different ways. Figures can be paired for sharper focus: "Cupid" will produce an unmanageably large number of hits, but "Cupid near Psyche," where "near" indicates a 10-word proximity, will be much more rewarding. The best-known figures can be refined in terms of activity or association. There is little point in searching simply for "Venus," but a recent project on "Venus Weeping" produced some excellent results, as well as providing a fascinating context – or series of intertexts – for Shakespeare's *Venus and Adonis*. Variations in early modern spelling need to be taken into account here. "Ganymede" will yield quite a lot of hits, but adding "Ganimede" and "Ganimed" produces even more. This particular example might also point toward other resources in the database. A disproportionate number of references come up for Richard Barnfield, so one would rightly infer that Barnfield had a particular interest in this figure. Searching for criticism on Barnfield will quickly take one on to the subject "Queer Theory" within the "Criticism and Reference" field, so the original myth becomes the gateway to a much larger area of inquiry.

The other projects provide different kinds of challenge. One problem with the "poets on their contemporaries" project is the relative sparsity of the material available and the rudimentary nature of the critical vocabulary used to describe poetic achievement in the period.

A way of dealing with this is to extend the historical scope so that it becomes more of a reception study: in the case of Shakespeare himself this might combine the main Chadwyck-Healey corpus with *Literary Theory* and *Editions and Adaptations of Shakespeare*. But it is also possible to do interesting work on this topic within the early modern period itself. A project on elegies for Sir Philip Sidney, for example, discussed the Renaissance language of eulogy and ideals of versatile accomplishment. A particularly musical student discussed representations of Elizabeth in songbooks (originally tagged on the database), though the difficulty here lay in penetrating the various mythological guises in which she may or may not have appeared. Projects involving the *Literary Theory* database, where the Renaissance is well represented, may also directly address the issue of the limited critical vocabulary of the period. But ideas about "artificiality," "liveliness," and "barbarism" can all be usefully pursued, bearing in mind that it is necessary to use wild-card characters (e.g. "barbar*") in order to find the range of variant forms of the selected terms. Intrepid students have also been known to enter the labyrinth of Renaissance rhetoric on this project.

The last of these four kinds of assignment, the editorial project, has produced some of the most impressive work, partly because an exceptionally accomplished edition of Shakespeare's "The Phoenix and the Turtle" was undertaken in the first year that these projects ran. Since this was subsequently held up as a model for emulation, ever more elaborately annotated and lavishly illustrated editions were produced to try and better it. With this project we also enter the territory covered elsewhere in this volume, and it seems worth pointing out that the ease with which the databases can produce parallel verbal usages from obscure sources does now call into question the function of this kind of annotation in prestigious editions such as the Arden Shakespeare and the Longman Annotated English Poets. Copiousness is less obviously a virtue in the digital age than it was for Erasmus and other humanist rhetoricians. The citation of parallel usages must genuinely illuminate the text that is being edited, and the success of editorial projects in the courses we teach has depended on students being able to distinguish between informative and uninformative material. Indeed, one might say that a central feature of all the *Literature Online* projects is selectivity, otherwise known as information processing. The power of the search engine and the potential limitlessness of hypertext need to be controlled if they are not to open up Escher-like prospects of interminability.

The Renaissance Booker Prize

The next project I want to describe, which we called – a little face-tiously – "The Renaissance Booker Prize" (in a US context this could become "The Renaissance Pulitzer Prize"), is designed to exploit the resources of the *ESTC* and *EEBO*. Although this is modeled as a literary competition, the primary object of the exercise is to construct an overview of British publishing in a single year from the period covered by the *ESTC*, 1475–1640. The project outline goes as follows:

You should bear in mind that the early years will be thin and the later years extremely dense: for example, the *ESTC* lists 123 titles for 1553, 179 for 1593, and 531 for 1633. You might choose to do this exercise as a way of mapping Shakespeare's publishing contexts, since the years covering his publications during his lifetime, 1593–1616, are each likely to produce a manageable number of results.

If you take this route, start by choosing a year in which Shakespeare has a play (or poem) published and, using the *ESTC*, see what competition he is up against in the book market. You can divide the material up by genre and also by publisher. How much of what was published in your chosen year was literature, and what different kinds of literature do we see? How much of this was drama? How much was Latin-language, how much foreign (either foreign-language or in English translation), and how much native English? If you want to look at publishers' lists – one of Shakespeare's own publishers, for example – bear in mind the distinction between publishers and printers: "by Valentine Sims, for Andrew Wise" means that Sims is the printer and Wise the publisher.

You may make your own rules for the competition itself. You might find it easier to construct it as a general literary prize, since playtext publication will not produce many results for a single year, but alternatively you might want to extend it to non-fictional texts. Disqualifying religious works certainly narrows the field. A further refinement would be to construct a panel of judges from your year and have them make their choices appropriate to their status and situation: for example, a nobleman, a middle-class woman, a Cambridge academic, a tradesman.

When you have made your shortlist (no more than six books) according to the criteria you have established, you should look at the books either on *EEBO*, which gives you facsimiles of the original editions, or, if available, on *LION*, which gives you modern, searchable texts. *LION* will also provide more information about the author, but if any of your texts are not available on *LION* you should try the *DNB* (*Dictionary of National Biography*) online for biographical information. For playtexts, the *Annals of English Drama* (Wagonheim 1989) is a useful resource for checking performance details and whether your text is a recent "book of the play."

In making your final verdict and awarding the prize, remember that this is an exercise in historical reconstruction and should not simply reflect the views and values of modern criticism.

One point that probably should be made about this project, on the basis of the ones that we have seen, is that it tends to take one of two forms: either a quite rigorous exercise in publishing history, with a high content of statistical material, or something that is closer to a piece of creative writing and reconstructs the jury's discussion of the books. An excellent piece of work in the second mode produced the following team: Jonah Martin, minister of a humble country parish in Gloucestershire and sometime poet; Quentin Martin, fellow of Christ's College, Cambridge, since 1575 and a regular publisher of pamphlets; and Lady Ermengarde Smith, respected wife of the earl of Earsham and patron of her nephew Adam Ardent, an aspiring poet. The year was 1592 and the shortlist consisted of John Lyly's *Gallathea*, Henry Constable's *Diana*, Philip Stubbes's *A Christal Glasse for Christian Women*, and *The Spanish Tragedy*, said to be by Thomas Kyd. One snag was that the author of *The Spanish Tragedy* was nowhere to be found, which led to Lyly's *Gallathea* being declared the winner.

Most people, however, understandably felt that they were on surer ground with a more purely bibliographical approach, and we have had some impressive results in this mode which nonetheless engaged with the spirit of the "Booker Prize" format. The competition for 1603 was one notable example. On this occasion the rules stipulated that the prize should be awarded to the work "which most commendably sets forth the eloquence of our native tongue." This device had the effect of removing the more pedestrian religious and moral tracts, academic textbooks, or purely informational works, and anything in Latin or a modern foreign language. At the same time it left open the possibility that a translation might win if it was able to demonstrate that the English version could match the expressive power of the original. This was an effective way of defining the "literary" without resorting to anachronistic genre categories.

A search for 1603 imprints on the *ESTC* produced 511 hits. This might at first have seemed daunting, but it was quickly reduced to a more manageable group of texts. A survey of the material recorded many welcomes to King James and to Scotland, as well as farewells to Elizabeth, treatises on the plague, proclamations, university publications, and a great deal of wholesome but dull religious matter. All this could be discarded. Eighty works were in a language other than English, almost always Latin (but in one instance Welsh), and these too disappeared from contention. In fact, a surprisingly small amount of "literature" in the modern sense was published in 1603, despite this year being at the very center of the Renaissance and of Shakespeare's own writing career. It was, however, a good year for translation, with new versions of Du Bartas, Plutarch's *Moralia*, and Montaigne's essays, alongside reissues of North's Plutarch, Hoby's Castiglione, Golding's translation of Ovid's *Metamorphoses*, and Marlowe's version of the *Elegies*. Reissues had been judged ineligible and this removed not only North's Plutarch and the Ovid, but also much of the writing of King James, which had been quickly reprinted in London after his accession to the English throne. An exception was made in the case of *Basilikon Doron* on the grounds that the original publication of 1599 was in Scots and had had a print run of only six copies. Also on the longlist was James's countryman William Alexander of Stirling for his *Tragedie of Darius*, Richard Knolles's *Generall Historie of the Turkes*, and Dekker's *Pleasant Comodie of Patient Grissill*.

The last three did not, however, make the shortlist, which consisted of *Basilikon Doron*, Florio's translation of Montaigne, Philemon Holland's translation of Plutarch's *Moralia*, Drayton's poem *The Barrons Wars*, John Davies of Hereford's poem *Microcosmos*, and Shakespeare's *Hamlet*. There was a great deal of disagreement among the judges, faced with comparing poetry, prose, and drama as well as translation and original work. At least two judges thought the prize should go to *Hamlet*, but a third complained that the published version was "not as he remembered it." Florio's Montaigne was vetoed on the grounds that a prize for English eloquence should not be given to an Italian, but double standards were applied in the case of the king, who was eventually (and judiciously) declared the winner. There was certainly no doubt that this was the bestseller of the year, but further disagreement flared up between the two English publishers, John Norton and Edward White, and the Scottish publisher, Robert Waldegrave, who had issued the book earlier in the year in Edinburgh, as to which of them should claim the credit.

Shakespeare's Publishers and Printers

The Renaissance Booker Prize is a project about early modern publishing which allows for some imaginative invention and which may or may not be given a Shakespearean slant, but we can of course construct an exercise focusing specifically on Shakespeare's publishers and printers. In this case a possible starting point would be Andrew Murphy's *Shakespeare in Print* (2003), which covers the history of Shakespeare publication up to the present day. For the purposes of the present exercise, though, we will confine ourselves to the period up to 1623, when the first collected edition of Shakespeare's plays was issued (the First Folio). The project outline runs as follows:

> You can find full publishing details of all Shakespeare editions up to 1623 in Murphy, so begin by choosing a publisher or printer whom you would like to find out more about, bearing in mind that books may have both a publisher and a printer but may also be published and printed by the same person. Once you have chosen your printer/ publisher you should consult R. B. McKerrow's *Dictionary of Printers and Booksellers* (McKerrow 1910) for general information about his (or, more rarely, her) career. Other useful resources are Clair (1965), Pantzer (1991), and the profiles of Renaissance publishers by Gerald D. Johnson which appeared in the *Library* in the early 1990s (especially Johnson 1992). The next step is to access *ESTC*, go to "Advanced Search," and search for your publisher/printer by "Imprint Word" (a simple "Imprint" search will not get you the information you need). Try putting in the full name first, and if that does not give you very many hits, try using the surname only, though you may need to filter out hits which are not your publisher/printer. *ESTC* should provide you with a full list of the books printed/published by your subject. Try to get a sense from this list of what kind of work he or she normally carried out. The *ESTC* listing will also give you a very rough sense of how many copies of each item still survive: a large number of location entries indicates a large number of surviving copies. You can then see any of the books listed in facsimile on *EEBO*, where you can, if you wish, print out any title-pages of particular interest to illustrate your project.
>
> The project itself should take the form of a short report on your chosen publisher/printer, using the evidence you have gathered to explain what you think is significant or interesting about this particular subject, especially in a Shakespearean context. Questions you might think about could include, but need not be limited to, the following:
>
> 1   How much Shakespeare did he or she publish?
> 2   How much drama did he or she publish?
> 3   How much literature did he or she publish?
> 4   Did Shakespeare texts/dramatic texts/literary texts constitute a large percentage of his or her total output?
> 5   What other kind of material did he or she publish?

6   How much English-language, foreign-language, and classical-language material did he or she publish – and how much in translation?

7   Did his or her publishing profile change over the course of his or her career? (For example, did he or she always publish the same kind of material? Did his or her rate of publishing go up or down significantly from year to year?)

8   Was he or she primarily a publisher or primarily a printer?

9   Is there anything in his or her output that seems strange, given that he or she was also a publisher of Shakespeare?

10   Did he or she include Shakespeare's name on the title-page of the Shakespeare texts that he or she published? (If he or she did this only occasionally, what percentage of the texts do carry Shakespeare's name?)

11   Do the books that he or she printed now survive in large numbers or are they very rare? What might this mean?

At the time of writing the *Stationers' Register* is coming online, and this will offer a further dimension to the exercise. The resource will enable extant publications of the period to be compared with a list of titles entered by publisher's name which were either never published or are now lost. The following outlines do not make use of this resource but do respond to some of the questions listed above. They are offered as examples, in abbreviated form, of what this assignment might yield.

Cuthbert Burby

Shakespeare texts published by Burby are listed in Murphy (2003) as numbers 11, *Edward III* Q1 [*The raigne of King Edward the third*], 1596; 18, *Love's Labour's Lost* Q1 [*A pleasant conceited comedie called, loues labours lost*], 1598; 24, *Edward III* Q2, 1599; 27, *Romeo and Juliet* Q2, 1599.

Most of the known facts about Burby's career can be found in McKerrow, with further bibliographical information available from *ESTC* and *EEBO*. He was a publisher and bookseller in London from 1592 until his death in 1607. The son of Edmund Burby of Ersley in Bedfordshire, a husbandman, he had been apprenticed to William Wright for eight years from Christmas 1583. On taking up his freedom in 1592, he published his first book, the *Axiochus* of Plato, translated by "Edw. [sic.] Spenser," which was entered on the *Stationers' Register* on May 1 and printed by John Charlewood and John Danter. But this was not quite the impressive debut it seems: *ESTC* tells us that the work is not in fact by Plato and that the translation has been attributed to Anthony Munday and (in the Pforzheimer catalogue [Unger and Jackson 1940]) to Lyly. Title-pages show us that his first shop was "the middle shop in the Poultry, under St Mildred's Church"; in 1594 he moved to premises near the Royal Exchange, and finally to St Paul's Churchyard "at the signe of the Swanne" (1603). He occasionally went into partnership: for example, with John Flasket for a translation from the Dutch in 1601, and with Edmund Weaver for a translation from the Latin attacking the Jesuit Edmund Campion in 1606. The *Stationers' Register* shows that he was admitted to the Livery on July 1, 1598. He died in August/September 1607, leaving his stock and premises to his apprentice, Nicholas Bourne, as well as a sum of money for loans to poor young booksellers. Nonetheless, his widow, Elizabeth, continued the business in her own right for two years after his death, publishing exclusively religious books.

Burby's publishing career spans roughly fifteen years and coincides with most of Shakespeare's own writing life, from the period of the early histories through to the first of the late romances. In terms of English literature this is the High Renaissance. *ESTC* lists 105 titles under Burby's name, and 9 under his widow's, but there are spikes and troughs in his output, with his most productive years being in 1592 (10 titles), 1594 (13 titles), and 1604 (11 titles), and his least productive in 1593 (3 titles), 1600 (2 titles), and 1605 (2 titles). Breaking down his output into categories we find that about half of his books are religious works, including sermons, Puritan "lectures," books of consolation, and (one of his first publications) a work on the evils of alcoholism. There are clusters of anti-Catholic works appearing in 1603 and 1606. At the same time there is quite a high proportion of translation from modern European languages, mainly French (12 titles) and Spanish (7 titles). In total, about 20 percent of Burby's output comes into this category, which is the same percentage that H. S. Bennett gives for translation as a whole during Elizabeth's reign (Bennett 1965: xvi); but Bennett's figures include translations from the classical languages, and Burby seems to have had a preference for modern-language works. This is also reflected in the steady production of current affairs and newsbooks about continental matters, with eight titles appearing between 1592 and 1604. What Burby does not seem to have much concerned himself with is books of a learned, technical, or scientific nature. He published one book on rhetoric, Angel Day's *The English Secretary*, in 1599, with another edition in

1607; a book on shorthand, John Willis's *The Art of Stenographie*, in 1602; and two editions of a timely medical book, Nicholas Bownd's *Medicines for the Plague*, in 1604. His single scientific book was *The Well Spring of Sciences* by Humfrey Barker, actually a book on arithmetic, which appeared in 1598, the same year as the first quarto of *Love's Labour's Lost*.

Literature and drama account for just under a quarter of Burby's list, some 25 titles, of which 13 are romances or other kinds of popular fiction and 12 are plays. Interestingly, there is no poetry; Burby seems to have taken the view of more modern publishers that poetry doesn't pay. But this part of his portfolio is suggestive from a Shakespearean point of view. Burby seems to have been attracted to the "University Wits," publishing Lyly's play *Mother Bombie*, two editions of Nashe's *The Unfortunate Traveller*, and Greene's play *Orlando Furioso*, all in 1594. He had published Greene's *The Thirde and Last Part of Conny-catching* and *The Repentance of Robert Greene* in 1592, the year of Greene's death following a notorious banquet of Rhenish wine and pickled herrings. In 1596 Burby brought out Lodge's Nasheian social satire, *Wits Miserie*. He did not publish Marlowe, but he did publish a work about "Doctor John Faustus" by an author describing himself as an "English gentleman student" in 1594. (Marlowe, Greene, and Nashe were students at Cambridge; Lyly and Lodge at Oxford.) What makes Burby's list distinctive is the combination of university wit, with a satirical, social, and controversial inflection, and romance fiction. Alongside Lyly, Greene, Nashe, and Lodge, Burby was publishing works such as *The Famous Historie of Chinon of England* by Christopher Middleton (1597), *Primaleon* (1596), and *Amadis de Gaul* (1595), translated by Anthony Munday (see Wright 1963).

As far as Shakespeare himself is concerned, each of the texts Burby published has been the subject of much debate. To these we should add the non-Shakespearean *The Taming of a Shrew* (1594), whose relationship to Shakespeare's play is still not firmly established. *Edward III* was long regarded as apocryphal, but has now been admitted rather cautiously into the canon. It did not appear in the original edition of the *Oxford Shakespeare*, but there is a 1988 New Cambridge edition by Giorgio Melchiori which makes a good case for Shakespeare's part (9–17), and it has now been included by Oxford. In 1596, the year of the first quarto of *Edward III*, Burby published four other works: Munday's translation of the romance *Primaleon*; a second edition of *A Shrew*; Lodge's *Wits Miserie*, and a chapbook by Richard Johnson, *The Seven Champions of Christendome*. This group of texts offers a view in miniature of the character of Burby's literary list. A further highly significant Shakespeare text published by Burby is the second quarto of *Romeo and Juliet* (1589). Although the status of this text has not been debated to the same extent as Q1, one of the so-called "bad quartos," it is now a key text in the debate initiated by Lukas Erne (2003) on whether Shakespeare wrote both "literary" (long versions) and oral (short versions) of his plays, with the former being the "True Originall Copies," as the First Folio was to put it, and the latter being abridged performance versions. Burby's *Romeo and Juliet* is the earliest "literary" version which also has a short counterpart, the 1597 quarto printed by John Danter (Murphy 2003: 15).

But perhaps the most interesting of Burby's Shakespeare publications, and the one that responds most suggestively to the mapping of Shakespeare's publishing contexts, is the 1598 quarto of *Love's Labour's Lost*. This may not have been the first printed text of the play (see Murphy 2003: 16), but it is the earliest to survive, and it is also the first of any of Shakespeare's plays to advertise his name on the title-page. Its combination of romance and satire aligns it perfectly with the rest of Burby's list, as does its showcasing of "wit" in the figure of Berowne. It is surely no coincidence that in the same year Burby published Francis Meres's *Palladis Tamia. Wits Treasury*, the second of the four "Wit" books which were designed to promote the new English literary Renaissance. This is where Shakespeare, whose name had just been claimed by Burby, was described as "among the English . . . the most excellent in both kinds [comedy and tragedy] for the stage," and where we are told that "the Muses would speak with Shakespeares fine filed phrase if they would speak English" (Smith 1937: II, 318). Meres's book is partly a celebration of the creative literary explosion of the 1590s, and *Love's Labour's Lost* is the play where Shakespeare is most self-consciously concerned with the business of literary expression. This is a theme that runs through Burby's other Shakespeare texts, in the scene which discusses the writing of love poetry in *Edward III*, and in *Romeo and Juliet* when the lovers join together in a sonnet at the masked ball. So Burby seems to have had a role in promoting Shakespeare as a name in this new literary environment. But his publishing activities intersect with *Love's Labour's Lost* in other interesting ways through the play's French connection. Among Burby's newsbooks and contemporary histories we find *An answere to the last tempest and villanie of the League . . . A declaration of the crimes whereinto the Catholikes do fall, in taking the king of Nauarre his part*

(1593), two books about the conquest of Savoy (1597 and 1601), an account of a battle at Villefranche (1597), and *The French Kings proclamation* (1604). These texts may have no direct connection with Shakespeare's play, but *Love's Labour's Lost* has no identifiable source and the prominence of this "news" from France in Burby's list is certainly suggestive. It helps to illustrate how *ESTC* searches, supported by the resources of *EEBO*, can bring different texts into new alignments, and how publishing conditions can tell us more about the origin of these texts.

Peter Short

Shakespeare texts printed by Short are listed by Murphy (2003) as numbers 8, *3 Henry VI* (variant) [*The True tragedie of Richard Duke of Yorke* . . .], 1595; 17, *1 Henry IV* (Q1) [*The history of Henrie the fourth* . . .], 1598; 19, *Lucrece* 2 [1598]; 29, *Venus and Adonis* 5 [1599]. Short is also listed as probably having printed the latter part of number 14, *Richard III* (variant) [1597].

Details of Short's career as a printer are supplied by McKerrow (1910), Clair (1965), and Pantzer (1991) and can be supplemented by information from *ESTC*. We first have sight of him when he becomes a freeman of the Stationers' Company on March 1, 1589, starting in business the following year with Richard Yardley, an arrangement that continued until 1593. Short and Yardley took over the stock of Richard Denham, whose list included staple works such as Thomas Tusser's *Five hundred pointes of good Husbandrie*, which had first appeared in 1557 and continued to be reissued long after Short's death. But Short's portfolio combined practical self-help with piety. In his first year in business (1590), Tusser's agricultural manual appeared alongside *Queen Elizabeth's Prayer Book* and an English version of the *Psalms of David* translated from the Latin of Théodore de Bèze. A much more unusual feature of Short's activities was his venture into music printing, a highly specialized activity on account of the special type required. This included an edition of the Psalms in English meter by Thomas Sternhold and John Hopkins, which came out in 1601. Two years later Short was dead and his widow, Elizabeth, was soon married to another printer, Humphrey Lownes. Many entries for Short in *ESTC* identify the location of his printing house as "Bredstreet Hill at the signe of the Star," and Elizabeth continued printing from that address. However, she seems not to have been highly regarded in the trade: one entry in the *Stationers' Register* for 1603 records that "Hump[h]rey Lowndes married Short's widdowe. Holds ye printing house though uncapable" (Clair 1965: 103). The final two post-humous entries for Short are a new edition (1605) of Stow's *Annals*, which he had first published in 1601, and a 1609 edition of William Hunnis's *Seven Sobs of a Sorrowful Soule*, including music, which may in fact have been Lownes's work.

A survey of the 173 imprints for Short in *ESTC* yields the following information. First, he was primarily a printer rather than a publisher, though he seems also to have been a bookseller: 74 of these editions show no other publisher or bookseller on the title-pages, and the advertisement of his business address in many of them implies that he was selling as well as producing books. He had a particular interest in the market for foreign books in translation. While only six of the books he printed were in a language other than English (Latin), 34 percent of his output was represented by translations either from Latin or from European languages. This is a higher proportion of translation than we saw in the case of Cuthbert Burby, and there are some interesting points of both similarity and difference when we compare the work of the publisher with that of the printer/bookseller.

In the first place, Short printed only a small amount of drama – so small, in fact, that it looks peripheral to his main business. In addition to *3 Henry VI* and *I Henry IV*, and his part in the publishing of *Richard III*, Short was responsible only for *A Shrew*, which he printed for Burby, Garnier's *Tragedie of Antonie* (1595), Daniel's *Cleopatra* (1598), and Jonson's *Euery Man Ovt of his Hvmovr* (1600), which appeared in three editions in the same year, one from a different printer (Andrew Islip). This might seem to illustrate Peter Blayney's argument that there was a limited demand for printed playtexts in the early modern period and that they cannot be regarded as a popular commodity, though the exchanges between Blayney and Farmer and Lesser should be borne in mind here (see Blayney 1997; Farmer and Lesser 2005a, 2005b). What is certainly true is that, unlike Burby, Short was interested in poetry. Daniel's *Cleopatra* was published as part of a collection which contained his sonnet sequence, *Delia*, and the poem *The Complaint of Rosamund*. This was in fact the fifth edition of *Delia* in six years, so it must have sold well, as did Daniel's historical poem *The Civile Wars*, which Short printed twice in 1595. The plays by Garnier and Daniel were in any case closet dramas, literary works not designed for the popular theater. Other major poetical works printed by

Short include Spenser's *Amoretti* and *Epithalamion* (1595) and Drayton's *Englands Heroical Epistles* (1598).

So Short's printing of Shakespeare fits into a wider literary profile of love poetry and verse history during the 1590s. Short's Shakespeare texts (three history plays and two narrative poems) fit this pattern exactly. They also link to a different kind of network from Burby's, though here too there is a French connection. This is the network of patronage operating from Wilton House in the person of Mary Sidney, countess of Pembroke. It was Mary Sidney who had translated Garnier's *Antonie* from the French in 1595 and also she who had been the dedicatee of Thomas Watson's *Amintae Gaudia* (1592), a collection of poems modeled on French and Italian verse, and the first volume of secular poetry to leave Short's workshop. This volume was published by William Ponsonby, who was a regular agent for work from the Sidney circle. Daniel himself was one of Mary Sidney's principal protégés and enjoyed her hospitality at Wilton: *Cleopatra* had been written in response to her English *Antonie*. There is evidence that Shakespeare was familiar with most of Daniel's poetry (Gillespie 2001: 122–32), not merely with *The Civile Wars*, which made an impression on his own history plays. It is Daniel who provides the principal link between both Short and Shakespeare and this other, distinctive phase of the English literary Renaissance: not the "University Wits," the London professionals favored by Burby, but the more aristocratic milieu of Wilton House and the kind of poetry (sonnets especially) produced by Spenser and Sir Philip Sidney, Daniel and Drayton.

This chapter has necessarily switched between descriptions of the database projects themselves and some reflections on how best to go about them and on what their purpose is, ending with two more detailed outlines from a project on Shakespeare's publishing contexts. I hope the transitions between these will have been reasonably clear. At the same time it has offered a very simple history of the development of new resources that can be used in teaching students about Shakespeare and the text and about his wider Renaissance contexts. During the time that we have been offering these projects, new resources have become available which have changed the character of the projects offered: the introduction of links to "Criticism and Reference" on *LION* opened up much wider possibilities for the original mythological figure searches; and the coming of *EEBO* has meant that it is no longer necessary to rely on print or microfilm copies of early

Shakespeare texts for the editing topic. The projects have evolved in tandem with the technological developments. What has remained constant is the fact that these exercises, though they demand different kinds of skill, all enable students to engage in exciting, original research that would not have been imaginable a decade earlier.

Afterword

John Drakakis

In the opening chapter of George Gissing's novel *New Grub Street* (1891), the literary entrepreneur Jasper Milvain offers his sister Maud some practical advice against her purist notions of the art of writing. He urges her to consider writing "Sunday-school prize-books" and when she regards this as "an inferior kind of work" he offers the following response:

> Inferior? Oh, if you can be a George Eliot begin at the earliest opportunity. I merely suggested what seemed practicable. But I don't think you have genius, Maud. People have got that ancient prejudice so firmly rooted in their heads – that one mustn't write save at the dictation of the Holy Spirit. I tell you, writing is a business. Get together half a dozen fair specimens of the Sunday-school prize; study them; discover the essential points of such composition; hit upon new attractions; then go to work methodically, so many pages a day. There's no question of the divine afflatus; that belongs to another sphere of life. We talk of literature as a trade, not of Homer, Dante, and Shakespeare. (Gissing 1985: 43)

Milvain's distinction between "literature as a trade" and figures of literary authority such as "Homer, Dante, and Shakespeare" raises, albeit inadvertently, the role of the writer in history, and the very cultural apparatus charged with the generation of the myth of authority. If the practice of writing entails a necessary engagement with the world of existing "texts," and if the market place is a determining

221

factor in their generation and dissemination, the writing "at the dicta-
tion of the Holy Spirit" is almost certain, as in the case of Milvain's
rival, Edwin Reardon, to lead to material impoverishment.

A *"Companion* to Shakespeare *and* the Text" (my italics) may seem
to gesture in the direction of a teleology that positions the production
of "text" as being somehow contingent upon the "divine afflatus" of
the writer. This is the myth that Tom Stoppard playfully entertains in
his script of the Michael Madden film *Shakespeare in Love* (2002): that
the ultimate guarantee of the provenance of a fictional Shakespearean
manuscript was a very personal experience. Such reassuring fictions
notwithstanding, our main point, if not our only point, of entry to
"Shakespeare" is through a series of printed texts, produced under
determinate conditions, and that have come down to us in various
states. Not only that, but, as Stephen Orgel has argued, such was the
nature of the "trade" that Shakespeare was largely involved in that
the very issue of "authority" is open to question. In a short and pithy
chapter entitled "What is a Text?" Orgel states that: "we assume,
in short, that the authority of a text derives from the author. Self-
evident as it may appear, I suggest that this proposition is not true: in
the case of Renaissance dramatic texts it is almost never true, and in
the case of non-dramatic texts it is true less often than we think"
(2002: 1). He is careful to emphasize that the "text" in this case was
"the *performing* text," that it was the property of the theater company,
and that the "authority" it represented was "that of the company, the
owners, not that of the playwright, the author" (2002: 2). In the case
of Ben Jonson, Orgel takes pains to point out that in the prefatory
material to *The Masque of Blackness*, a distinction is made between the
poet's own "invention" and the ascription of "authority" to Queen
Anne (2002: 2–3), although even here the water is a little muddied
with the admission that "Hence (because it was her Maiesties will, to
haue them *Black-mores* at first) the inuention was derived by me, and
presented thus" (Herford et al. 1941: VII, 169). Jonson's concern with
publication may well have represented an attempt to establish the
writer's own authority, and certainly, by the early 1630s, one "son of
Ben," the royalist playwright Shackerley Marmion, could fashion a
prologue to *The Fine Companion* (1633) that was a dialogue between
a "Critick" and the "Authour." Here the author is cast by the Critic as
the object of a popular contempt the source of which is the "ignorance" of an audience, and whose habitual consolation resides in the
dual compensation of the protective power afforded by patronage and
the possibility of self-justification afforded by publication:

> I should be loath to see you mooue their spleenes
> With no better successe, and then with some
> Commendatory Epistles flie to the Presse,
> To vindicate your credit.
>   (Marmion 1633: Prologue. ll. 14–17)

In the case of Shakespeare, Orgel's argument remains powerful in the face of recent attempts to reclaim the dramatist as a "literary" figure (Erne 2003), a process that, as Anthony James West and Andrew Murphy outline in chapters 4 and 5, began in the late seventeenth century, and that editorial tradition has done much to sustain (de Grazia 1991a: 14–48, 177–222).

These are just a few of the problems that any engagement with Shakespeare's "texts" present, and there are many more. The present *Companion* confronts three important overlapping areas of concern, "Histories of the Books," "Theories of Editing," and "Practicalities," that correspond to a trajectory that most contemporary students of Shakespeare will recognize. Putting it another way, we might say that this tripartite division corresponds to the emphasis on the conditions under which the books themselves are made, the manner of their preparation for circulation in the market place, and their subsequent use-value for readers and interpreters. Much has happened in these three areas during the past half-century that revisionist accounts, seeking to challenge the prevailing emphases, have thus far done little to overturn. In the wake of particular developments within current literary theory that have focused upon what we might call "the materiality of the text," and by extension "the materiality of culture," the extension of scholarly interest to encompass "the history of the book" is of crucial significance. What had become the purview of a self-enclosed, rigorously defended field of textual bibliography has now been extended into all areas of the study of Shakespeare, in a way comparable to the acceleration of interest in the performance dynamics of the plays. It is also the source of a problem, a problem surrounding the weight that is given to the epithet "material" in these formulations.

In their introduction to an adventurous set of essays on *Subject and Object in Renaissance Culture* (1996), Margreta de Grazia, Maureen Quilligan, and Peter Stallybrass attempt to rethink what they perceive to be "a long and monotonous history of the sovereignty of the subject" by re-establishing the primacy of "the object." Their insistence that "the object be taken into account" continues to be a welcome adjustment to an otherwise skewed historical perspective. But in their haste to link "the object-as-thing" to "Marx's (uncommodified) product" (1996: 4), they risk effecting a simple inversion of the categories of subject and object for which they seek a semantic license:

> Reading "ob" as "before" allows us to assign the object a prior status, suggesting its temporal, spatial, and even causal *coming before*. The word could thus be made to designate the potential priority of the object. So defined, the term renders more apparent the way material things – land, clothes, tools – might constitute subjects who in turn own, use and transform them. The form/matter relation of Aristotelian meta-physics is thereby provisionally reversed: it is the material object that impresses its texture and contour upon the noumenal subject. And this reversal is curiously upheld by the ambiguity of the word "sub-ject," that which is *thrown under*, in this case – in order to receive an imprint. (1996: 5)

The rhetoric here is cautious, and the aim is clearly to correct the ascription of an absolute volitional power to the noumenal subject; and in many of the fascinating essays that follow, attempts are made to tease out various historical engagements through which received objects bear the marks of essentially political transformation. Their commitment to a Foucauldian account of periodization, and to a post-modern investment in the fragmented surfaces of culture, is uncomfort-ably aligned with the residual structuralism that was a mainstay of New Historicism. This circle is very difficult to square, especially when many of the "objects" isolated for analysis have already themselves become commodities, and are, therefore, in the classical Marxist sense, the results of the transformative power of labor. To assert the priority of the object is to risk the misrecognition of the process whereby labor becomes objectified, even though this rhetorical maneuver appears to disclose the object in its material existence.

We can see what this has become in Patricia Fumerton's introduc-tion to a jointly edited collection, *Renaissance Culture and the Everyday* (Fumerton and Hunt 1999), in which the claim to have founded "A New New Historicism" takes its cue from a series of studies in the 1990s, including the de Grazia–Quilligan–Stallybrass collection, that signal "the shift from old political historicism to a new social histori-cism of the everyday" (1999: 4). Fumerton sees this as being "not an absolute break but in many ways a continuum, a filling out, and also a dispersal of the earlier methodology" (1999: 4), with a new emphasis upon a "*sense* of the everyday" that is "very much caught up in sensuality or physicality" (1999: 5).

The history of this appropriation of the concept of materialism for a form of politically docile cultural inquiry, which dilutes the preoccupation with what Marx formulated as the connection between "the production relations" of an "economic community" and the simultaneity of "its specific political form" (Marx 1981: 927), has yet to be written. But it is this version of "materiality" that has sometimes been allowed to inflect "the history of the book" with a certain kind of emphasis. At their very root, the earliest printed texts of Shakespeare's plays and poems are commodities: that is to say, they were produced using available technologies, and within a particular set of productive relations that were in process rather than fixed or stable. The construction of presses, the molding of type, the making of paper, the business of printing – all of the things that we might designate the commodity's "use-value" – are transformed into "exchange-value," from their existence as expressions of human labor, which, in Marx's terms, gives them "an objective character as values" that are "purely social" (Marx 1982: 138–9), to the process of their circulation in exchange for money. We might ask the question – which textual scholars occasionally, and literary critics rarely, ask – what does it *mean* to exchange a particular sum of money, say 4 pence or 6 pence, for a copy of Middleton's *A Mad World My Masters* (1608) (Blayney 1982: 391), or some 15 shillings for a copy of Shakespeare's First Folio, and what might that exchange represent (Blayney 1996: xxviii)?

Peter Blayney is one of the most reliable sources of information about late sixteenth- and early seventeenth-century printing-house and publishers' practice, and the consequences of his contention that playbooks during this period were not a source of "quick profit" or that "the demand for printed plays greatly exceeded the supply" should not pass unheeded (Blayney 1997).[1] There is much to ponder in the carefully sifted evidence that Blayney amasses, and Helen Smith in chapter 1 of this volume alludes to it. For example, if, as Blayney demonstrates, the printing of plays was a long-term investment (1997: 410–13), then we need to rethink radically the model of commercial and social relations by which we evaluate the business of producing playbooks during the period. As Peter Stallybrass and Roger Chartier observe in their excellent account of the publication of Shakespeare's poems (chapter 2 in this *Companion*), there is little evidence that the dramatist's name was considered to be important as a playwright. This raises the question of what we might call the "cultural capital" of plays compared with other forms of published output, and stakes out the ground of the stern resistance to those revisionist voices that seek to recuperate Shakespeare for a "literary" establishment. The words of Mercury are harsher than they could possibly be aware after the songs of Apollo.

As the first four chapters in this *Companion* emphasize repeatedly, the book as object or commodity was an inherently unstable phenomenon, and its radical instability was derived from what we know of the complexities of printing-house practice. Charlton Hinman was among the earliest to note the extent of this radical instability when he produced his first facsimile reprint of the First Folio in 1968, and, as subsequent commentators have noted, this enterprise represents not an actually extant but an "ideal" copy insofar as that is practically possible (de Grazia 1991a: 17–18). We owe much to Hinman's monumental two-volume *The Printing and Proof-Reading of the First Folio of Shakespeare*, and subsequently to the radical assaults of D. F. McKenzie on the so-called "New Bibliography" (Hinman 1963; McKenzie 1966, 1969). We can account for some of the variations in books that emanate from what is now taken to be the normal practice of concurrent printing, and from the identification of damaged typefaces and what they reveal about compositorial habits; and recently, we have discovered some of the unexpected consequences of type-shortages, the behind-the-scenes effects of censorship. In addition, histories of the book have begun to direct our attention to what Gerard Genette has labelled "peritexts," the "spatial and material" features of the book (1997: 16) that have for some time interested textual bibliographers, and also "paratexts," which encompass all of the ancillary material that surrounds the text, such as dedications, inscriptions, epigraphs.[2]

Leah Marcus, in *Unediting the Renaissance: Shakespeare, Marlowe, Milton*, has speculated on some of the reasons for the renewed interest in textual studies. She believes that there may be two not entirely compatible reasons for it. One reason emanates from a sense of the relative permanence of books and manuscripts "in a world of typographic instability and lightning change" (1996: 26). But also, she thinks that with the advent of computer technology students are more receptive to the instabilities of early print insofar as they replicate the ever-changing nature of computer-generated "text" in the modern world. Certainly the process of easy and endless reduplication deprives "original" texts (and other artifacts) of their "aura," as Walter Benjamin famously observed (Benjamin 1969). But with the Renaissance we are, in fact, at one end of a process that we now experience as the democratization of meaning. Faced with unstable linguistic forms, and the technological constraints of the printing house, the early modern compositor can be made to look very much like a Saussurean structuralist *and* a Derridean deconstructionist *avant la lettre*. He selected and combined pieces of type in order to form words and sentences, and he made adjustments to spelling either out of personal idiosyncrasy, or out of the need to justify lines of type; and at various (usually fairly regular) points he dismantled the type that he had set, returned sorts to their appropriate place (sometimes making errors) in his type-cases, and then proceeded to reassemble his types in new combinations. Because he may have been involved in more than one project the compositor's practice may have been dispersed across a range of texts, thus making it extremely difficult at times to trace all of the evidence that has survived. For example, it is clear that James Roberts's compositors began setting *The Merchant of Venice* Q1 (1600) with depleted supplies of italic, and of some roman, type, and that this seriously affected the setting of speech prefixes throughout a large part of the quarto (see Kennedy 1998, Drakakis 2000, and my edition of *Merchant*). Setting and printing were often interrupted or slowed down for a variety of reasons about whose causes we can sometimes evolve plausible speculations, and these form just a part of those multiple agencies at work, to which Thomas L. Berger draws our attention in chapter 3 above.

The "facts" of presswork and the mechanics of the circulation of books in the market place, as well as the various controls to which these processes were more or less subject during and after Shakespeare's lifetime, feed nicely into the next part of this *Companion*, which brings the "material" life of books into contact with the business of editing. Modern editors have come to rely on the empirical work of textual bibliographers to furnish them with reasons for the readings that they choose. Editors mediate texts, they decide on what should appear in print, and the choices they make are often informed by aesthetic as well as "scientific" principles. We might consider the following line from *Othello*, which appears in the Folio as: *"Des.* No, vn-pin me here, / This *Lodouico* is a proper man. / *Aemil.* A very handsome man" (TLN 3005–7). This is substantially the reading that has come down to us through the editorial tradition. But if we compare it with Ernst Honigmann's reading in the Arden 3 *Othello*, the following alternative is offered:

DESDEMONA   No, unpin me here.
EMILIA   This Lodovico is a proper man. A very handsome man.
                         (4.3.33–5)

Honigmann is no stranger to the careful "scientific" practices of the textual bibliographer; indeed, his book *The Instability of Shakespeare's Text* inveighs against what he calls "a new enthusiasm for corrective editing comparable in many ways to the excesses of Pope and Warburton" (1965: 153). M. R. Ridley's Arden 2 *Othello* follows F1, but asks: "What did Shakespeare intend by this sudden transition to Lodovico? Is Desdemona for a moment 'matching Othello with her country forms'? One is tempted to wonder whether there has not been a misattribution of speeches, so that this line as well as the next should be Emilia's" (166, n. 35). Ridley links the figure of Emilia in this example with the case of Juliet's Nurse in *Romeo and Juliet*, who has "the same matter-of-fact materialism" (lxvii), although he does not proceed to any corrective editing. Despite his earlier caution, Honigmann flies in the face of his own counsel and emends, offering the following reasoning: "I follow Ridley's conjecture in moving the SP [speech prefix]. For Desdemona to praise Lodovico at this point seems out of character" (291). The "authority" for this emendation is not strong, but the idea that it should rest upon a perception of Desdemona's "character" serves to pinpoint the dilemma of the editor, caught between two distinct but connected discursive fields. Andrew Murphy's chapter 5 in this *Companion* charts the evolution of a role whose identity traverses the dividing line between the process of literary evaluation, on the one hand, and on the other the "science" (to use Paul Werstine's term in chapter 6 above) that furnishes the protocols by which we might judge the practical logic of the text's evolution. It is the difference between what Jerome McGann has identified as "the bibliographical codes" enshrined within the materiality of the book, and the "linguistic codes" that constitute "the work's locus of meaning." McGann's concern is with texts for which an identifiable manuscript exists; he argues:

> If the presence of other textual authorities is apparent in the bibliographical codes, it frequently invades the linguistic codes as well. We observe these kinds of invasions most often, perhaps, when we notice the part which certain readers and editors play in the production of an author's work: when we look, for instance, at Faulkner's printer's copy manuscripts, with their three-way dialogue of textual changes carried on by Faulkner and two of Random House's copy editors. These kinds of collaborative efforts attract our attention because they generally concern the text's linguistic code, which we commonly treat as the work's locus of meaning. In fact, however, the most important "collaboration"

process is that which finds ways of marrying a linguistic to a bibliographical text. (1991: 60–1)

Of course, with only the dubious evidence of Hand D in the extant manuscript of *Sir Thomas More*, Shakespearean textual scholars are deprived of the luxury afforded to textual scholars of Faulkner.

But two further issues intervene in the process of Shakespeare editing, and they reflect more general epistemological and technological changes. The first is concerned with the question of the accurate evaluation of those multiple agencies that Werstine identifies as contributing to the existence of particular versions of the text. Werstine's own conclusion is that because of a radical uncertainty that haunts the practice of textual editing, the business of distinguishing "what Shakespeare wrote" is rendered all but impossible, so that editors can do no more than offer "editions of individually printed versions." Werstine, of course, is writing in the wake of the re-evaluation of the so-called "bad quartos," and of the uncertainty of the identification of Hand D in the manuscript of *Sir Thomas More*. But his strictures notwithstanding, we might ask whether it is not possible to make educated guesses concerning what a manuscript copy that provided the basis for the printed text of a Shakespeare play might contain.

Two instances come to mind, one from *The Merchant of Venice* and a second from *Much Ado About Nothing*. The effects of the type-shortages revealed in the setting of *The Merchant of Venice* appear to have produced some intriguing – and for a modern readership controversial – compositorial choices. Many editors have detected in the play certain inconsistencies that may have been the result of the abandoning of ideas at an early stage in the writing of the play. Circumstantially we can chart the introduction of the speech prefix "*Shy(l).*" at points where those shortages are most acute. Also, the introduction of "Lancelet Iobbe" at 2.2, and the truncation of the surname to "*Iob*" in F3 (1663), with the speech prefix "*Clown*" used frequently, may also, as I have argued elsewhere (forthcoming edition of *The Merchant of Venice*), have been affected; in any event the name "*Gobbo*" looks increasingly unstable. In the matter of "*Iew(e)/Shy(l)*" the question we may ask is whether this variation existed in the manuscript copy – which many editors agree appears to have emanated from foul papers – or whether the speech prefix "*Iew(e)*" was consistent. Given the modern tendency to normalize speech prefixes, resting, as it appears to, upon some stable conception of dramatic "character," the editor is faced with a choice: either *"Shylock"* or *"Jew."* No edition yet has been prepared to follow the instability of Q1 (1600) *and* F1 (1623) in representing *both*.

In the case of *"Lance(let)/Launcelet/Clown"* within the editorial tradition only Capell opted for *"Clown,"* and among modern editions thus far only the Folger has opted for *"Lancelet,"* with editors generally preferring *"Lancelot/Launcelot."* In Q1 the alternation between role and name raises some interesting questions about the nature of composition. In what we might consider as a more extreme case, the figure of Dogberry in *Much Ado About Nothing* is, at various points, indicated in Q1 (1600) by no fewer than four names: *"Const.," "Dog.," "Andrew,"* and *"Kempe."* Three of Dogberry's names emanate from the role itself: he is a "Constable," and he is the "Clown" or "Merry Andrew"; the fourth, "Kempe," is the name of the actor who impersonated "Dogberry." It would be reasonable to speculate that "Kempe" appeared in the manuscript, and if so, then what might we deduce from this as regards the business of composition? Did Shakespeare compose the dialogue in isolation but with particular actors firmly in mind? Was this a joint effort in which Shakespeare simply transcribed Will Kempe's extemporized lines? We simply do not know, just as we don't know whether the silent figure of "Innogen," whose name appears in two early scene headings, is an unrealized character that editors are justified in excising, or a persistent testimony throughout to the process of the silencing of the woman. We may recall that in Q1 the line: "Peace. I will stop your mouth" (5.4.97) is attributed to Leonato, Hero's father, but that F1 attributes it to Benedick.[3] We are left to wonder what the impact might have been had the line been attributed to Leonato, vocalized in the presence of the silent "Innogen" who stands as a rebuke to the masculine folly that the play persistently ridicules. In these examples from both plays editorial choices materially affect the business of interpretation, and in Anthony James West's tracing of the "histories" of the First Folio in chapter 4 we can see the fortunes of a particular influential text as it travels through time.

The second issue is a much more difficult one to deal with and arises from a significant epistemological shift within the sphere of culture generally and literary criticism in particular, of which the fluidity of electronically assembled texts is a major symptom. In *Unediting the Renaissance: Shakespeare, Marlowe, Milton*, Leah Marcus attempts to chart what she calls "shifting conceptualisations of the text" (1996: 22). Resisting a curious, and manifestly American, reading of the formalism of Roland Barthes, she argues for a radical dislocation of the figure of the "author" in favor of an investigation of rhetorical and textual difference, "with a keen eye on other elements in the network that may have impinged upon them." In the new paradigm, she continues:

> Where different versions of a given work differ markedly, the areas of instability tend to be interpreted in terms of multiple factors rather than single ones: deviant versions of a given text are not the mere by-product of institutional "corruptions" impinging upon some texts but not on others; nor are they only a record of the author's developing powers, although writers may indeed change over time. Rather, areas of instability are interpreted in terms of alterations in the text's complex network of contemporaneous events, institutions, and potential audiences – not because more traditional explanations are always entirely mistaken, but because they have been overemphasised to the neglect of other factors. (1996: 23–4)

"Unediting" in this context means for Marcus undoing "at least temporarily some of that era's own innovative assumptions about the exalted status of literature, its timelessness and transcendence"; it means also resisting traditional attempts "to purge the text of the impurities it has gathered over time and restore its original elevation and splendour" (1996: 32).

This demystification of the process of assembling any text from the past must be welcomed. It follows on from Gary Taylor and Michael Warren's innovative attempt in 1983 to resurrect the question of whether *King Lear* existed in one or two texts deriving, as a number of their contributors to *The Division of the Kingdoms: Shakespeare's Two Versions of "King Lear"* (1983) argue, from different theatrical traditions. Such arguments have long been a matter of debate in relation to the A and B texts of Marlowe's *Doctor Faustus*, and the solution that the Oxford editors of *William Shakespeare: The Complete Works* (1986) hit upon was to publish both the quarto text of *The History of King Lear* and the folio text of *The Tragedy of King Lear*. This has begun something of a fashion, and in the Arden 3 edition of *Hamlet*, in addition to an "edited" text, all three texts, Q1 (1603), Q2 (1605), and F1 (1623), have been published.

In her contribution to this *Companion* (chapter 7), Marcus takes her argument a little further in opposing the task of editing as the "choosing among available alternatives, a setting of limits upon a range of possible forms and meanings" to a postmodern "restless kineticism." Where stability once reigned, what is now favored, indeed "celebrated," is "patchwork, palimpsest, and textual hybridizations of various kinds." If we follow this to its logical conclusion then the process of "unediting" is not simply the evolution of a practice that respects the multiform overdeterminations of the text, but can only acknowledge, and presumably celebrate, a radical indeterminacy. That this is itself a "politics" that will admit of revolutionary *and* reactionary interpretations does seem to get a little lost in the excitement of an alleged liberation, albeit one that re-inscribes the autonomous liberal subject as the locus, not just of meaning, but of the responsibility for assembling all of the materials that might contribute to the construction of meaning. Demystifying editorial practice is one thing; demanding that editors disclose the grounds of their editorial judgments is perfectly in keeping with a laudable process of democratization that acknowledges the grounds for communal judgment while at the same time leaving room for dissent. Celebrating the plethora of material detail, without considering the conditions under which that celebration is both encouraged and takes place, risks undermining the very rhetoric deployed to establish the text's historical veracity in the first place. If, for example, Marcus wishes to argue for the speech prefix "*Jew*" in *The Merchant of Venice* on cultural and not on bibliographical grounds, then is not editing in danger of becoming a matter of supermarket choices? Both quarto and folio of *The Merchant of Venice* contain a mixture, as we suggested earlier; but if we cannot first establish a plausible explanation for the *material* appearance of both forms of this speech prefix in particular formes in the quarto, preference on "cultural" grounds is likely to be unconvincing, unless we can overcome the distortions that our own historically situated perspectives impose (whether consciously or not) upon the culture that we have identified as the object of our inquiry. It is no good our appealing to the "local" and the "specific" *unless and until* we can separate out clearly the various bibliographical and linguistic codes that traverse *all* published versions of Shakespearean texts. But this is a different kind of epistemological discourse from that traversed by Michael Best, who in chapter 8 above is concerned to identify what is available electronically to readers of Shakespeare's texts.

The theory of editing is, of course, tied in with the practices of establishing the provenance of texts, and we should be careful to distinguish, wherever we can, what a writer like Shakespeare *wrote* – however we might speculate about the conditions under which he wrote – from what he *intended*. To return to Werstine's question of multiple agencies, when a writer *writes* then the act embodies an agency, but what happens when the fact of agency is entwined with the question of intention? For example, in the Oxford *History of Henry IV* (*1 Henry IV*) the editors substitute the name "Sir John Oldcastle" for the one that appears in all printed texts, "Sir John Falstaff." The editors argue that although the earliest title-page refers to "the humorous conceits of Sir John Falstaff," the surname was changed "as a result of the protests from Oldcastle's descendants, the influential Cobham family, one of whom – William Brooke, 7th Lord Cobham – was Elizabeth I's Lord Chamberlain from August 1596 till he died on 5 March 1597" (Wells and Taylor 1987: 509). They admit that they are restoring "Sir John's original surname for the first time in printed texts" and they believe that "even after 1596 the name 'Oldcastle' was sometimes used on the stage" (1987: 509). "Oldcastle" is Falstaff's name in the anonymous *The Famous Victories of Henry V* (1594), and the speech prefix "*Old*" appears at 1.2.119 of *2 Henry IV*. In F1 the speech prefix is normalized throughout as "*Fal./Falst.*" Historically the Oxford editors' case for saying that the *intended* figure was "Sir John Oldcastle" is a strong one, supported by most modern editors,[4] but the case for *printing* the speech prefix "*Old.*" in *1 Henry IV* is far from convincing, since no manuscript exists to verify this particular piece of either imposed or self-censorship. The question is: did Shakespeare *write* "Oldcastle," and was he forced at some time between the composition of the manuscript and its printing to alter it? Or did he sail knowingly as near to the political wind as he dared by writing "Falstaff" and incorporating a few references to the model for the dramatic character in the dialogue of the play?

The resolution of this conundrum relies heavily upon rival theories of editing; if we begin from the standpoint of the materiality of the book then we are forced to come down in favor of "Falstaff," since there is no copy of the earliest edition of *1 Henry IV* in which "Oldcastle" appears, even though a less than convincing case is made out on the basis of metrics that implies that in certain instances the disyllabic "Falstaff" replaced the trisyllabic "Oldcastle." In this example, historical, linguistic, *and* bibliographical codes intersect with each other, but the overriding emphasis remains on the "authority" of the "author." We are still at the beginning of a process of exploring the ways in which the figure of "the author" is inscribed in the overdetermining practices of writing, history, and culture, as the locus of a series of particular discourses rather than as the origin of them. Here, material bibliographical "fact" acts as a brake upon historical and literary speculation, and historical information facilitates speculation on some of the ways in which the writer's consciousness (and possibly, even, the writer's "unconscious") is shaped by a range of overdetermining external forces.

The Taylor and Warren volume (1983), coming in the wake of major shifts of emphasis within the discursive field of textual bibliography, has helped to accelerate the radical questioning of a number of accepted explanations concerning the genesis of Shakespearean texts. The traditional hierarchy to which Leah Marcus referred sought to establish a distinction between "good" and "bad" quartos, whose definitions remain, though much weakened. With the advent of a new theoretical emphasis upon ambiguity and ambivalence, those features of so-called "bad" quartos that displayed what Laurie Maguire has called "heterogeneity" and "accumulation" now require re-evaluation (1996: 152). The specific focus of Maguire's account is W. W. Greg's listing of the differences between the quarto and folio *Lear* in his influential *The Editorial Problem in Shakespeare* (1942), and his linking them to memorial reconstruction based on performance. Greg contends:

> Besides frequent and often indifferent variants, we find in the quarto all the usual stigmas of a reported text: redundancy, whether through the actors' introduction of vocatives, expletives, or connective phrases, or through their lapsing into looser and more commonplace phraseology, merging into paraphrase; anticipation, recollection, and assimilation; vulgarisation, and mere breakdown through failure of memory. (1942: 90)

Greg offers a comparison between two lines in quarto and folio *Lear*:

F: I am made of that self metal as my sister. . . .
Q: Sir, I am made of the selfsame metal that my sister is. . . .

and he comments:

> The loosening of the texture is obvious: the vigorous phrase "that self metal" suggests to the actor's mind the familiar "selfsame" that comes glibly from his tongue. The verse itself stamps the folio as correct, and surely original: it seems incredible that the Globe edition (though not the Cambridge) should have preferred the quarto reading. (1942: 90)

The advent of literary theory has taught us to be on our guard against a lexicon whose rhetorical power depends upon appeals to "correctness" and "originality." But although it is a little less assertive than Greg, we might consider Giorgio Melchiori's Arden 3 edition of *The Merry Wives of Windsor* (2000), which investigates very fully the differences between the 1602 quarto and the folio versions of the play. Like the *Henry IV* plays, this appears to have been sensitive to problems surrounding the figure of Falstaff, and also, according to Melchiori, "Brooke" (51). But Melchiori's general conclusion is that all of the inconsistencies between the quarto and folio texts of the play, and the consequent balance of editorial choice in favor of the folio and not the quarto as copy text, is because the latter is thought to have been "a memorial reconstruction of an authorial acting version of the play" (109). The evidence for such a claim, enticing though Melchiori makes it sound, is circumstantial, depending upon a host of assumptions about how performance versions might have been prepared. It is the work that the epithet "authorial" performs in this explanation that demonstrates the persistence of tradition.

With these examples we move to the third part of the *Companion*, which deals very specifically with the practice of editing and concludes with some suggestions from Neil Rhodes about how, in the classroom and with the aid of information technology and the progressive digitalization of the archive, students might be persuaded to emulate the processes of the text's genesis. We have seen how very quickly discussion traverses the boundary between bibliographical and linguistic codes, between the collection and evaluation of the material evidence left by the traces of printing-house practice, on the one hand, and on the other the literary interpretation of the words on the page. Part III opens with David Bevington's judicious account of the actual practice of editing, with how the editor contributes to the making of meaning, and in particular, with some examples of the kinds of intransigent problems that theoretical analysis does not explain. He alludes to the "Falstaff/Oldcastle" dilemma, and notes, impishly, that although the *Norton Complete Shakespeare* (1997c) adopts the *Oxford Complete Shakespeare* text, it reverts in the *Henry IV* plays to "Falstaff." There is still a residual faith in the "author" as origin, rather than locus, of textual production, but it is fascinating to observe the ways in which – even in the case of an immensely experienced and cautious editor of Bevington's reputation – the concept of the "two-text play" infiltrates the discourse of authorship; in addition to the cases of *Hamlet* and *Lear*, Bevington speculates that *Troilus and Cressida* in its 1609 quarto and 1623 folio versions might also be considered under this heading. This is not unlike the move from consistent to concurrent printing. Here the model of compositorial practice that assigned compositors to single tasks in the printing house gradually gave way, in the wake of Hinman, McKenzie, and Blayney, to the theory of multiple setting and the concurrent production of a number of books. The renewed interest in the protocols and economics of early modern theatrical practice has effected a comparable shift in the re-evaluation of the provenance of playhouse texts. This threatens to undermine the practice of editing as a process involving the making of decisions about what to print and what not to print, what to include and what to exclude, a dilemma sharpened by the growing awareness that modern annotated editions are, in effect, "steam-age" hypertexts that digitalization and the powerful capacities of computers can effect with greater efficiency.

Whether this leads to "plural texts," to adopt Sonia Massai's phrase in chapter 10 of this *Companion*, and what the precise nature of that plurality might amount to, is another question altogether. Massai's "history" of the genesis of the various edited "texts" of *King Lear*, albeit one that eschews teleology, owes more to Foucault's conception of genealogy than it does to any recognizable historicism, hence her wish to resist the evolutionary claims emanating from editorial tradition. The desire to break with that tradition coexists in the manner of Foucault with the power that tradition asserts upon editorial practice generally, and the ways in which the conjectures of one generation of editors can sometimes harden into the "truths" of its heirs. As what Massai calls "a highly contested cultural field" a non-teleological account of editorial practice seems a distinct possibility, although it is then incumbent upon the commentator to account fully for those social, economic, epistemological, and professional pressures that lie behind any decision to emend a text. Stephen Orgel, in his pithy essay "What is an editor?" is surely correct to resist the editorial impulse to produce a "notional platonic ideal" (1999: 16). But how an editor can do justice to "[t]he in flux, the text in process" (1999: 15), when this interventionist role is, perhaps, more akin to the act of translation rather than to faithful reproduction, challenges the limitations of print itself. Of course, it is important to preserve as much as we can of the text's "archaeology," to use Orgel's term, and to expose the sedimentation of successive generations of editors.

We should, perhaps, take care not to overstate the "instability" of Shakespearean texts in their original published forms as documents emanating from the printing house, since in every print run there would have been copies that were roughly identical, even if they have no longer been preserved. Such changes in these copies may not have been immediately perceptible to the naked eye: slight variations of inking, minuscule movements of lines of type, and so on. The variations that are claimed to derive from different theatrical practices simply add one more layer, albeit an important one, to "process." To sanitize these texts of what an eighteenth-century editor such as Lewis Theobald might have regarded as their "impurities" (Seary 1990: 132ff), or what according to modern typographical or literary practice are their instabilities, or to conflate different versions whose provenance has been properly established, is to translate them for a modern readership. An appropriate, though not entirely exact, analogy might be the film version of a Shakespeare play, which usually irritates textual purists more even than modern performance, since it invariably departs from a deeply held platonic "truth," while at the same time rendering it fit for modern consumption. It would be a pleasing fantasy, but a fantasy no less, to imagine Jaggard's compositors leaving alternative versions of particular folio texts of individual plays on the printshop floor in much the same way that film directors discard particular unwanted rushes.

Montaigne asserted that "Friendship is nourished by communication," and it is the function of a *Companion to Shakespeare and the Text* to provide precisely the companionship that will stimulate communication. Interest in textual matters is compulsive, some might feel, obsessively neurotic, but it is upon texts that are, in Shakespeare's case in particular, elevated to canonical status that our shared culture depends for its complex identity. The traversing of the full gamut of textual matters, the re-situating of some of them in the electronic age, and the rehearsing of a range of issues that, taken together, constitute the prehistory of the act of interpretation are the hallmarks of this particular *Companion*. As with all companionship, there are occasions when the individual emphases of particular chapters rub together pleasingly to expose the archeology of a series of related but distinct discourses that have now, thankfully, come more into the mainstream of Shakespeare studies. Whether we can "unedit" Shakespeare in a very radical sense is, of course, open to question. Whether the implied invitation to the reader to perform their own acts of editing makes the process more democratic is also open to question. What is important, however, is that readers can see how editorial power works, and what it does, and perhaps the most exciting element in current studies of Shakespeare's texts is the challenge that it throws up to edit otherwise. This carefully edited collection, a blend of conservative thinking, cautious reservation, and adventure, each contribution in dialogue with the others, organizes a very complex field into manageable compartments that, together, open out onto a panoramic view of exciting possibilities. What more can one ask from a Companion?

Notes

1 Blayney's contention has been subject to a recent challenge by Alan B. Farmer and Zachary Lesser in *Shakespeare Quarterly* (2005a) and by an equally robust refutation in the same volume by Peter Blayney (2005).

2 For an even more radical rethinking of these issues extended to the practice of writing, see Jonathan Goldberg (1990, 2003).

3 See McEachern's 2006 edition of *Much Ado About Nothing* (316), where the Q1 reading is restored, but where "Innogen" has been excised from the text.

4 See A. R. Humphreys's 1966 edition of *1 Henry IV* (xii): "It is well known that Falstaff's original name was Oldcastle and that this was changed because Sir Henry, or his father Sir William Brooke, or both, being descendants of the historical Oldcastle, objected to their ancestor's mishandling."

Bibliography

Shakespeare editions

For electronic editions, see under "Shakespeare, William" in "Websites and other electronic resources" below.

The following offer standard facsimiles of the earliest texts:

Allen, Michael J. B., and Kenneth Muir (eds.) 1981: *Shakespeare's Plays in Quarto: A Facsimile Edition*. Berkeley and Los Angeles: University of California Press.

Hinman, Charlton (ed.) 1996: *The Norton Facsimile: The First Folio of Shakespeare*. Second edition; originally published in 1968. New York: W. W. Norton.

PRE-1900

These are arranged chronologically. For an extensive listing of editions, with full publishing details, see the chronological appendix to Murphy (2003).

1593: *Venus and Adonis*. London: Richard Field.

1594: *Lucrece*. London: Printed by Richard Field for John Harrison.

1597a: *The Tragedy of King Richard the Third*. London: Valentine Sims [and Peter Short] for Andrew Wise.

1597b: *An Excellent Conceited Tragedie of Romeo and Iuliet*. London: printed for Iohn Danter.

1599: *The Most Excellent and Lamentable Tragedie, of Romeo and Iuliet*. London: by Thomas Creede, for Cuthbert Burby.

1603: *The Tragicall Historie of Hamlet Prince of Denmarke.* London: printed [by Valentine Simmes] for N[icholas] L[ing] and John Trundell.

1604: *The Tragicall Historie of Hamlet Prince of Denmarke.* London: printed by J[ames] R[oberts] for N[icholas] L[ing].

1605: *The Tragedie of King Richard the Third.* London: by Thomas Creede, and are to be sold by Mathew Lawe.

1609: *The Most Excellent and Lamentable Tragedie, of Romeo and Juliet.* London: Printed for Iohn Smethwick.

1623: *Mr. William Shakespeares Comedies, Histories, & Tragedies. Published According to the True Originall Copies.* London: Isaac Iaggard and Ed. Blount.

1632: *Mr. William Shakespeares Comedies, Histories, and Tragedies. Published According to the True Originall Coppies. The Second Impression.* London: by Tho. Cotes for Robert Allot (and other imprints).

1637: *The Most Excellent and Lamentable Tragedie of Romeo and Juliet.* London: by R. Young for John Smethwicke.

1663: *Mr. William Shakespeares Comedies, Histories, and Tragedies. Published According to the True Original Copies. The Third Impression.* London: for Philip Chetwinde.

1664: *Mr. William Shakespear's Comedies, Histories, and Tragedies. Published According to the True Original Copies. The Third Impression. And unto this Impression is Added Seven Playes, Never Before Imprinted in Folio. viz. Pericles Prince of Tyre. The London Prodigall. The History of Thomas Ld. Cromwell. Sir John Oldcastle Lord Cobham. The Puritan Widow. A York-shire Tragedy. The Tragedy of Locrine.* London: for P[hilip] C[hetwinde].

1676: *The Tragedy of Hamlet Prince of Denmark.* London: by Andr. Clark, for J. Martyn, and H. Herringman.

1685: *Mr. William Shakespear's Comedies, Histories, and Tragedies. Published According to the True Original Copies. Unto Which is Added, Seven Plays, Never Before Printed in Folio: Viz. Pericles Prince of Tyre. The London Prodigal. The History of Thomas Lord Cromwel. Sir John Oldcastle Lord Cobham. The Puritan Widow. A Yorkshire Tragedy. The Tragedy of Locrine. The Fourth Edition.* London: H. Herringman, E. Brewster, and R. Bentley (and other imprints).

1709: Nicholas Rowe (ed.). *The Works of Mr. William Shakespear; in Six Volumes. Adorn'd with Cuts. Revis'd and Corrected, with an Account of the Life and Writings of the Author.* 6 vols or 9 vols. London: Jacob Tonson.

1725: Alexander Pope (ed.). *The Works of Shakespear. In Six Volumes. Collated and Corrected by the Former Editions, by Mr. Pope.* 6 vols. London: Jacob Tonson.

1728: Alexander Pope (ed.). *The Works of Mr. William Shakespear. In Ten Volumes. Publish'd by Mr. Pope and Dr. Sewell.* 10 vols. London: J. and J. Knapton et al.

1733: Lewis Theobald (ed.). *The Works of Shakespeare: in Seven Volumes. Collated with the Oldest Copies, and Corrected; with Notes, Explanatory, and Critical: By Mr. Theobald.* 7 vols. London: A. Bettesworth et al.

1743–4: Thomas Hanmer (ed.)., *The works of Shakespear. In six volumes. Carefully revised and corrected by the former editions, and adorned with sculptures designed and executed by the best hands*. 6 vols. Oxford: Printed at the Theatre – for the university press.

1747: William Warburton (ed.). *The Works of Shakespeare in Eight Volumes*. 8 vols. London: J. and P. Knapton et al.

1765: Samuel Johnson (ed.). *The Plays of William Shakespeare, in Eight Volumes, with the Corrections and Illustrations of Various Commentators; to Which are Added Notes by Sam. Johnson*. 8 vols. London: J. and R. Tonson et al.

1768: Edward Capell (ed.). *Mr William Shakespeare his Comedies, Histories, and Tragedies, Set out by Himself in Quarto, or by the Players his Fellows in Folio*. 10 vols. London: Dryden Leach for J. and R. Tonson.

1785: Samuel Johnson, George Steevens and Isaac Reed (eds.)., *The plays of William Shakespeare. In ten volumes. With the corrections and illustrations of various commentators; to which are added notes by Samuel Johnson and George Steevens. The third edition, revised and augmented by the editor of Dodsley's collection of old plays*. 10 vols. London: C. Bathurst et al.

1790: Edmond Malone (ed.). *The Plays and Poems of William Shakespare, in Ten Volumes*. 10 vols. London: J. Rivington and Sons et al.

1793: Samuel Johnson, George Steevens and Isaac Reed (eds.). *The Plays of William Shakespeare. In Fifteen Volumes*. 15 vols. London: T. Longman et al.

1807: [Henrietta Bowdler (ed.)]. *The Family Shakespeare*. 4 vols. Bath: R. Cruttwell, Bath, for J. Hatchard, London.

1826: Samuel Weller Singer (ed.). *The Dramatic Works of William Shakespeare*. 10 vols. Chiswick: Charles Whittingham.

1832–4: A. J. Valpy (ed.). *The Plays and Poems of Shakespeare*. 15 vols. London: Valpy.

1842–4: Charles Knight (ed.). *The Pictorial Edition of the Works of Shakspere*. 12 vols. London: Charles Knight & Co.

1863–6: W. G. Clark, J. Glover, and W. A. Wright (eds.). *The Works of William Shakespeare*. 9 vols. Cambridge: Macmillan.

1864: W. G. Clark and W. A. Wright (eds.). *The Works of William Shakespeare*. 1 vol. London: Macmillan.

1871–: Furness, H. H., Sr., H. H. Furness, Jr., et al. (eds.). *The Variorum Shakespeare*. Philadelphia: J. B. Lippincott, later, New York: Modern Language Association.

1880–1: Henry N. Hudson (ed.). *Works of Shakespeare*. 20 vols. Boston and Cambridge, MA: Ginn & Heath.

POST-1900

These are arranged chronologically.

1901: W. J. Craig (ed.). *The Tragedy of King Lear*. London: Methuen.

1908: F. J. Furnivall and John Munro (eds.). *The Century Shakespeare*. 40 vols. London: Cassell.

1910: W. W. Greg (ed.). *The Merry Wives of Windsor 1602*. Oxford: Clarendon Press.

1921: Arthur Quiller-Couch and J. Dover Wilson (eds.). *The Tempest*. Cambridge: Cambridge University Press.

1934: John Dover Wilson (ed.). *Hamlet*. Cambridge: Cambridge University Press.

1952: John Dover Wilson (ed.). *Henry VI, Parts 1–3*. Cambridge: Cambridge University Press.

1965: M. R. Ridley (ed.). *Othello*. London: Methuen.

1966: A. R. Humphreys (ed.). *1 Henry IV*. London: Methuen.

1974: G. Blakemore Evans (ed.). *The Riverside Shakespeare*. Boston: Houghton Mifflin. Second edition 1997.

1980: Mark Eccles (ed.). *Measure for Measure*. New York: Modern Language Association.

1982: Harold Jenkins (ed.). *Hamlet*. London: Methuen.

1985: Eric Sams (ed.). *Shakespeare's Lost Play Edmund Ironside*. London: Fourth Estate.

1986: Stanley Wells and Gary Taylor, with John Jowett and William Montgomery (eds.). *The Complete Works*. Oxford: Oxford University Press.

1987: David Bevington (ed.). *Henry IV, Part 1*. Oxford, Clarendon Press. Reissued in the World's Classics series 1994 and as an Oxford World's Classics paperback 1998.

1989: Michael Warren (ed.). *The Parallel King Lear, 1608–1623*. Berkeley: University of California Press.

1991: Paul Bertram and Bernice W. Kliman (eds.). *The Three-Text Hamlet: Parallel Texts of the First and Second Quartos and the First Folio*. New York: AMS Press. Second edition 2003.

1993: Barbara Mowat and Paul Werstine (eds.). *Othello*. New York: Washington Square Press.

1996: E. A. Honigmann (ed.). *Othello*. Walton-on-Thames: Thomas Nelson.

1997a: A. R. Braunmuller (ed.). *Macbeth*. Cambridge: Cambridge University Press.

1997b: R. A. Foakes (ed.). *King Lear*. Walton-on-Thames: Thomas Nelson.

1997c: Stephen Greenblatt (ed.). *The Norton Shakespeare*, based on the Oxford edition. New York: Norton.

1998a: David Bevington (ed.). *Troilus and Cressida*. Walton-on-Thames: Thomas Nelson.

1998b: Giorgio Melchiori (ed.). *King Edward III*. Cambridge: Cambridge University Press.

2000a: Jill L. Levenson (ed.). *Romeo and Juliet*. Oxford: Oxford University Press.

2000b: Giorgio Melchiori (ed.). *The Merry Wives of Windsor*. Walton-on-Thames: Thomas Nelson.

2001: Richard Proudfoot, Ann Thompson, and David Scott Kastan (eds.). *The Arden Shakespeare: Complete Works*. London: Thomson Learning.

2002: Colin Burrow (ed.). *Complete Sonnets and Poems*. Oxford: Oxford University Press.

2006a: Claire McEachern (ed.). *Much Ado About Nothing*. Walton-on-Thames: Thomas Nelson.

2006b: Neil Taylor and Ann Thompson (eds.). *Hamlet*. 2 vols. Walton-on-Thames: Thomas Nelson.

2006c: Leah S. Marcus (ed.). *The Merchant of Venice*. New York: Norton.

Forthcoming: John Drakakis (ed.), *The Merchant of Venice*. Walton-on-Thames: Thomas Nelson.

Websites and other electronic resources

ArdenOnline. 1997–8. Website no longer available. The current Arden Shakespeare site is found at www.ardenshakespeare.com.

Arden Shakespeare CD ROM. Thomas Nelson, 1997.

Bartleby.com. *The Oxford Shakespeare*, ed. W. J. Craig. Bartleby.com, 2000. Accessed September 2006. www.bartleby.com/70.

Best, Michael. Forswearing Thin Potations: The Creation of Rich Texts Online. Paper presented at the meeting of the Consortium for Computing in the Humanities/Social Sciences and Humanities Research Council of Canada, 2002. Accessed September 2006. http://ise.uvic.ca/Annex/Articles/tapor/hamAnimated.html.

Best, Michael. Standing in Rich Place: Electrifying the Multiple-Text Edition: Or, Every Text is Multiple. Paper presented at the Shakespeare Association of America, 2002. Accessed September 2006. See especially http://ise.uvic.ca/Annex/Articles/SAA2002/rich4.html.

EEBO (*Early English Books Online*). wwwlib.umi.com/eebo.

EMLS (*Early Modern Literary Studies*). Sheffield Hallam University, 1995–2006. Accessed September 2006. http://purl.org/emls.

ESTC (*English Short Title Catalogue*). http://eureka.rlg.org.

Google Earth. 2005. Computer application. http://earth.google.com.

Gray, Terry A. *Mr. William Shakespeare and the Internet*. 1995–2005. Last modified June 2005. Accessed September 2006. http://shakespeare.palomar.edu.

Hamlet on the Ramparts, dir. Peter S. Donaldson. MIT and the Folger Shakespeare Library. Accessed September 2006. http://shea.mit.edu/ramparts.

Internet Shakespeare Editions, coordinating ed. Michael Best. University of Victoria. Created 1996. Last modified September 2006. Accessed September 2006. http://ise.uvic.ca.

Internet Shakespeare Editions, coordinating ed. Michael Best. Links. University of Victoria. Created 1996. Last modified September 2006. Accessed September 2006. http://ise.uvic.ca/Annex/links/index.html.

Internet Shakespeare Editions, coordinating ed. Michael Best. Shakespeare in Performance. Web database. Created 2005. Last modified September 2006. Accessed September 2006. http://ise.uvic.ca/Theater/sip/index.html.

Lancashire, Ian (ed.). *Early Modern English Dictionaries Database* (*EMEDD*). University of Toronto, 1999. Accessed September 2006. www.chass.utoronto.ca/english/emed/emedd.html. Updated July 2006 to the *Lexicons of Early Modern English* (*LEME*): http://leme.library.utoronto.ca.

Lancashire, Ian. The Public-Domain Shakespeare. Paper presented at the Modern Language Association, New York, December 29, 1992. Reprinted as Renaissance Electronic Texts Supplementary Studies 2. Accessed September 2006. www.library.utoronto.ca/utel/ret/mla1292.html.

LION (Literature Online). Individual databases: *Editions and Adaptations of Shakespeare; Literary Theory*. http://lion.chadwyck.com.

McGann, Jerome J. The Rationale of Hypertext. Institute for Advanced Technology, University of Virginia, 1995. Accessed January 2006. http://jefferson.village.virginia.edu/public/jjm2f/rationale.html.

Modern Language Association. Guidelines for Editors of Scholarly Editions. Last updated May 15, 2006. Accessed September 2006. www.mla.org/resources/documents/rep_scholarly/cse_guidelines.

Oxford Text Archive. Last updated August 2006. Accessed September 2006. http://ota.ahds.ac.uk.

Rasch, Chris. A Brief History of Free/Open Source Software Movement. Last modified December 2000. Accessed January 2006. Unavailable September 2006. www.openknowledge.org/writing/open-source/scb/brief-open-source-history.html.

Raymond, Eric Steven. The Cathedral and the Bazaar. Version 3.0, 2002. Accessed September 2006. www.catb.org/~esr/writings/cathedral-bazaar/cathedral-bazaar.

Renaissance Forum: An Electronic Journal of Early-Modern Literary and Historical Studies, ed. Andrew Butler. University of Hull, 1996–2004. Updated December 2004. Accessed September 2006. www.hull.ac.uk/renforum.

Rusche, Harry. *Shakespeare Illustrated*. Emory University. Accessed September 2006. http://shakespeare.emory.edu/illustrated_index.cfm.

Shakespeare Collection, The. Thomson-Gale, 2005. Website, access by subscription. Information page: www.galegroup.com/shakespeare.

Shakespeare, William. *Macbeth*, eds. A. R. Braunmuller and David S. Rhodes. CD-ROM, Macintosh. Voyager, 1994.

Shakespeare, William. *The Arden Shakespeare CD-ROM: Texts and Sources for Shakespeare Study*, consultant ed. Jonathan Bate. Version 1.0. Thomas Nelson, 1997.

Shakespeare, William. *The Cambridge King Lear CD-ROM: Text and Performance Archive*, eds. Jackie Bratton and Christie Carson. Cambridge University Press, 2001.

Shakespeare, William. *Comedies, Histories, & Tragedies: First Folio, London, 1623*. Octavo, 2001.

Shakespeare, William. *The Complete Works of William Shakespeare*, created Jeremy Hylton. 1993. Accessed September 2006. www-tech.mit.edu/Shakespeare/works.html.

Shakespeare, William. *The Enfolded Hamlet*, ed. Bernice Kliman. 1996. WWW interface by Jeffery and Charlotte Triggs. Part of the larger site, *HamletWorks*. Accessed September 2006. www.leoyan.com/global-language.com/ENFOLDED.

Shakespeare, William. *The Nameless Shakespeare*, eds. Craig Berry, Martin Mueller, and Clifford Wulfman. Joint project of the Perseus Project at Tufts University, the Northwestern University Library, and NU-IT Academic Technologies. 2003. Now part of the larger project WordHoard. Accessed September 2006. http://wordhoard.northwestern.edu/userman/index.html.

Shakespeare, William. *The Open Source Shakespeare*, created Eric Johnson. Bernini Communications LLC, 2003–6. Accessed September 2006. www.opensourceshakespeare.org.

Shakespeare, William. *The Works of the Bard*, created Matty Farrow. 1993. Accessed September 2006. www.cs.usyd.edu.au/~matty/Shakespeare.

Shakespeare, William. *William Shakespeare: The Complete Works, Electronic Edition*. Oxford University Press, 1988. CD-ROM. Based on the 1986 edition by Stanley Wells and Gary Taylor, with John Jowett and William Montgomery.

Siemens, Raymond. Disparate Structures, Electronic and Otherwise: Conceptions of Textual Organisation in the Electronic Medium, with Reference to Editions of Shakespeare and the Internet. In Michael Best (ed.), *The Internet Shakespeare: Opportunities in a New Medium. Early Modern Literary Studies* 3.3 / Special Issue 2 (1998). Accessed September 2006. http://purl.oclc.org/emls/03–3/siemshak.html.

Siemens, Raymond, Michael Best, Alan Burk, and others. *The Credibility of Electronic Publishing: A Report to the Humanities and Social Sciences Federation of Canada*. May 12, 2001. Accessed September 2006. http://web.mala.bc.ca/hssfc/Final/Credibility.htm.

TAPoR. Text Analysis Portal For Research. McMaster University. 2003. http://tapor.humanities.mcmaster.ca. University of Victoria node: http://web.uvic.ca/hrd/tapor.

TEI (Text Encoding Initiative). Accessed September 2006. www.tei-c.org.

TEI (Text Encoding Initiative). SIG [Special Interest Group]: Overlap. For the ISE's solution to the problem of overlapping hierarchies, see entry 2.1.5, "Treespaces," contributed by Peter van Hardenberg. Accessed September 2006. www.teic.org/wiki/index.php/SIG:Overlap.

WordCruncher Bookshelf Shakespeare. Electronic Text Corporation, 1988.

Books and articles

Alexander, Peter 1928–9: *Troilus and Cressida*, 1609. *Library* 4th ser., 9, 267–86.

Alexander, Peter 1929: *Shakespeare's Henry VI and Richard III*. Cambridge: Cambridge University Press.

Allott, Robert 1600: *Englands Parnassus: or the Choysest Flowers of our Moderne Poets*. London: N[icholas] L[ing], C[uthbert] B[urby] and Th[omas] Hayes.

Allott, Robert 1913: *Englands Parnassus*, ed. Charles Crawford. Oxford: Clarendon Press.

Andrews, John F. 2002: Textual Deviancy in *The Merchant of Venice*. In John W. Mahon and Ellen MacLeod Mahon (eds.), *The Merchant of Venice: New Critical Essays*. New York and London: Routledge, 165–77.

Anon. 1606: *The Returne from Pernassus: or the Scourge of Simony*. London: Printed by G. Eld for John Wright.

Anon. 1724: *Thesaurus Dramaticus*. London: printed by Sam[uel] Aris, for Thomas Butler.

Arber, Edward 1967: *A Transcript of the Registers of the Company of Stationers of London*. 4 vols. Gloucester, MA: Peter Smith.

Barnard, John 2002: Introduction. In John Barnard and D. F. McKenzie (eds.), and Maureen Bell (assistant ed.), *The Cambridge History of the Book in Britain. Vol. IV: 1557–1695*. Cambridge: Cambridge University Press, 1–27.

Barnard, John and Maureen Bell 2002: Appendix 1: Statistical Tables. In John Barnard and D. F. McKenzie (eds.), and Maureen Bell (assistant ed.), *The Cambridge History of the Book in Britain. Vol. IV: 1557–1695*. Cambridge: Cambridge University Press, 779–93.

Benjamin, Walter 1969: The Work of Art in the Age of Mechanical Reproduction. In *Illuminations*, trans. Harry Zohn. New York: Shocken, 217–52.

Bennett, H. S. 1965: *English Books and Readers 1558 to 1603*. Cambridge: Cambridge University Press.

Bevington, David 1987: Determining the Indeterminate: The Oxford Shakespeare (a review of *William Shakespeare, The Complete Works*, Vol. 1, *Old Spelling*, Vol. 2, *Modern Spelling*, and *William Shakespeare: A Textual Companion*. General editors, Stanley Wells and Gary Taylor). *Shakespeare Quarterly* 38, 501–19.

Bevington, David and Eric Rasmussen (eds.) 1993: *Doctor Faustus: The A and B Texts (1604, 1616)*. Manchester and New York: Manchester University Press.

Black, N. W. and Matthias Shaaber 1937: *Shakespeare's Seventeenth-Century Editors, 1623–1685*. New York: Modern Language Association.

Blayney, Peter W. M. 1982: *The Texts of King Lear and their Origins. Vol. I: Nicholas Okes and the First Quarto*. Cambridge: Cambridge University Press.

Blayney, Peter W. M. 1991: *The First Folio of Shakespeare*. Washington, DC: Folger Library Publications.

Blayney, Peter W. M. 1996: Introduction to the Second Edition. In *The Norton Facsimile of the First Folio of Shakespeare*. New York and London: Norton, xxvii–xxxvii.

Blayney, Peter W. M. 1997: The Publication of Playbooks. In John D. Cox and David Scott Kastan (eds.), *A New History of Early English Drama*. New York: Columbia University Press, 383–422.

Blayney, Peter W. M. 2005: The Alleged Popularity of Playbooks. *Shakespeare Quarterly* 56, 33–50.

[Bodenham, John and Anthony Munday] 1600: *Bel-vedére, or, The Garden of the Muses*. London: F[elix] K[ingston] for Hugh Astley.

Bodley, Thomas 1926: *Letters of Sir Thomas Bodley to Thomas James, First Keeper of the Bodleian Library*, ed. G. W. Wheeler. Oxford: Clarendon Press.

Bolter, Jay David 1991: *Writing Space: The Computer, Hypertext, and the History of Writing*. Hillsdale, NJ: Lawrence Erlbaum.

Bolton, W. H. 1990: The Bard in Bits: Electronic Editions of Shakespeare and Programs to Analyse Them. *Computers and the Humanities* 24.4, 275–87.

Bourus, Terri 2001: Shakespeare and the London Publishing Environment: The Publisher and Printer of Q1 and Q2 *Hamlet*. *Analytical and Enumerative Bibliography* n.s. 12, 3–4, 206–28.

Brockbank, Philip 1991: Towards a Mobile Text. In Ian Small and Marcus Walsh (eds.), *The Theory and Practice of Text-Editing: Essays in Honour of James T. Boulton*. Cambridge: Cambridge University Press, 90–106.

Chakrabarty, Dipesh 2000: *Provincializing Europe: Postcolonial Thought and Historical Difference*. Princeton, NJ: Princeton University Press.

Chambers, E. K. 1923: *The Elizabethan Stage*. 4 vols. Oxford: Clarendon Press.

Chambers, E. K. 1930: *William Shakespeare: A Study of Facts and Problems*. Oxford: Clarendon Press.

Chartier, Roger 2003: Foucault's Chiasmus: Authorship Between Science and Literature in the Seventeenth and Eighteenth Centuries. In Mario Biagioli and Peter Galison (eds.), *Scientific Authorship: Credit and Intellectual Property in Science*. New York: Routledge, 13–31.

Clair, Colin 1965: *A History of Printing in Britain*. London: Cassell.

Clark, W. G. and H. R. Luard 1860: *The First Act of Shakespeare's "King Richard II." Intended as a Specimen of a New Edition of Shakespeare*. Cambridge: Cambridge University Press.

Collinson, Patrick 1967: *The Elizabethan Puritan Movement*. London: Cape.

Cotgrave, John 1655: *The English Treasury of Wit and Language Collected out of the Most, and Best of our English Drammatick Poems; Methodically Digested into Common Places for Generall Use*. London: Humphrey Moseley.

Crawford, Charles 1932a: *England's Parnassus*, 1600. In C. M. Ingleby, L. Toulmin Smith, and F. J. Furnivall (eds.), *The Shakespeare Allusion-Book*. 2 vols. London: Oxford University Press, vol. 2, appendix B, 470–9.

Crawford, Charles 1932b: J. Bodenham's *Belvedere*. In C. M. Ingleby, L. Toulmin Smith, and F. J. Furnivall (eds.), *The Shakespeare Allusion-Book*. 2 vols. London: Oxford University Press, vol. 2, appendix D, 489–518.

Daniel, Samuel [1594]: *Delia and Rosamond Augmented* [by] *Cleopatra*. London: [James Roberts and Edward Allde] for Simon Waterson.

de Grazia, Margreta 1991a: *Shakespeare Verbatim: The Reproduction of Authenticity and the 1790 Apparatus*. Oxford: Clarendon Press; New York: Oxford University Press.

de Grazia, Margreta 1991b: Shakespeare in Quotation Marks. In Jean I. Marsden (ed.), *The Appropriation of Shakespeare: Post-Renaissance Reconstructions of the Works and the Myth*. New York: St Martin's Press, 57–91.

de Grazia, Margreta 1994: Sanctioning Voice: Quotation Marks, the Abolition of Torture, and the Fifth Amendment. In Martha Woodmansee and Peter Jaszi (eds.), *The Construction of Authorship: Textual Appropriation in Law and Literature*. Durham, NC: Duke University Press, 281–302.

de Grazia, Margreta and Peter Stallybrass 1993: The Materiality of the Shakespearean Text. *Shakespeare Quarterly* 44.3, 255–83.

de Grazia, Margreta, Maureen Quilligan, and Peter Stallybrass 1996: *Subject and Object in Renaissance Culture*. Cambridge: Cambridge University Press.

Donaldson, Peter S. 1997: Digital Archive as Expanded Text: Shakespeare and Electronic Textuality. In Kathryn Sutherland (ed.), *Electronic Text: Investigations in Method and Theory*. Oxford: Clarendon Press, 173–98.

Drakakis, John 2000: *Jew.* Shylock is My Name: Speech-Prefixes in *The Merchant of Venice* as Symptoms of the Early Modern. In Hugh Grady (ed.), *Shakespeare and Modernity*. New York and London: Routledge, 105–21.

Duthie, G. I. 1949: *Elizabethan Shorthand and the First Quarto of King Lear*. Oxford: Blackwell.

Dutton, Richard 1996: The Birth of the Author. In R. B. Parker and S. P. Zitner (eds.), *Elizabethan Theater: Essays in Honor of S. Schoenbaum*. Newark, DE: University of Delaware Press, 71–92.

Eastman, Arthur M. 1950: Johnson's Shakespeare and the Laity: A Textual Study. *Publications of the Modern Language Association* 65, 1112–21.

Erne, Lukas 2003: *Shakespeare as Literary Dramatist*. Cambridge: Cambridge University Press.

Farmer, Alan B. and Zachary Lesser 2005a: The Popularity of Playbooks Revisited. *Shakespeare Quarterly* 56, 1–32.

Farmer, Alan B. and Zachary Lesser 2005b: Structures of Popularity in the Early Modern Book Trade. *Shakespeare Quarterly* 56, 206–13.

Fletcher, John (n.d.): *Bonduca Queene of Brittaine*. Additional MS. 36758, British Library.

Foakes, R. A. and R. T. Rickert (eds.) 1961: *Henslowe's Diary: Edited with Supplementary Material, Introduction and Notes*. Cambridge: Cambridge University Press.

Foucault, Michel 2003: What Is an Author? In Paul Rabinow and Nikolas Rose (eds.), *The Essential Foucault: Selections from the Essential Works of Foucault 1954–1984*. New York: New Press, 101–20.

Friedlander, Larry 1991: The *Shakespeare Project*: Experiments in Multimedia Education. In George Landow and Paul Delany (eds.), *Hypermedia and Literary Studies*. Cambridge, MA: MIT Press, 257–71.

Fumerton, Patricia and Simon Hunt 1999: *Renaissance Culture and the Everyday*. Philadelphia: University of Pennsylvania Press.

Galey, Alan 1999: Probing Shakespeare's Idiolect in *Troilus and Cressida* I.3.1–29. *UTQ* 68.3, 728–67.

Galey, Alan 2005: "Alms for Oblivion": Bringing an Electronic New Variorum Shakespeare to the Screen. Paper presented to the Shakespeare Association of America, Bermuda].

Genette, Gerard 1997: *Paratexts: Thresholds of Interpretation*, trans Jane E. Lewin. Cambridge: Cambridge University Press.

Gillespie, Stuart 2001: *Shakespeare's Books: A Dictionary of Shakespeare's Sources*. London: Athlone Press.

Gissing, George 1985: *New Grub Street*, ed. Bernard Bergonzi. Harmondsworth: Penguin.

Goldberg, Jonathan 1990: *Writing Matter: From the Hands of the English Renaissance*. Stanford: Stanford University Press.

Goldberg, Jonathan 2003: *Shakespeare's Hand*. Minneapolis and London: University of Minnesota Press.

Greg, W. W. 1908: On Certain False Dates in Shakespearian Quartos. *Library* 2nd ser., 9, 113–31, 381–409.

Greg, W. W. 1922: *Two Elizabethan Stage Abridgements: The Battle of Alcazar & Orlando Furioso*. London: Malone Society.

Greg, W. W. 1926: Prompt Copies, Private Transcripts, and the "Playhouse Scrivener." *Library* 4th ser., 6, 148–56.

Greg, W. W. 1927: Shakespeare's Hand Once More. *Times Literary Supplement*, November 24 and December 1, 871, 908.

Greg, W. W. 1931: *Dramatic Documents from the Elizabethan Playhouses: Stage Plots, Actors' Parts, Prompt Books*. 2 vols. Oxford: Clarendon Press.

Greg, W. W. 1933: The Function of Bibliography in Literary Criticism Illustrated in a Study of the Text of King Lear. *Neophilologus* 18, 241–62.

Greg, W. W. 1936: King Lear, Mislineation and Stenography. *Library* IV.17, 172–83.

Greg, W. W. 1939–59: *A Bibliography of the English Printed Drama to the Restoration*. 4 vols. London: Bibliographical Society.

Greg, W. W. 1940: *The Variants in the First Quarto of King Lear, a Bibliographical and Critical Inquiry*. London: Bibliographical Society.

Greg, W. W. 1942: *The Editorial Problem in Shakespeare*. Oxford: Clarendon Press. Second edition 1951, third edition 1954.

Greg, W. W. 1949: Bibliography – A Retrospect. In F. C. Francis (ed.), *The Bibliographical Society 1892–1942*. London: Bibliographical Society, 23–31.

Greg, W. W. 1950–1: The Rationale of Copy-Text. *Studies in Bibliography* 3, 19–36.

Greg, W. W. 1951a: The Printing of Shakespeare's *Troilus and Cressida* in the First Folio. *Papers of the Bibliographical Society of America* 45, 273–82.

Greg, W. W. (ed.) 1951b: *Bonduca*. Malone Society Reprints. London: Malone Society.

Greg, W. W. 1955: *The Shakespeare First Folio: Its Bibliographical and Textual History*. Oxford: Clarendon Press.

Greg, W. W. (ed.) 1961: *The Book of Sir Thomas More*. Malone Society Reprints. Oxford: Malone Society.

Greg, W. W. 1966: What is Bibliography? In *Collected Papers*, ed. J. C. Maxwell. Oxford Clarendon, 75–88.

Greg, W. W. (n.d.): The Final Revision of *Bonduca*. MS RB112111 PF, Huntington Library.

Hammond, Antony 1994: The Noisy Comma: Searching for the Signal in Renaissance Dramatic Texts. In Randall McLeod (ed.), *Crisis in Editing: Texts of the English Renaissance*. New York: AMS Press, 203–49.

Herford, C. H., Percy Simpson, and Evelyn Simpson 1941: *Ben Jonson*. 11 vols. Oxford: Oxford University Press, VIII.

Hill, T. H. [Howard-Hill, T. H.] 1963: Spelling and the Bibliographer. *Library* 5th ser., 18, 1–28.

Hinman, Charlton 1963: *The Printing and Proof-Reading of the First Folio of Shakespeare*. 2 vols. Oxford: Clarendon Press.

Holinshed, Raphael 1587: *The Third Volume of Chronicles*. Second edition. London: At the Expenses of J. Harison, G. Bishop, R. Newberie, H. Denham, and T. Woodcocke.

Honigmann, E. A. J. 1965: *The Instability of Shakespeare's Text*. London: Edward Arnold.

Honigmann, E. A. J. 1985: The Date and Revision of *Troilus and Cressida*. In Jerome J. McGann (ed.), *Textual Criticism and Literary Interpretation*. Chicago: University of Chicago Press, 38–54.

Honigmann, E. A. J. 1996: *The Texts of "Othello" and Shakespearian Revision*. London: Routledge.

Honigmann, E. A. J. 2004: The New Bibliography and its Critics. In Lukas Erne and Margaret Jane Kidnie (eds.), *Textual Performances: The Modern Reproduction of Shakespeare's Drama*. Cambridge: Cambridge University Press, 77–93.

Hoppe, Harry 1946: *John of Bordeaux*: A Bad Quarto that Never Reached Print. In Charles T. Prouty (ed.), *Studies in Honor of A. H. R. Fairchild*. Columbia, MO: Curators of the University of Missouri, 119–32.

Hoy, Cyrus (ed.) 1979: *Bonduca*. In Fredson Bowers (gen. ed.), *The Dramatic Works in the Beaumont and Fletcher Canon*. Cambridge: Cambridge University Press, IV, 149–259.

Hunter, G. K. 1951–2: The Marking of *Sententiae* in Elizabethan Printed Plays, Poems, and Romances. *Library* 5th ser., 6, 171–88.

Ingleby, C. M., L. Toulmin Smith, and F. J. Furnivall (eds.) 1932: *The Shakespeare Allusion-Book*. 2 vols. London: Oxford University Press.

Ioppolo, Grace 1990: The Final Revision of *Bonduca*: An Unpublished Essay by W. W. Greg. *Studies in Bibliography* 43, 62–80.

Jackson, MacDonald P. 1988: Editions and Textual Studies. *Shakespeare Survey* 40, 224–36.

Jackson, William A. (ed.) 1957: *Records of the Court of the Stationers' Company, 1602 to 1640*. London: Bibliographical Society.

Jaggard, William 1911: *Shakespeare Bibliography: A Dictionary of Every Known Issue of the Writings of Our National Poet*. Stratford-upon-Avon: Shakespeare Press.

Jardine, Lisa and Anthony Grafton 1990: "Studied for Action": How Gabriel Harvey Read His Livy. *Past and Present* 129, 30–78.

Jarvis, Simon 1995: *Scholars and Gentlemen: Shakespearian Textual Criticism and Representations of Scholarly Labour, 1725–1765*. Oxford: Clarendon Press.

Jensen, Phebe 1995: The Textual Politics of *Troilus and Cressida*. *Shakespeare Quarterly* 46, 414–23.

Johnson, Gerald D. 1985: Nicholas Ling, Publisher 1580–1607. *Studies in Bibliography* 38, 203–16.

Johnson, Gerald D. 1992: Thomas Pavier, Publisher, 1600–25. *Library* 6th ser., 14, 12–50.

Jonson, Ben 1616: *The Workes of Beniamin Jonson.* London: Printed by W. Stansby; to be sould by Rich. Meighen.

Kastan, David Scott 2001: *Shakespeare and the Book.* Cambridge: Cambridge University Press.

Kelliher, Hilton 1989: Contemporary Manuscript Extracts from Shakespeare's *Henry IV, Part 1. English Manuscript Studies 1100–1700* 1, 144–81.

Kelliher, Hilton 1990: Unrecorded Extracts from Shakespeare, Sidney and Dyer. *English Manuscript Studies* 2, 163–87.

Kennedy, Richard F. 1998: Speech-Prefixes in Some Shakespearean Quartos. *Publications of the Bibliographical Society of America* 92.2, 177–209.

Kiessling, Nicholas K. 1988: *The Library of Robert Burton.* Oxford: Oxford Bibliographical Society.

King, Edmund 2004: "Small-Scale Copyrights?" Quotation Marks in Theory and Practice. *Papers of the Bibliographical Society of America* 98.1, 39–53.

Kirschbaum, Leo 1938: A Census of Bad Quartos. *Review of English Studies* 14, 20–43.

Kirschbaum, Leo 1945a: *The True Text of King Lear.* Baltimore: Johns Hopkins University Press.

Kirschbaum, Leo 1945b: *The Faire Maide of Bristow* (1605), Another Bad Quarto. *Modern Language Notes* 60, 302–8.

Kirschbaum, Leo 1955: *Shakespeare and the Stationers.* Columbus: Ohio University Press.

Knapp, Jeffrey 2005: What is a Co-Author? *Representations* 89, 1–29.

Knowles, Richard 2003: *Shakespeare Variorum Handbook.* Second edition. New York: Modern Language Association.

Lancashire, Ian 1989: The Dynamic Text: ALLC/ICCH Conference. *Literary and Linguistic Computing* 4.1, 43–50.

Landow, George P. 1992: *Hypertext: The Convergence of Contemporary Critical Theory and Technology.* Baltimore: Johns Hopkins University Press.

Landow, George P. 1994: *Hyper / Text / Theory.* Baltimore: Johns Hopkins University Press.

Landow, George P. and Paul Delany (eds.) 1991: *Hypermedia and Literary Studies.* Cambridge, MA: MIT Press.

Langbaine, Gerard 1691: *An Account of the English Dramatick Poets.* Oxford: LL for G. West and H. Clements.

Lee, Sidney 1902a: *Shakespeares Comedies, Histories, & Tragedies: A Census of Extant Copies.* Oxford: Clarendon Press.

Lee, Sidney 1902b: *Shakespeares Comedies, Histories, & Tragedies: Being a Reproduction in Facsimile of the First Folio Edition 1623.* Oxford: Clarendon Press.

Lee, Sidney 1906: *Notes & Additions to the Census of Copies of the Shakespeare First Folio.* Reprinted from the *Library*, April 1906, and revised to May 24, 1906. Oxford: Oxford University Press.

Lee, Sidney 1924: A Survey of First Folios. In Israel Gollancz (ed.), *1623–1923: Studies in the First Folio Written for the Shakespeare Association in Celebration of the First Folio Tercentenary.* London: Oxford University Press.

Leishman, J. B. (ed.) 1949: *The Three Parnassus Plays.* London: Nicholson and Watson.

Lesser, Zachary 2004: *Renaissance Drama and the Politics of Publication: Readings in the English Book Trade.* Cambridge: Cambridge University Press.

[Ling, Nicholas and John Bodenham] 1597: *Politeuphuia. Wits Common Wealth.* London: Printed by J[ames] R[oberts] for Nicholas Ling.

London, William 1657: *A Catalogue of the Most Vendible Books in England.* London: William London.

Long, William B. 1985: "A bed / for woodstock": A Warning for the Unwary. *Medieval and Renaissance Drama in England* 2, 91–118.

Lyotard, Jean-François 1993: *The Postmodern Explained: Correspondence, 1982–85,* eds. Julian Pefanis and Morgan Thomas, trans. Don Barry, Bernadette Maher, Julian Pefanis, Virginia Spate, and Morgan Thomas. Minneapolis and London: University of Minnesota Press.

Macdonald, Robert H. (ed.) 1971: *The Library of Drummond of Hawthornden.* Edinburgh: Edinburgh University Press.

McGann, Jerome J. 1991: *The Textual Condition.* Princeton, NJ: Princeton University Press.

McKenzie, D. F. 1966: *The Cambridge University Press 1696–1712: A Bibliographical Study.* 2 vols. Cambridge: Cambridge University Press.

McKenzie, D. F. 1969: Printers of the Mind: Some Notes on Bibliographical Theories and Printing-House Practices. *Studies in Bibliography* 22, 1–75.

McKenzie, D. F. 1992: The London Book Trade in 1644. In John Horden (ed.), *Bibliographia: Lectures 1975–1988 by Recipients of the Marc Fitch Prize for Bibliography.* Oxford: Leopard's Head Press, 130–52.

McKerrow, R. B. (gen. ed.) 1910: *A Dictionary of Printers and Booksellers in England, Scotland and Ireland, and of Foreign Printers of English Books 1557–1640.* London: Bibliographical Society.

McKerrow, R. B. 1924: Reviews. *Library* 4th ser., 4, 238–42.

McKerrow, R. B. 1933: *The Treatment of Shakespeare's Texts by his Earliest Editors, 1709–1786.* London: British Academy.

McKerrow, R. B. 1935: A Suggestion Regarding Shakespeare's Manuscripts. *Review of English Studies* 11, 459–65.

McKerrow, R. B. 1937: A Note on the "Bad Quartos" of *2* and *3 Henry VI* and the Folio Text. *Review of English Studies* 13, 64–72.

McKerrow, R. B. 1939: *Prolegomena for the Oxford Shakespeare: A Study in Editorial Method.* Oxford: Clarendon Press.

McKitterick, David 1997: "Ovid with a Littleton": The Cost of English Books in the Early Seventeenth Century. *Transactions of the Cambridge Bibliographical Society* xi.2, 184–234.

McLeod, Randall (contents page) / Cloud, Random (chapter heading) 1997: What's the Bastard's Name? In George Walton Williams (ed.), *Shakespeare's Speech-Headings: Speaking the Speech in Shakespeare's Plays*. Newark: University of Delaware Press, 133–209 (actually 131–207).

McMillin, Scott 1987: *The Elizabethan Theatre and the Book of Sir Thomas More*. Ithaca, NY: Cornell University Press.

Maguire, Laurie E. 1996: *Shakespearean Suspect Texts: The "Bad" Quartos and their Contexts*. Cambridge: Cambridge University Press.

Marcus, Leah 1996: *Unediting the Renaissance: Shakespeare, Marlowe, Milton*. London: Routledge.

Marmion, Shackerley 1633: *The Fine Companion*. London: Aug. Mathewes for Richard Meighan.

Marprelate, Martin (pseud.) 1588: *Oh Read Over D. John Bridges, for it is a Worthy Worke*. . . . Fawsley (?): Printed on the other hand of some of the priests.

Marx, Karl 1981: *Capital. Vol. 3*, trans. David Fernbach. Harmondsworth: Penguin.

Marx, Karl 1982: *Capital. Vol. 1*, trans. Ben Fowkes. Harmondsworth: Penguin.

Massai, Sonia 2007: *Shakespeare and the Rise of the Editor*. Cambridge: Cambridge University Press.

Melchiori, Giorgio 2003: The Continuing Importance of New Bibliography. In Ann Thompson and Gordon McMullan (eds.), *In Arden: Editing Shakespeare: Essays in Honour of Richard Proudfoot*. London: Thomson Learning,? 17–30.

Meres, Francis 1598: *Palladis Tamia. Wits Treasury being the Second Part of Wits Common Wealth*. London: Printed by P. Short for Cuthbert Burbie.

Middleton, Thomas 1608: *The Familie of Loue*. London: [by Richard Bradock] for Iohn Helmes.

Modern Language Association 1996: *Using TACT with Electronic Texts*. New York: Modern Language Association.

Moss, Ann 1996: *Printed Commonplace-Books and the Structuring of Renaissance Thought*. Oxford: Clarendon Press.

Mowat, Barbara A. 1994: Nicholas Rowe and the Twentieth-Century Shakespeare Text. In Tetsuo Kishi, Roger Pringle, and Stanley Wells (eds.), *Shakespeare and Cultural Traditions*. Newark, London and Toronto: University of Delaware Press and Associated University Presses, 314–22.

Mowat, Barbara A. 2001: The Reproduction of Shakespeare's Texts. In Margreta de Grazia and Stanley Wells (eds.), *The Cambridge Companion to Shakespeare*. Cambridge: Cambridge University Press, 13–29.

Mowat, Barbara A. 2003: *Othello* and the 1606 Act to Restrain Abuses of Players. Unpublished essay.

Moxon, Joseph 1958: *Mechanick Exercises on the Whole Art of Printing*, eds. Herbert Davis and Harry Carter. London: Oxford University Press.

Mueller, Martin and Bill Parod 2005: The Word Hoard Project: Final Report to the Andrew W. Mellon Foundation. Private communication (to Michael Best).

Munby, A. N. L. and Lenore Coral (eds.) 1977: *British Book Sale Catalogues 1676–1800: A Union List*. London: Mansell Information Publishing.

Murphy, Andrew (ed.) 2000: *The Renaissance Text: Theory, Editing, Textuality*. Manchester: Manchester University Press.

Murphy, Andrew 2003: *Shakespeare in Print: A History and Chronology of Shakespeare Publishing*. Cambridge: Cambridge University Press.

Nashe, Thomas 1592: *Strange Newes, of the Intercepting Certaine Letters*. London: J. Danter.

Nashe, Thomas 1594: *The Terrors of the Night or, A Discourse of Apparitions*. London: Printed by Iohn Danter for William Iones, and are to be sold at the signe of the Gunne nere Holburne Conduit.

Nelson, Alan H. 2005: Shakespeare and the Bibliophiles: From the Earliest Years to 1616. In Robin Myers, Michael Harris, and Giles Mandelbrote (eds.), *Owners, Annotators and the Signs of Reading*. Newcastle, DE: Oak Knoll Press; London: British Library, 49–73.

Nosworthy, J. M. 1965: *Shakespeare's Occasional Plays: Their Origin and Transmission*. London: Edward Arnold.

Orgel, Stephen 1999: What Is an Editor? In Stephen Orgel and S. Keilen (eds.), *Shakespeare and the Editorial Tradition*. New York and London: Garland, 117–23.

Orgel, Stephen 2002: *The Authentic Shakespeare and Other Problems of the Early Modern Stage*. New York: Routledge.

Pantzer, Katharine F. (ed.) 1991: *A Short-Title Catalogue of Books Printed in England, Scotland, & Ireland 1475–1640. Vol. 3: Printers' and Publishers' Index*. London: Bibliographical Society.

Patrick, D. L. 1936: *The Textual History of Richard III*. Stanford: Stanford University Press.

Pollard, Alfred W. 1909: *Shakespeare Folios and Quartos: A Study in the Bibliography of Shakespeare's Plays 1594–1685*. London: Methuen.

Pollard, Alfred W. 1917: *Shakespeare's Fight with the Pirates and the Problems of the Transmission of his Text*. London: Moring.

Pollard, Alfred W. (ed.) 1923: *Shakespeare's Hand in Sir Thomas More*. Cambridge: Cambridge University Press.

Pollard, Alfred W. and J. Dover Wilson 1919: *Romeo and Juliet. Times Literary Supplement*, August 14.

Pollard, Alfred W. and G. R. Redgrave, with the help of G. F. Barwick and others (compilers) 1926: *A Short-Title Catalogue of Books Printed in England, Scotland, & Ireland and of English books Printed Abroad 1475–1640*. London: Bibliographical Society.

Prynne, William 1633: *Histrio-Mastix. The Players Scvrge, or Actors Tragœdie, Divided into Two Parts*. London: W. A. and W. I. for M. Sparke.

Ranganathan, S. R. 1931: *The Five Laws of Library Science*. Madras: Madras Library Association.

Reid, S. W. 1974: Justification and Spelling in Jaggard's Compositor B. *Studies in Bibliography* 27, 91–111.

Rhodes, Neil 1998: Teaching with the Chadwyck-Healey Literary Databases. *Computers and Texts* 16–17, 6–8.

Roberts, Sasha 2003: *Reading Shakespeare's Poems in Early Modern England*. Basingstoke: Palgrave.

Rothwell, Kenneth 1990: *Shakespeare on Screen: An International Filmography and Videography*. New York: Neal Schuman.

Schoenbaum, Samuel 1977: *William Shakespeare: A Compact Documentary Life*. Oxford: Oxford University Press.

Seary, Peter 1990: *Lewis Theobald and the Editing of Shakespeare*. Oxford: Oxford University Press.

Shaaber, Matthias A. 1935: The Furness Variorum Shakespeare. *Proceedings of the American Philosophical Society* 75, 281–5.

Sherman, William forthcoming: *Used Books: Marking Readers in the English Renaissance*. Philadelphia: University of Pennsylvania Press.

Smith, G. Gregory (ed.) 1937: *Elizabethan Critical Essays*. 2 vols. London: Oxford University Press.

Stallybrass, Peter forthcoming: "Little Jobs": Broadsides and the Printing Revolution. In Sabrina Baron, Eric Lindquist, and Eleanor Shevlin (eds.), *The Printing Revolution Revisited*. Amherst: University of Massachusetts Press.

Steevens, George 1766: Proposals for a New Edition of Shakespeare. (No place of publication or publisher.)

Stephens, John 1613: *Cinthia's Revenge*. London: Roger Barnes.

Stern, Virginia 1979: *Gabriel Harvey: His Life, Marginalia and Library*. Oxford: Clarendon Press.

Stone, P. W. K. 1980: *The Textual History of "King Lear."* London: Scolar Press.

Tate, Nahum 1681: *The History of King Lear. Acted at the Duke's Theatre. Reviv'd with Alterations*. London: E. Flesher.

Taylor, Gary 1980: The War in *King Lear*. *Shakespeare Survey* 33, 27–34.

Taylor, Gary 1982: *Troilus and Cressida:* Bibliography, Performance, and Interpretation. *Shakespeare Studies* 15, 99–136.

Taylor, Gary 1985: The Fortunes of Oldcastle. *Shakespeare Survey* 38, 85–100.

Taylor, Gary 1987: General Introduction. In Stanley Wells and Gary Taylor, *William Shakespeare: A Textual Companion*. Oxford: Clarendon Press, 1–68.

Taylor, Gary 1990: *Reinventing Shakespeare: A Cultural History from the Restoration to the Present*. London: Hogarth Press.

Taylor, Gary and Michael Warren (eds.) 1983: *The Division of the Kingdoms: Shakespeare's Two Versions of "King Lear."* Oxford: Clarendon Press.

Theobald, Lewis 1726: *Shakespeare Restor'd: or, A Specimen of the Many Errors as well Committed, or Unamended, by Mr. Pope in his Late Edition of this Poet....* London: R. Francklin, J. Woodman and D. Lyon, and C. Davis.

Thompson, Edward Maunde 1916: *Shakespeare's Hand*. Oxford: Clarendon Press.

Trousdale, Marion 1986: A Trip Through the Divided Kingdoms. *Shakespeare Quarterly* 37, 218–23.

Trousdale, Marion 1990: A Second Look at Critical Bibliography and the Acting of Plays. *Shakespeare Quarterly* 41, 87–96.

Unger, E. V. and W. A. Jackson (compilers) and F. Warde and B. Rogers (designers and arrangers) 1940: *The Carl H. Pforzheimer Library: English Literature, 1475–1700*. 3 vols. New York: privately printed.

Urkowitz, Steven 1980: *Shakespeare's Revision of King Lear*. Princeton, NJ: Princeton University Press.

Vickers, Brian (ed.) 1995: *Shakespeare: The Critical Heritage*. 6 vols. London: Routledge.

Wagonheim, Sylvia Stoler (ed.) 1989: *Annals of English Drama, 975–1700*. London: Routledge.

Walker, Alice 1953: *Textual Problems of the First Folio: Richard III, King Lear, Troilus and Cressida, 2 Henry IV, Hamlet, Othello*. Cambridge: Cambridge University Press.

Walker, William Sidney 1860: *A Critical Examination of the Text of Shakespeare*. 3 vols. London: (no publisher).

Warren, Michael J. 1978: Quarto and Folio *King Lear* and the Interpretation of Albany and Edgar. In David Bevington and Jay L. Halio (eds.), *Shakespeare: Pattern Excelling Nature*. Newark: University of Delaware Press, 95–107.

Webster, John 1623: *The Tragedy of the Dutchesse of Malfy*. London: N. Oakes for J. Waterson.

Wells, Stanley and Gary Taylor 1987: *William Shakespeare: A Textual Companion*. Oxford: Clarendon Press.

Wells, Stanley and Gary Taylor 1990: The Oxford Shakespeare Re-viewed by the General Editors. *Analytical and Enumerative Bibliography*, n.s. 4, 6–20.

Werstine, Paul 1988a: "Foul Papers" and "Promptbooks": Printer's Copy for Shakespeare's *Comedy of Errors*. *Studies in Bibliography* 41, 232–46.

Werstine, Paul 1988b: McKerrow's "Suggestion" and Twentieth-Century Shakespeare Textual Criticism. *Renaissance Drama* 19, 149–73.

Werstine, Paul 1990: Narratives About Printed Shakespearean Texts: "Foul Papers" and "Bad" Quartos. *Shakespeare Quarterly* 41, 65–86.

Werstine, Paul forthcoming: Margins to the Centre: REED and Shakespeare. In Sally-Beth Maclean and Audrey Stanley (eds.), *REED in Review*. Toronto: University of Toronto Press.

Werstine, Paul and Edith Snook 2000: Under the Spell. Paper presented at the conference on Shakespeare Authorship and the Canon. University of Toronto, October 20–1.

West, Anthony James 1995: Two Early Gifts of the First Folio., *Library*, 6th ser., 17, 270–1.

West, Anthony James 2001: *The History of the First Folio. Vol. I: An Account of the First Folio Based on its Sales and Prices, 1623–2000*. Oxford: Oxford University Press.

West, Anthony James 2003: *The History of the First Folio. Vol. II: A New World-wide Census of First Folios*. Oxford: Oxford University Press.

West, Anthony James 2005: The Case of the Mysterious Folio. *Fine Books & Collections*, March–April, 33–5.

Williams, G. J. 1948: *Traddodiad Llenyddol Morgannwg*. Caerdydd: Gwasg Prifysgol Cymru.

Williams, George Walton 1979: Second Thoughts on Falstaff's Name. *Shakespeare Quarterly* 30, 82–4.

Williams Jr., Philip 1949–50: The "Second Issue" of Shakespeare's *Troilus and Cressida*, 1609. *Studies in Bibliography* 2, 25–33.

Williams Jr., Philip 1950–1: Shakespeare's *Troilus and Cressida*: The Relationship of Quarto and Folio. *Studies in Bibliography* 3, 131–43.

Wilson, F. P. 1945: *Shakespeare and the New Bibliography*, rev. and ed. Helen Gardner, 1970. Oxford: Clarendon Press.

Wilson, J. Dover 1934: *The Manuscript of Shakespeare's Hamlet and the Problems of its Transmission*. 2 vols. Cambridge: Cambridge University Press.

Wilson, J. Dover 1935: *What Happens in "Hamlet."* Cambridge: Cambridge University Press.

Wither, George 1624: *The Schollers Purgatory*. Imprinted for the Honest Stationers, [London: George Wood].

Wright, Celeste Turner 1963: "Lazarus Pyott" and Other Inventions of Anthony Munday. *Philological Quarterly* 42, 532–41.

Yamada, Akihiro 1998: *The First Folio Shakespeare: A Transcript of Contemporary Marginalia in a Copy of the Kodama Memorial Library of Meisei University*. Tokyo: Yushodo Press.

Index